Project Management

I would like to dedicate this book to Shai and Niels. Thank you for your unconditional love and the support you have given me.

Iris Eshel

Project Management

A Professional Approach to Events

Jan Verhaar & Iris Eshel

Second edition

Eleven International Publishing
The Hague
2010

Published, sold and distributed by Eleven International Publishing
P.O. Box 85576
2508 CG The Hague
The Netherlands
Tel.: +31 70 33 070 33
Fax: +31 70 33 070 30
Website: www.elevenpub.com

Cover design: Cunera Joosten, Amsterdam
Cover picture: © ID&T (Mysteryland festival)
Layout: H&R, Purmerend
Translation first print: Wouter & Cath de Been
Translation second print: To the letter: Michelle Mellion & Woutera Willemsen

ISBN 978-90-473-0150-9
NUR 801

Contents

Appendices

—

Recommendation

During the past few years, the contact between the Amsterdam College of Arts and the Utrecht School of Arts has become much closer in regards to cultural management. This is no surprise, given the fact that both schools have each been training students from their own particular perspective to become managers in the creative industry. Ever since the publication of *Project Management 1* by Jan Verhaar, the contact between the two training courses has become tangible in such a way that it will continue to lead towards future cooperation. After all, the book written by Jan Verhaar, which was partly realised on the initiative of the European League of Institutes of the Arts, was not only geared to the world of practice, but it is also significant in that it contributes to the general quality of professionalisation in the creative industry.

In our opinion, this book should be on the reading list of all those who want to become competent in the professional management of an event, and this includes most cultural projects. Both schools, however, made the book core reading in the course on project management. Many schools, including those outside the creative industry, have already followed our example. After all, in this day and age no course can afford to keep students in the dark about project management. In this respect, not only the professional approach to a project, but also the part played by the project leader deserves much attention.

As an independent consultant and manager for a wide range of projects, both within and outside the creative industry, the authors have gained a wealth of experience. Their methodical approach is suitable for the professional management of projects in a wide range of industries. The book provides the student with a solid foundation in the field, while at the same time, it leaves room for a more personal touch.

To guarantee the quality and applicability of *Project Management* in a wide range of topics the undersigned have installed a supporting committee consisting of:
- Eva van der Molen, a teacher of project management (Center for Art & Media Management at the Utrecht School of Arts)
- Frans Schouten, a teacher of heritage-management (NHTV Breda University)

Despite the great care that has been taken while working on this publication, there is always room for improvement. Therefore, we would like to invite the reader, also on behalf of the author, to send us his or her comments on the book, both with regard to its content and to its usage.

We congratulate the authors and the publisher with the publication of this volume and hope that 'The Verhaar' will be used as an instrument at events and projects, both within and outside of higher education.

Meine Fernhout, MA
Director of the Department of Cultural Management of the Amsterdam College of Arts
Professor Giep Hagoort, Master in Law, PhD. Economics
Director of the Center for Art & Media Management of the Utrecht School of Arts

Preface

The book that you have in front of you is a completely revised edition. This edition has been adapted regarding both the contents and the form that were altered in the Dutch version of the book *Project Management: Een professionele aanpak van evenementen*, the 8th edition. This revision has been carried out by the first author, Jan Verhaar and Iris Eshel, who has now become the co-author of this book.

In the past few years, we received interesting comments from the readers of this book. We would like to thank everyone for their feedback and whenever it was possible, we incorporated these comments into the text of this new edition.

The most obvious change is that the sequence of the chapters has been arranged in a more logical way. In Part A, the chapters have been included which guide you through the methodology and which should first be studied. Once you have this basic knowledge, you can subsequently proceed further by using the step-by-step plan in Part B, with your own event or conference project. In Part C, all of the chapters have been bundled together so that you can gain theoretical insight into the different techniques and models, to which you are referred to in one of the step-by-step plans in Part B.

The most important *internal* change has to do with the extension of the step-by-step plan in the initiative phase of an events project. Chapter 5 now includes a complete step-by-step plan, which can serve as a checklist for all of the phases of an events project. The step-by-step plan for a conference project has been completely revised and readjusted to that of a step-by-step plan to be used for an event in regard to content and form. The separate chapter about decision documents has been integrated in this edition in the step-by-step plans for both an event and a conference. At the end of each phase, the corresponding decision document is dealt with. The extensive models for a *project proposal*, a *project plan and a production programme* are included in Appendices C.

Besides the obvious changes and placing the book in an international context, smaller changes have been made throughout the entire book.

We trust that we have once again served you well as a reader by offering you this completely revised edition of a tried and tested book.

Santpoort, 1st of May 2010
Iris Eshel and Jan Verhaar

1

Introduction

Events have been with us since time immemorial; think of gladiator fights, jousts, fairs and markets. Now, professional events, such as trade fairs, expositions, conventions, festivals, sport matches, and all sorts of stage and film productions enjoy extraordinary attention. Moreover, events companies have really taken off in the past years. The event has proven to be an effective medium to come into direct contact with the target group. From an economical point of view, as well as from the perspective of culture and tourism, events have become projects of great significance.

Another social trend has also focused attention on these projects. Many creative institutions, but also companies, have to deal with momentous changes in their environment. Cut-backs and a receding state have confronted these institutions with budget financing, self-administration, privatisation and mergers. State control that is increasingly focused on output, growing competition and an ever more critical public, confront both institutions and companies with problems that demand more than merely an adjustment of the procedures or the organisational structure. More often, these developments are demanding a market- and public-oriented approach, quality control, attention to company management, and efficient transformation of creative ideas into interesting and high-quality products. Today, companies frequently set up projects to achieve their targets and manufacture their products in a flexible way.

1.1 Why Project Management?

Regularly projects, whether they deal with events or something else, result in failure, because the finances cannot be arranged, deadlines or quality standards cannot be met, budgets are overrun, or communication problems disrupt the collaboration to such an extent that the project has to be cancelled. Professional management of a project can prevent many of these problems and can ensure that high-quality events and other kind of projects are set up efficiently. In this way it is possible to respond quickly and flexibly to the demands of the internal and external environment of an organisation.

1.2 What is Project Management?

In general, management deals with controlling all sorts of processes within an organisation. This can refer to, for instance, the production processes, communication processes, the flow of written or oral information, the cooperation between people, or the control of budgets and time. The manager makes sure that the company activities remain focused on the target of the organisational unit (institution, company, section, group). He is the air traffic controller who coordinates and directs the flow of traffic in the busy air space.

Roughly, a manager can work for two types of organisation. The first type is the permanent organisation. In the culture and leisure industries, this could be, for instance, a museum, a stage company, an orchestra, a theatre group, a sports organisation, a convention centre, a recreational facility, or a tourist information office. Outside of these industries it could be a ministry, a factory, a school, or a retail organisation. The second type of organisation is a project organisation. This type is aimed at the realisation of a certain product or result, and is, therefore, only of temporary nature. In the cultural and events industry we can distinguish, for instance, festivals, public events, cinema, music and theatre productions, expositions, conventions, new attractions, sports events, conferences, publications, complex restorations, cultural programmes, and company events. Outside of these industries it might involve an IT project, real estate development, a complex move, or a policy development project.

Project management is the control of processes within a temporary organisation. The employees of different departments within a permanent organisation can also form a temporary organisation to achieve a certain target. Project management is characterised by the systematic and integral control of the development process from a creative idea to a concrete product or result.

With respect to the input of the manager, a distinction can be made between his *specific skills in the field of project management* and his *general management skills*. The first relate to activities that are necessary for structuring and controlling the project, phased management, management of time, money, etc. and the adjustment of the project to its environment.

With regards to the second, important skills are meeting and negotiation skills, social skills to deal with the client and other interested parties, motivating team members, handling of conflicts, solution of problems, applying effective management styles, the division of tasks within the team and team development.

Of these two categories of skills the first is described in this textbook *Project Management: A Professional Approach to Events*.

This book describes a concept of project management for general application, and the organisational, financial and planning aspects of a project. It focuses on a specific type of project, namely events, but can also be used for different kinds of projects. In the final chapter issues are discussed that go beyond the individual project, an area referred to as multi-project management. Among other things, it discusses some very practical phase models, step-by-step plans and checklists for different types of events.

1.3   Organisation of the Book

Project management, a professional approach to events, has been divided into three parts, namely:
Part I   A theoretical introduction
Part II   Getting Started
Part III   The project leader's toolbox

Part I A theoretical introduction consists of three introductory chapters. Chapter 2 is of a somewhat philosophical nature and explains how a project comes into being. A project always starts with a problem or an idea. In this chapter it is also indicated which approach is best to use for which question or for which problem. From this point of departure, the preliminary questions, which might be asked at the start, have been divided into six categories. An event can be a response to such a preliminary question. The choice to have an event should still, however, be carefully considered in lieu of other alternatives in order to achieve the objective.

In Chapter 3 all kinds of event forms are discussed. The different objectives that can be achieved by having an event are examined. The stakeholders are mentioned as well, which are involved in setting up events. Chapter 4 forms the theoretical core of the book. In this chapter the project management concept is presented, which is summarised in Figure 4.1. Afterwards, the product orientation, the control orientation and the communicative activities, which are seen as the different 'tracks' of the project, are described in detail. This results in the detailed model that is depicted in Figure 4.6. This model forms the core of the book!
Part I. You can view this as a necessary intrinsic introduction, if you decide to develop your own event when using Part II Getting Started.

Part II. Getting Started can be used in a very practical way. After having read the introductory chapter of Part A, you can start immediately. In Chapter 5, a detailed step-by-step plan is given for the phases of an events project and the same is true of Chapter 6 in which a similar plan is presented that shows the phases of a conference project. This step-by-step plan can be used as a checklist when developing your own event or conference. At the end of a phase, each step-by-step plan develops into a decision document. The chapters indicate where detailed models can be found for these decision documents, namely the project proposal, the project plan and the production programme, which have all been included in Appendix C.

Part III. The project leader's toolbox consists of chapters that are related to the most important business aspects of (events) projects. In Chapter 7 the area of tension between the project organisation and the permanent organisation is described. In this chapter the general aspects regarding the organisation of projects is also discussed. In Chapter 8, among others, the drawing up of project estimates, monitoring the budget and budget reports are examined. Chapter 9 deals with the funding of events projects, including sponsoring. In Chapter 10 different planning techniques are presented and a step-by-step plan is given which can be used to structure the project process and to set up a GANNT chart planning. In Chapter 11, an overview is given of all the activities that will need to be carried out during the different phases, within the track of the (marketing) communication. In this chapter is also described, in detail, how to set up and carry out a public survey for an event.
The book is concluded by a chapter on the multi-project organisation and the multi-project management. In this chapter all kinds of project aspects are covered that go beyond what was discussed. For example, a so-called project protocol is described, an instrument in which the project infrastructure can be used to describe your own organisation.

In Appendix A, a number of practical tools are provided. This concerns the forms that can be used for making a time schedule, for monitoring the budget and for arranging the project organisation. In addition, a test has been included on organisational culture, but also models have been included that can be used for drawing up different contracts.

In Appendix B, phase models are presented for a number of events projects, namely for conferences, exhibitions, trade fairs, festivals and manifestations, stage productions and video/film productions. These phase models can be used as a manual when developing these events projects. The Phase Model Festivals and Manifestations (Appendix B.3) and the Phase Model Conferences (Appendix B.1) lay the foundation for the step-by-step plans in Part B Getting Started. In Appendix C three detailed models have been included for the three decision documents for an events project which were mentioned earlier.

From a didactical point of view, the most important aspects have been repeated in various parts of the book. In order to make it easy to study, references are often made to the relevant sections found elsewhere in this book.

1.4   Who is this Book for?

This book on a professional approach to events is primarily aimed at undergraduate and graduate education. It offers students in any field that touches the subject of project management (of events) the opportunity to get acquainted with a professional approach to projects.
Moreover, it can also help professionals who have to develop a project with an important reference.
For the sake of readability the book has been written using the male pronoun. Yet, where 'he' is used, one can, of course, also read 'she'.

1.5   How to use this Book?

This book is meant to make you, as a reader, familiar with different aspects of professional management that involve fairly complex events projects. You can use the book in one of the following two ways. In either case, the idea is that the best learning outcome can be achieved when both theory and practice go hand in hand.

1   From theory to practice

First you should read through the book completely and possibly participate in supporting lectures which cover the different themes that are discussed in the book. Once you have become familiar with the subject matter, the book can subsequently be used as a guide with its step-by-step plans and checklists that can help you to pilot through the process of project development during a learning project.

2   From practice to theory

The following route has been recommended by the authors in view of the experience they acquired while teaching in Higher Professional Education (HBO- higher vocational studies). You should first only study Part I, in which an introduction is given and in which the project management concept is presented. Afterwards, you should immediately start working in a team composed of your fellow students on a (practice) project. This can be done by following one of the step-by-step plans found in Chapter 5 (for an events project) or from Chapter 6 (for a conference project). While working together with fellow students on the project, you should begin with the first idea via the plan to develop the final product, and then you can consult other chapters in the book by following the references give in the step-by-step plan. It is advisable that while working on the project, you receive a series of accompanying lectures which go further into the aspects which are involved at this stage of the project.

These lectures could possibly be partially substituted by receiving intensive coaching by an experienced teacher (a project coach). Experience has shown that in this way the student can become very skilled in applying a professional project-based approach in a fairly short time.

If you would like to apply this book regarding the project-based approach of an events project directly to your own professional practice, you can also choose one of these two methods. You will have to make do without the supervision that such a study can offer, but then on the other hand, you will have the advantage of possessing a great deal of work experience. It is also possible to compensate for the lack of support by participating in a project management workshop.

Just as we mentioned before, the books about the project-based approach have been written as textbooks for (future) professional project managers. This book is therefore not meant to be used as a tool for setting up 'an event project'. To achieve this, the set of instruments in many cases would actually be too complicated. If you still would like to use the book for this purpose, then it is recommended that one of the step-by-step plans in Part II be used and that this be applied with the necessary flexibility.

In conclusion, still two remarks should be made:
When you, as a student, apply the method for the first time you will probably think this is done in quite a farfetched way. Nevertheless, it is a professional skill, just like driving a car and playing the piano, and it will have to be practiced. Experience has, however, shown that when someone consistently approaches a project by using this method, he or she will only need to use the book as a reference when doing projects in the future.

It is certainly not the intention that a too rigid application of the method is used. You are advised to use the method described and the step-by-step plans and models as a guideline, and subsequently adjust them to your own way of working and to meet the specific demands that your project requires.

PART 1
A theoretical introduction

The Application

Small things can have big consequences. The organiser of events L.v.B. knows all about this. 'One time I organised two events in a single weekend to which Murphy's Law applied.'

Instant Improvisation

'It all started on the Saturday when I organised a day for the pensioners of an oil company in Schoonebeek in the east of the Netherlands. From all corners of the country buses transported 2,500 guests to a party with an Arabic theme. When guests have been on the road for a long time, you know that they want two things when they arrive: a sanitary break and coffee. I had prepared myself extremely well for this ceremony, as shortly before Nestlé had provided me with the use of a new, truly superb, coffee maker. In half a minute it could produce twenty litres of coffee. Three quarters of an hour before the first bus was due to arrive, I checked everything one more time: the electricity and water were okay and proudly I pushed the button of the splendid machine. The result was a spark, a puff of smoke and a feeling of panic. We had no coffee! I immediately sent out a number of assistants to get coffee from all the pubs in the area. This was quite tricky, because not a single pub had opened yet. In the end we managed, ten minutes after the first bus arrived we had coffee. I had learned my first lesson that day: Always make sure you have a contingency plan.

Who does what?

Having barely recovered from all the commotion, the next day, a Sunday morning, L.v.B. travelled to Utrecht for an event at the Academic Hospital. 'An event for four thousand people on the completion of a building project; the employees of a construction company including partners,' says L.v.b. 'My assistants had organised everything, except for the toilet facilities. As it happened, the customer had offered to organise those himself, because of his good relationship with the rental company.

To be sure, on arrival a long row of mobile toilets stood in an orderly formation in the mud. It looked like a modern object of art. While I was drinking a cup of coffee together with the customer, by chance I saw an early guest going to the toilet unit. A moment later the man left the toilet again, looked around nervously, walked to the buffet quasi-discreetly, and grabbed a pile of paper napkins glancing guiltily around as he walked back to the toilets again!

At that moment the customer and I looked at each other and thought exactly the same thing: Weren't you going to.... There I was: just try to organise toilet paper for four thousand people on a Sunday morning! In the end I succeeded, but ever since that day I always organise each part of my events myself and never leave anything to the customer.'

Realise what you say

The same events manager spoke of another example that took place during the same event. 'There were beautiful flower arrangements on the tables. All of a sudden the customer decided that it was a good idea to give the flowers away to the guests at the end of the day.

I was doing something completely different at that moment and agreed without giving it much thought. Boy, did we ever regret it! Suddenly I saw the client on stage telling the guests that they could take the flowers home with them. However, there were four thousand guests and only five hundred flower arrangements. The guests immediately took action and plundered everything they could get their hands on. Not only flower arrangements, but even complete flower boxes and palm trees were carried out! It was a stampede that was uncontrollable!'

(From: High Profile Events, edited by the authors)

2

The Creative Process

Projects can develop in many different ways. Many projects originate from the need to change something in our environment. When that happens, everything can be seen from a different point of view, from what we would actually prefer to happen (our objective) to what we are seeing in all actuality. Here, a 'problem' is defined as 'the difference between objective and reality.' Projects can also arise from someone's inner need to realise an idea (objective). Hence, both an internal and external need can give rise to the realisation of something. The realisation of an objective can occur in the shape of a project.

In some cases projects originate from the (long-term) policy of an institution or company in the creative or leisure industry. This policy can require, for instance, that each year one or more big productions, expositions, festivals, sports events, courses or conferences be organised, and that they be referred to as an annual programme. Incidental projects can also be part of the annual programme, such as the development of a new attraction, an extensive alteration or restoration, the automation of a department, a grand launch of a new product, an opening or another celebration. Furthermore, as a manager or an employee we are frequently confronted with problems and needs of various natures. New ideas and initiatives could emerge for which a project approach might be considered.

Moreover, people outside organisations are confronted with questions that demand a solution, or they have ideas that they would very much like to see executed.

2.1 The Start of the Creative Process

How can questions be dealt with and how can problems be solved? Management, in general, means the guiding of processes. The question at hand is how can the process of problem-solving be managed or the idea realised? To be able to manage a process, first, it is important to gain insight into the nature of the process concerned.

This chapter provides a general understanding of the different types of questions that confront us and of the process of problem-solving and the realisation of ideas. Next, a concrete method will be presented in Chapter 4 which will deal with certain types of questions and problems.

To provide insight into the emergence of a project, a real-life situation is described below which gives an example of a project that arose out of the practical need for an event.

The Start of an Event Project

It is the end of 1994 in Berlin. The participants of a conference organised by the European League of Institutes of the Arts (ELIA) are having lunch in the beautiful garden of the Hochschule der Kunste on wooden benches at long tables. At one of the tables a small group of men are talking loudly. A woman is wandering around looking for a place to sit and finally she sits down on the end of the bench near the group, who is speaking a language she does not understand. Suddenly, the men next to her stand up, which causes the bench to tip like a seesaw and the woman falls down. A funny incident had happened that in the end will prove to have great consequences. The woman and the men start talking. The men tell her they are from Albania. One is an actor, but he has recently become the principal of a school for dramatic art; another is a violin player and for a short time he has been principal for the school of music; a third is a painter and recently he became the principal of an art academy. The woman is a policy maker at the Amsterdam College of Arts. The men tell her that they are artists and that they know nothing about management. They feel that they lack the necessary know-how in this respect. The woman remarks that at least it is better than the opposite: managers of art schools that know nothing about art. When she returns to Amsterdam she tells her colleagues about the incident. It seems to fit surprisingly well with all of the signals that ELIA and others have received about art schools in that region. A small group of colleagues decide to organise an event for managers of art schools in Central and Eastern Europe who would like to participate in an international exchange. Few words are neces-

Frame 2.1

sary to negotiate an agreement. During informal conversations in a bar, a plan to organise a seminar on 'The Managing of International Projects in Arts Education' takes shape. The seminar will take place during the International Theatre Festival. ELIA coincidentally has a trainee who is perfect for organising the seminar. Hoping for the best, a brief announcement is sent to all the members of ELIA, which results in a huge response: 28 registrations from 17 different countries. A choice of speakers and discussion leaders immediately offer their cooperation, despite the – for many – unusual date (the end of June). A teacher from the Department of Cultural Management always wanted to compile his notes and teaching material and, within weeks, he provides an English syllabus.

The participants receive notice that they can apply for a visa, while in the meantime funding is secured. Financial contributions are made by the Dutch Ministry of Education, Culture and Science, the Ministry of Foreign Affairs, the Nuffic and the European Union. The city of Amsterdam offers a boat trip through the canals and the Dutch Theater Institue offers a farewell reception. Within four months a project was set up.

When we analyse the story above, we notice several stages. Someone observes, merely by chance and only partially aware of a need in her environment. This keeps haunting her, she thinks about it, she talks to other people about it, gets a flash of inspiration and starts to shape the project with the help of others.

After a problem, or need, has been observed and the will to do something about it has been created, people evidently generate all the necessary support. When it is a good idea, an idea that people and institutions become excited about, then, obviously, things can move fairly quickly. Yet, it does take a lot of time.

The spontaneous creative process unfolds between the world of daily practice, where the problem or need arises, and the world of ideas. We are hardly aware of the different stages involved in the process; the different activities almost seem to occur in natural succession.

2.1.1 The World of Ideas

From within the framework of this book the previously mentioned world of ideas, or spiritual dimension of existence, can be represented as a reservoir from which we draw – mostly subconsciously – our ideas, intuitions and inspiration. Everything around us originates from an idea or a principle. The ideas that form the foundation of everything that exists around us now, but also of everything that has existed before and of everything that will exist in the future, all make up the world of ideas. Real new ideas, therefore, are not the result of mental activity in our minds; they are not invented. When the time is right an idea will trickle down from the world of ideas into the world of our perception. That is when we become aware of it. The world of ideas, also known as our collective unconsciousness, does not belong to the world of our immediate perception. Maybe we can illustrate this in the next example.

Try to imagine the following: before people had invented the wheel, which made it easier to transport heavy loads, the 'principle' or 'idea' of the wheel had already existed. If we were to forget the principle or idea that lies at the founda-

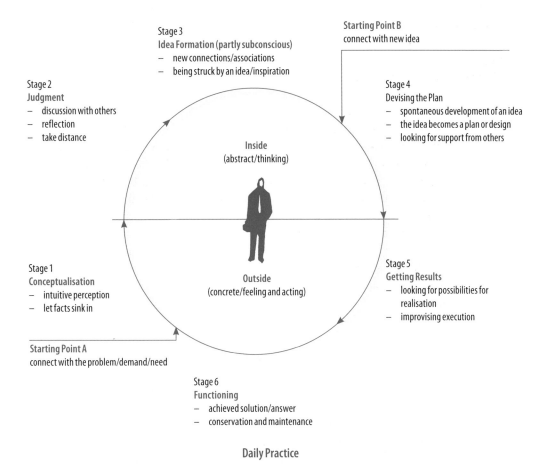

Figure 2.1   Model of the Spontaneous Creative Process

tion of the wheel, then the idea would naturally continue to exist. From this we can deduct that everything that will ever be discovered or developed, exists already as an 'idea' in the world of ideas. We are just not yet aware of them. When a need exists in our daily lives, this creates a space that allows 'fitting' for ideas, in the shape of hunches and intuitions, to fill the void. This process can be stimulated somewhat by using creative techniques. Even if the reader does not share the view presented here, this does not make the practical relevance of the book any less.

In Figure 2.1 the spontaneous creative process (also referred to as the intuitive process) and the different stages that can be distinguished are represented.

In general terms, the spontaneous process all boils down to the following sequence. We are confronted with a situation that we experience as uncomfortable. It affects and preoccupies us (Starting Point A). It appears that at the heart of this situation there is a problem, demand or need which acts upon us and with which we can connect emotionally. We talk about it with others and we ponder the issue. Often, we distance ourselves temporarily from it, or sleep on it, when we cannot yet find a way to resolve it. Sooner or later (often unexpectedly or at night) an idea about what should be done, presents itself. This is usually followed by a release of energy and the development of the idea, largely on the foundation of our intuition. We search for support, often quite naturally, from people who can, and who will, help us. We also start looking for the ways and means to start realising our idea through improvisation and experimentation. The process unfolds naturally, and for the most part, transpires spontaneously, without any conscious guidance.

The cyclical model in Figure 2.1 is a simplified representation of this process. The process starts with a need in daily practice (or inspiration from the world of ideas) and returns with a response to that need. In the meantime, however, time has elapsed, something which is not depicted in the model as it is shown here. To represent the aspect of time, a third dimension should be added to the cyclical model. The circle should really be shown as part of a three-dimensional spiral.

| Excercise | Read the case about how the international seminar developed again and try to distinguish the different abstract stages of the cyclical model described above. |

As mentioned before, projects can also develop from an inner need to realise an idea (starting point B). When this happens, the process does not start with a problem. An artist simply gets an idea, for instance to make a movie or a play. This means that the creative process starts with inspiration from the world of ideas, for example in the form of a mental picture of how the result will appear. This inspiration emerges, because the person concerned is receptive to it. On closer inspection, the inspiration was caused by an association with something in the surrounding area or with an idea in mind, or, all the same, by a confrontation with a need or demand that was important in daily life. Yet, at the crucial moment one was unaware, or perhaps only partially aware of this being the cause. Nevertheless, this association sparked the creative process and resulted in the sudden development of the idea.

2.1.2   *The Spiral-Shaped Development Process*

Interestingly, the result of the international seminar on 'The Managing of International Projects in Art Education,' described above, was the emergence of a new demand. At the end of the seminar the author of this book, who wrote the syllabus for the seminar, was approached by several participants. He was asked to develop the syllabus into a manual for professional management of event projects. The book in front of you now is the result of that request. The publication of that book, in turn, led to a new demand for training courses and workshops on project management. The international seminar itself was also preceded by an initiative. It was conceived during another conference, namely the gathering in Berlin, which was also an event.

Solutions and answers apparently evoke new problems, demands or ideas. This shows that the cyclical process, as it was represented, should really been seen as part of a series of analogous processes. Such a series can be imagined as a spiral-shaped development process, in which after each cycle something new is added or learned. Because of this qualitative improvement through new experiences, the spiral is shaped like 'a snail's shell,' as represented in Figure 2.2. In each cycle the six stages that were mentioned before can be distinguished.

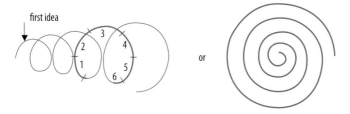

Figure 2.2   The Principle of the Spiral-Shaped Development Process

2.2   A Tailor-Made Approach for Each Problem

Section 2.1 provided an insight into the creative process from which projects can arise. The process can be driven by a problem (Starting Point A) and/or by an idea (Starting Point B). What is being stressed in Section 2.2 is the fact that the problems that confront us at work and in our daily lives are not all of the same nature. For each category of problems, another approach is preferred.

2.2.1   *Problems Connected to the Life-Cycle*

The nature of a problem and, therefore, the preferred approach, is somewhat related to the life-cycle of the product or system (such as an organisation, group, or relationship) the problem is related to.

Every phenomenon, whether it is a human being, a computer, a thought, an organisation, a tree, or an event, passes through different stages during its existence. In the natural world we can distinguish: conception, growth, flourishing, decay and extinction. With respect to intelligent systems a radical 'transformation' can occur during the stage of decay, in which the system radically renews itself, and, thus, saves itself from extinction (for the time being).

The process in which a phenomenon takes a certain form and then, after a while, loses this form again, consists of a number of zones. These zones have the following characteristics (see Figure 2.3):
– Zone 1: Spiritual Zone or Zone of Formlessness (world of ideas);
– Zone 2: Mental Zone (thought);
– Zone 3: Practical or Physical Zone (creation);
– Zone 4: Zone of Manifest Form (the world we live in with all its phenomena)

In Zone 1 the form is only latent, as a subconscious principle or idea. Zone 1 can be compared to the world of ideas that has been described before. In Zone 2 the form appears in our consciousness and becomes somewhat defined. Then, in Zone 3 the form develops into a clear notion, which becomes manifest in Zone 4. Eventually, in the natural course of events, decline will set in. The form starts to show defects, begins to malfunction and embarks on its way back through the zones.

Eventually, there will be a real loss of shape or decay. When a fundamental process of renewal is not started on the foundation of a new idea or principle, then in due course only the outmoded idea will remain, which, after a while, will completely disappear from our consciousness. You could say that the idea slides back into the world of ideas or into the collective unconsciousness. The principle that a needle of a record player produces music, was very special in everyday life a number of years ago, but now we have almost forgotten that principle. Other principles have surplanted this function. Of course, the principle survives as an idea, whether we are aware of it or not.

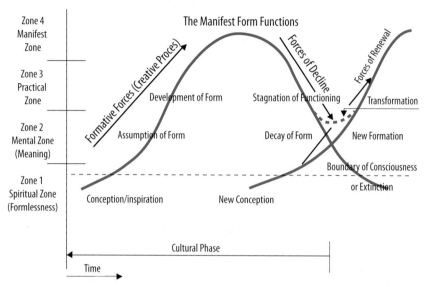

Figure 2.3   The Life Cycle of a Phenomenon

The course of an idea through the zones moves from formlessness to maximal form or structure and subsequently attains maximal functionality. After that, the stability of the form and its functionality gradually starts to decrease. At first, the form can still be salvaged, but when the process continues, the loss of form and functionality becomes unstoppable.

Intelligent systems, such as a relationship, a team, or an organisation, can become aware of this process and transform themselves in time. Transformation implies that a fundamental renewal of form occurs, which in turn means that the system restructures itself on the foundation of a fundamental new idea or principle. Technical systems and pure biological systems are incapable of doing that, and after some time they will ultimately fall apart. Transformation is often accompanied by crises. Old ideas and principles have to be abandoned to be replaced by something radically new, of which we are usually hardly aware, if at all. This creates a great deal of insecurity and confusion and makes it difficult to give up the familiar, even if it is outmoded. The handling of processes of renewal and innovation is a true art and demands a deep insight into the nature of living systems. 'Biomimicry' is an emerging discipline and an ancient concept which has recently returned to scientific thought and it examines nature, its models, systems, processes, and elements- and emulates or takes inspiration from them to solve human problems sustainably.

There is a beautiful quotation by the painter Kandinsky (1942) concerning this ongoing process of creating forms, with respect to an intrinsic quality, but also with regard to the renewal of these forms on the basis of an awareness in which new qualities appear from beneath the surface.

> *Every spiritual age expresses its particular substance in a form that matches that substance exactly. Thus, every age acquires its own true 'physiognomy,' full of power and expression, and, thus, 'yesterday' changes in 'today' on all spiritual levels. Art, however, also exclusively possesses the power already to see in the 'today' the quality of what 'tomorrow' will bring – a creative and prophetic power.*
>
> (Quotation from: *Kandinsky*, Ulrike Becks-Malorny)

The project approach is a way to turn the individual process of creation into something collective.

When we study the history of a project, we can discern the same stages as in the individual creative process. Because of the specific nature of each zone, each stage suffers from its own characteristic problems and demands its own particular approach (See Figure 2.4).

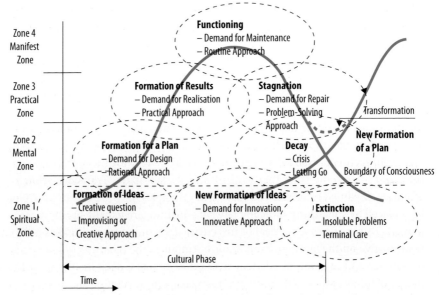

Figure 2.4   *The Nature of Problems during the Life-Cycle of a Product or System*

In the stage of the Formation of Ideas (Go to Stage 3 in the outline represented in Figure 2.1) a new idea will be born either spontaneously, or as a result of a struggle with a problem that calls out for innovation. In both cases, the need to create something new is central. Most of this takes place within Zone 1. The tension between the real situation and the situation we would actually like to have, could be the breeding ground for the creation of a new idea. In this first stage the emphasis is on association, creativity and improvisation. A 'creative question' asks for a creative approach that takes the improvisational character of this phase into account, because it is hard to grasp the implications of the process. The creative process is (partly) hidden from observation. We receive a flash of inspiration, or make a mental leap, seemingly by coincidence. The intuitive or improvisational approach to a creative question belongs to what is known as *heuristic* activities. The creative process, which mainly takes places in the right half of our brain, is difficult to control. In other words, heuristic activities cannot be programmed, but they can be stimulated. Creativity techniques for searching solutions or handling information, based on heuristic activities, are for instance brainstorming and brainwriting, visualisation, synectics, and mind-mapping.

In the stage of the Formation of a Plan we are confronted with 'design questions.' These are situated within Zone 2, the zone in which mental activity is usually predominant. Here we deal with the development and design of an idea that has already emerged. This stage demands a more rational approach, even though a great deal of creativity is still called for. The rational approach moves along a planned route, step by step, towards the objective. This step-by-step method is also known as the *algorithmic* method. it is a rational process, which primarily takes place in the left part of the brain and can be controlled and programmed. It is about the classification of information in a framework, for instance in a phase model or step-by-step plan. Morphological analysis is an instrument that also belongs to this category. Moreover, the project approach central to this book emphasises this path.

With respect to 'questions of realisation' in the stage of the Formation of Results a practical approach is called for, characterised by a great deal of arranging and organising. This stage, in which an idea has already been developed, will have to be realised, and fits within Zone 3. This is called the zone of physical activity, or 'action.' The project approach, the focus of this book, refers to questions within the second and third zone and is, therefore, characterised by a rational and practical approach. By this stage, the idea of the project's end result already exists. The question at hand in the project approach is, for instance: How do we develop and realise the idea of the new attraction, the exhibition, the festival, the film production, the international competition, the course or the building?' But there is also the question: How do we develop and implement the operational schedule or the automation plan in our organisation?'

As shown by Figure 2.4 the stage in which an idea is realised is followed by the stage of functioning, in which the realised product or system will be maintained. This stage is situated in Zone 4, the zone of the manifest, or crystallised, fixed form. At this stage we are confronted with 'maintenance demands.' These can usually be dealt with in a routine fashion, i.e. according to fixed guidelines and procedures.

When a product or system has been operating for some time, sooner or later operational hiccups will set in and 'repair demands' will emerge. Here, the point is to find a solution to a problem that has come up within the existing system. The old situation has to be restored. The underlying principle or idea of the system or product will be preserved, which means that essentially nothing has changed. Therefore, these problems are of the same nature as the problems found within Zone 3 and, usually, amenable to a practical, problem-solving approach, characterised by arranging or organising intervention.

Finally, Figure 2.4 makes it clear that within Zone 1 a certain class of problems remains. These are problems that even fundamental innovation cannot solve, the 'Insoluble Problems.' The product or system is doomed to come to an end, or to fall apart completely. The underlying idea, and therefore the reason, has expired. The old principle can no longer keep up with new developments. Think, for instance, of the earlier example of the record player. It could no longer perform its function, because its underlying principle or idea has been superseded by new developments. The CD-player, based on a new idea, took its place and had its own life-cycle and is being pushed of the market by digital downloading and mp3 devices; see the next 'cultural phase' in Figure 2.4. This principle of decay, which follows from the loss of the reason, does not only apply to technical or inanimate systems, but it also applies to living systems. Take, for example, an organisation which has lost its rationale for existence and has consequently gone bankrupt. In addition, a project team that no longer functions or has accomplished its task, or a relationship between two people that has lost its 'vitality', has returned to the first zone and will soon disappear. This natural phenomenon is very difficult for people to accept and they usually resist it; often without results, because nature has its own dynamics and will not be dictated by human beings. In this case, terminal care is the appropriate line, aimed at a conscientious dismantlement of the system, with respect for what used to be.

Above we saw that problems within the second and third zone (the mental and the physical or practical zone) more or less demand a rational and practical approach, because of their peculiar nature. The concept of a project approach, as it will be presented in Chapter 4, specifically covers these zones and it is derived from these approaches. Therefore, the nature of the rational process will first be highlighted below. Insight into the characteristics of this process is necessary so that it can be consciously controlled (managed).

2.2.2   The Rational Step-by-Step Method

If, within everyday practice, we are confronted with a problem or a question that fits within the second or third zone, and we want to deal with this problem, several steps will have to be taken. What can be helpful in this situation is the step-by-step method, which is based on the rational approach to problems. The rational process stands out from the spontaneously associative and creative process that was described in Section 2.1, because we can exert some conscious influence on the spontaneous process of thoughts. In the rational or systematic process, however, a 'conscious navigator' is added to the spontaneous process. It is has not been left to fate to decide what enters our vision and whether we will develop intuition in order to solve a problem or to see which direction the process should take. Within the systematic approach, steps are taken and choices are made consciously to come to a solution or to realise a product. To be sure, the process can start with a rational analysis, as well as a more associative analysis of the situation in which we are confronted with an idea, question, or problem. For the primarily associative analysis we can use the technique of the *mind-map*.

If we trace the individual rational process of thoughts, we can roughly distinguish the stages represented in Figure 2.5. Figure 2.5 relates to the same process as Figure 2.4, but from a different perspective. Figure 2.5 shows how we, as human beings, monitor the life processes represented in Figure 2.4. The zones mentioned earlier can also be found in Figure 2.5.

Just like every model, the model of the rational process of thoughts is a simplification of living reality. This implies that we have to be conscious of the fact that solutions to the problems within the second and third zone will rarely fit perfectly within the different stages. The decision-making process for these kinds of problems is more like drifting through unknown territory, than walking towards a clear destination. This is because the different steps are in constant interaction with each other, but also because all sorts of non-rational motives play a role in the decision-making process. Nevertheless, the step-by-step method has turned out to be an acceptable tool for the systematic approach to most of the problems found within this category.

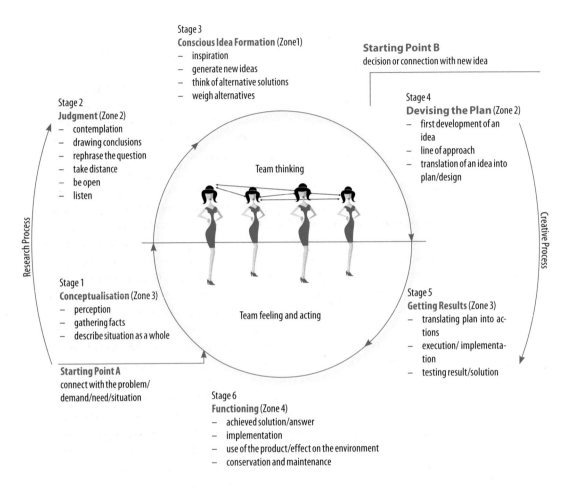

World of Ideas

Stage 3
Conscious Idea Formation (Zone1)
– inspiration
– generate new ideas
– think of alternative solutions
– weigh alternatives

Starting Point B
decision or connection with new idea

Stage 2
Judgment (Zone 2)
– contemplation
– drawing conclusions
– rephrase the question
– take distance
– be open
– listen

Stage 4
Devising the Plan (Zone 2)
– first development of an idea
– line of approach
– translation of an idea into plan/design

Team thinking

Research Process

Creative Process

Stage 1
Conceptualisation (Zone 3)
– perception
– gathering facts
– describe situation as a whole

Team feeling and acting

Stage 5
Getting Results (Zone 3)
– translating plan into actions
– execution/ implementation
– testing result/solution

Starting Point A
connect with the problem/demand/need/situation

Stage 6
Functioning (Zone 4)
– achieved solution/answer
– implementation
– use of the product/effect on the environment
– conservation and maintenance

Daily Practice

Figure 2.5   The Rational Thought Process for the Solution of Problems

We have lived for more than two years in this new neighbourhood and we have only met a few people in our street. (Stage 1. Conceptualisation) Yesterday I was waiting at my daughter's school and started talking to one of the other parents. I noticed that everyone in the neighbourhood still keeps very much to themselves. The others agreed and thought that it was actually a pity. They said that they would like to have more contact with others in their own street or in the neighbourhood. (Stage 2. Judgment) James, Harry's father, who lives at number 76, came up with the idea of organising a neighbourhood party. The others responded very enthusiastically.

(Stage 3. Conscious Idea Formation). James did not lose any time. Before the week was over, we were sitting down at our place with four of the neighbours from our street drinking wine and brainstorming about how the neighbourhood party should be. By the end of the fun evening, we had already decided how the event should look. As a location, the park at the end of the street seemed to be the obvious choice. The second Saturday in June was set as the date. For the youngest children we would have a bouncer, for the somewhat older children we would have a sport event and a lottery, and for the adults we would have a game of skills and volley ball. In addition, we planned to have a barbecue and everyone was supposed to bring their own bottle. Moreover, it was agreed that the costs would be shared among the adults who showed up. (Stage 4. Devising the Plan). On Friday afternoon, 12 June, a section of the park was roped off and preparations were made for holding the sport activities. A few people went shopping for the barbecue. On Saturday morning the bouncer was delivered and blown up, and the barbecue was set up. At one o'clock everything was all set to go, just as planned. (Stage 5. Getting Results). At one thirty, the first neighbours arrived carrying chairs and umbrellas. The party was in full swing. Both young and old had themselves a great time. We spoke to more people then, than we have in the past two years. (Stage 6. Functioning).

Frame 2.2

The project-oriented approach is focused on taking ideas that emerge in our mind in Stage 3 and transforming them into a concrete product that can function in Stage 6. Hence, the project approach can be of service in relation to Stages 4 and 5 of this process. This, again, shows that the project way of working is a way to deploy the individual creative process in order to tackle problems and to design an idea.

In practice, we often see that ideas take shape in companies and institutions long before a project gets on its way. For instance, the policy plan of a theme park will mention that a new attraction will have to be realised in the coming year. In the course of the year a project team will be assigned the task to develop and realise that idea. When this happens, the project team starts with what is known as the 'design question'. The idea of the new attraction, of the opening festivities, or the music festival has often already been conceived and the question that remains is how can it be developed and realised. In this case, what the end result of the project will look like is clear from the start.

In other cases an initiating group or a project team can be presented with a 'creative question'. In contrast to a design question, a creative question does not yet have an idea as to how the problem can be solved, or the area in which an answer can be found. Then, Stage 3, the stage of idea formation, will also become part of the project. Below an example of each of these two types of questions will follow.

A An example of a *creative question*:
   'How can I teach my students how they can deal with problems in practice?'

B An example of a *design question*:
   'How do I structure a workshop aimed at teaching students how to deal with problems in practice?'

The creative question starts with a problem or a vague idea. In short there is no concrete image of the result of the project, yet. The design question starts at a notion of the result of the project, in this case the workshop. So, in the design question we are one stage ahead in the process. We have already brainstormed, mapped all the alternative solutions, and, eventually, chosen the workshop as the best medium. Other alternatives were, for instance: lectures, compulsory reading material, a lab, or an internship with an organiser of events.

When a project starts with a creative question, then the creativity techniques can be useful in the first phase of the project, the so-called initiative phase.

2.2.3   *Thinking from a Market or from a Product Perspective?*

Previously we saw that projects can come into being in different ways. An artist gets an idea and decides he would like to design and realise it, without immediately asking the question who might take an interest in the end product. In most cases, however, projects spring from a certain need that we perceive in our surroundings, for instance with (potential) clients, or they result from a problem that confronts us, or our client.

In the case of the artist we start out from an idea that is turned into a product for which we find a market (client) later. For a long time this product-centred approach also dominated the private industry. Manufacturers designed and produced products that, because of an insatiable demand, would somehow always be purchased in the marketplace. When the supply grew on many different terrains, producers had to start competing for the consumer. They were forced to give up their orientation towards the product and to focus on the market, instead.

Today, a thriving leisure industry is unthinkable without that market-orientated approach, i.e. demand is central: 'What does our (potential) customer want?' In the creative industry, however, there is still a strong urge towards product orientation. A stage director often starts out with an idea of the end product when he works on a theatre production. Artists often resist the notion that the product of their artistic endeavours derives its justification from the functionality of and/or appreciation for that product in the social environment. That appreciation can be expressed by the willingness of the public to watch exactly *that* programme on television, or to buy a ticket for exactly *that* performance, but also by the willingness of the government or the private industry to subsidise or sponsor a certain production. When they have to concern themselves with the social relevance of their product, artists sometimes feel limited in their autonomy and creative freedom. The great risk in taking a market-orientated approach is, indeed, the loss of identity and autonomy. When the activities of a company or institution are completely guided by the wishes of their clients, and they are focused solely on facts such as turnover, high ratings and box office successes, that company or institution could risk losing its identity.

Now the one-sidedness of each approach becomes more clear. With a product orientation, one's identity and autonomy are guaranteed to a maximum degree, but social relevance is minimal. With market orientation, on the other hand, social relevance is ensured, but one's identity and freedom are placed under pressure.

The project approach, as it is presented below, does justice to the identity and freedom of the initiators, but it also assumes that the initiative addresses a social need and is therefore socially relevant. Hence, the method is not aimed at projects that are set up by an individual or group purely to express their own creativity, without any regard for its social relevance. The conclusion that can be drawn from this is that we do not choose one of these approaches, but that we assume a dynamic balance between both orientations.

The project approach starts from the concept of balanced product-market combinations, or PMCs. With this approach an organisational unit, for instance a company, institution, or group, formulates its own identity, ambition *and* the foundation of its existence in a 'mission statement,' which is coupled with an 'image.' The mission statement indicates what the unit wants to achieve and for whom. By doing that, the unit positions itself and distinguishes itself from competitors. In every mission statement two elements can always be distinguished, i.e. a general description of the target groups and a general description of the duties that need to be performed for those target groups. The image, subsequently, tells us something about how a company or institution wants to present itself, in other words, which image a company or institution wants to send out. The mission statement of a centre for visual arts could be:
'We want to preserve and develop the cultural values within the region by being a low threshold centre which
- *capitalises on the need of artists to show their work to the general public and the need of the general public to actively as well as passively participate in art*
- *functions as a meeting place for artists and the general public.'*

The mission is also linked to an image. The choice to have a low threshold shows what kind of message the centre wants to convey.
Not only institutions and companies can state their mission, but also projects that emerge within them and independent projects should formulate a project mission and a project image. The mission of a project is the source as well as the touchstone of all the activities that derive from it.
Within the centre mentioned above, for instance, a project could be developed with the following mission:

'This project wants to organise an art auction in which professional artists from the region can sell appliances made specifically for the occasion, for the benefit of the regional population.'
The image, which tells us something about the feel of the project, can be conveyed as follows:

'The atmosphere of the art auction should be intimate and should appeal to the whole family.'

In practice, sometimes first an idea for a product will surface, after which possible target groups will be sought that might be interested in that product. At other times a need or problem generated by the environment or the market will be the point of departure and a fitting product or answer is sought.

2.2.4   Defining the Starting Question of a Project

If we combine the earlier distinction between creative questions and design questions, with the distinction between a market orientation and a product orientation, we arrive at four different ways in which a project can get started. These starting positions are represented in Figure 2.6.

	1 Project Idea Idea of mine about a product is the point of departure.	**2 Market Project** External problem or question (market) is the point of departure.	**3 Project Assignment** Concrete question posed by customer is the point of departure.
A **Creative Question** (basic shape is not yet clear)	**A2 Product-oriented Creative Question** I have an urge to express something or a vague idea and I am looking for a form to express this. Afterwards, I plan to search for someone who might be interested in the product. (Neither the end result of the project, nor the target group are clear yet).	**A1 Market-Oriented Creative Question** I am faced with a problem or demand in my environment/market and that is why I am looking for a suitable answer or product. (The end result of the project is not yet clear, but the target group is).	**A3 Customer-oriented Creative Question** I am faced with a concrete question from a customer or client, and I am looking for a suitable answer or product. (The end result of the project is not yet clear, but the objective and possible user (target group) is clear).
B **Design Question** (basic shape is clear)	**B2 Product-oriented Design Question** I have a clear idea or concept of the product or end result of the project that I want to carry out. Afterwards, I plan to search for someone who might be interested in the idea. (The end result of the project is clear, but the target group is not yet clear).	**B1 Market-Oriented Design Question** I have a clear idea of the product or end result of the project for that particular problem in my environment that I would like to use to solve it with. (Both the end result of the project and the target group are clear).	**B3 Customer-oriented Design Question** I have a clear idea of the product or the end result of the project that should be achieved in order to solve the question or to meet the client's demand. (Both the project result and the user (target group) are clear).

Figure 2.6   Overview of Starting Positions of a Project

In the first phase of the project approach, which is known as the initiative phase, we will have to keep these different starting positions in mind. If there is clarity about the end result the project will aim for, if we are dealing, in other words, with a design question, we can move directly to the project approach. However, if the start question has all the characteristics of a creative question, i.e. if there is a question but not yet an image of the end result of the project, then a preliminary creative step will precede the rational approach. In that preliminary step an inventory will have to be made of the alternative solutions and one of them will have to be chosen, before the actual project approach can get started. One of the most important criteria that determine whether a job is suitable for a project approach is a clear view of the end result of the project. The end result of a project can be a certain type of event. Before the method of the project approach is presented in Chapter 4, the next chapter will first discuss how the event can be seen as a specific kind of project.

3

The Event

As it was mentioned in the introduction, events are not a new phenomenon. Yet, nowadays, events attract a lot of attention. Every year, hundreds of thousands of revellers descend on fields, parks, beaches and castles all over Europe to sleep in tents, shower in glorified baked bean tins and listen to some of the best known, unknown and most talented artists on the planet, who perform in front of small or huge audiences. They come in all shapes and sizes, from a fair to a World Exhibition, from a pop festival to an experimental theatre performance and from a party for employees to a stockholders' meeting and an international conference. Sometimes the following classification is made in regard to the size of an event:

1 small-scale: up to 500 visitors a day
2 medium-size: around 500-5,000 visitors a day
3 large-scale: more than 5,000 visitors a day
4 mega event: more than one million visitors

When seen from an economic or touristic perspective, events are of great importance. Take, for example, the spin-off produced by a mega event such as the Olympic Games. From a (socio-)cultural perspective events are also of great significance. An event can serve many functions, but it is not the only way to achieve an objective.

3.1 What is an Event?

The dictionary defines an event as an 'occurrence,' but it can also be defined as a 'weighty or remarkable occasion' These are very broad definitions that need to be tailored to our purposes.

One could think of many more definitions to describe the phenomenon of an event. Most of the definitions found in professional literature apply only to a restricted group of events. For example, in a book about business events the following definition can be found:

> An event is an activity of a particular nature where a group of invited guests is present.
>
> (Herlé)

This definition does not cover all events. Public events, for instance, are often open to anyone who wants to attend.

If a book covers events in the field of leisure and tourism, you could come across the following definition:

> A special event is a one-off happening designed to meet specific needs at any given time.
>
> (Wilkinson)

But what about public events that appear periodically in a new edition, such as *the Olympics*, or annual *Summer Festivals*, or the annual sports tournament of a company? Other definitions, still, refer to only a limited category of events, for instance:

> Local community events may be defined as an activity established to involve the local population in a shared experience to their mutual benefits.
>
> (Wilkinson)

This definition only focuses on a specific type of event, which is also true of the following definition:

> Sports events are characterised by an active participation of the spectators in sports, they are heavily focused on exercise, taking the needs and abilities of the participants as the point of departure.

To cover the entire range of events we need to define them broadly. I suggest the following definition:

> *An event is a special occurrence tied to a certain time and place,*
> *consciously planned by an initiator (individual, group, or organi-*
> *sation) and aimed at a certain target group, in order to achieve a*
> *certain objective through consciously selected means.*

Hence, it is not about some ordinary, *accidental* occurrence, but about a special occurrence that has been *planned* by an initiator, because he wants to achieve a (commercial, communicative, idealistic) objective (primarily for a certain target group and/or himself). Attention has also been focused on whether certain means are the most effective way to achieve the objective.

Thus, this broad definition also covers fairs and conferences, in addition to all company and public events. Furthermore, one-off as well as serial events can be found within the definition and also very broad events like multi-faceted happenings (for instance with workshops, expositions, performances, television recordings, etc.) and very specific or singular events.

3.2   Every Objective Requires Its Own Form

Obviously the form of a project assumes depends on its objective. Hence, it is very important to have a clear notion of the objective or mission of a project, before its form is chosen.

In the case described earlier (See Section 2.1) the actual question was: 'How can we make a contribution to an improved exchange of experiences, especially when our EasternEuropean colleagues are involved?' In spontaneous processes sometimes the answer is easy: 'By organising a seminar on the management of international projects in arts education.'

When a response to a question is made too soon, or an all too quick solution to a problem is found, one pitfall might be that alternative solutions and answers, each with their own consequences, are not taken into consideration and compared. As a result, the choice made in regard to a certain form, in this case a seminar, cannot be conclusively argued. A study tour consisting of visits to organisations or the recording and publishing experiences could have provided other solutions to the question posed in this case. Why were these options not chosen?

When the basic form of a project is undetermined, it is of the utmost importance that, before anything else, the central question or problem is formulated clearly. The mission statement will follow from this central question, and will indicate what the project intends to signify and to whom. The mission statement of the project described earlier, for instance, could have been: 'The project seeks to offer a solution for the need to exchange experiences, among our Eastern European colleagues.'

When the mission or objective is formulated in this way, there is still room to weigh and compare different alternatives. An event does not necessarily have to be the outcome of this process. Because this book is about the project management of events, these types of projects will be discussed.

3.2.1 Which Purpose Should the Project Fulfil?

Projects in the field of leisure and culture, such as events, can fulfil many different purposes. Below a number of categories are listed that show what the possible objectives of an event might be. The objectives can range from one hundred per cent commercial to one hundred per cent idealistic, from personal to communal.

Objectives	
Sales	**Communication**
– direct, on-the-spot sales (showroom, gallery, fair)	Increasingly, the purpose of business events is communication, i.e. companies treat events more and more as a marketing tool to get a (commercial) message across to the clients and other relations. An event has, therefore, become part of the communication mix, which is a specific form of advertising, in addition to more traditional media like advertisements, etc. In this respect, events are often seen as three-dimensional communication media.
– establish contact with potential buyers (trade fair)	
Promotion	
– stimulation of purchases and sales (city marketing events)	
– name recognition of the product/service/company (open day, promotion campaign, presentation, festival)	
– acquaintance with new product/company (application for a stock-market quotation, product launch)	**Meeting Place**
– call attention to a certain subject (conference, symposium, event)	– place of orientation for potential buyers (ideal home exhibition, trade fair)

Frame 3.1

Frame 3.1 Continuation

- networking between participants, lobbying and political pressure (contact day)
- exchanging information/experiences between participants (conference)
- discussing pinions/points of view (conference, symposium)
- making contact with relations and (potential) clients, (reception, open day, tour, opening of a building, company anniversary)

Education
- education and development of people (course, seminar, stage/film production, educational attraction)
- transfer of (scientific) knowledge and opinion (study day, publication, conference)
- improve skills (workshop, seminar)
- introduction, exploration, or solution of a problem (work conference)
- study issues (seminar)
- brainstorming and the development of ideas (conference as generator of ideas)
- policymaking (work conference)
- forming or changing of opinion (conference in support of a process of transformation)

- accelerate ongoing or new processes (conference as 'pressure cooker' like the Climate Change Conferences)

Motivation
- motivation of employees (incentives, kick-off meeting at the start of a project or campaign, party for employees, company anniversary, employee sports day)

Information
- transmit or make information available (exposition based on a concept, publication, instruction film/video, conference or lecture, press conference, stockholder's meeting)

Consumption
- entertainment (stage or film production, novel, attraction, game shows)
- pastime (idem)
- relaxation (idem)
- social gathering (reception)

Fund Raising
Many events in the socio-creative industry are planned to raise funds. Take, for example a lottery or jumble sale. Hence, they have a charitable purpose.

Often an event project aims at different target groups (primary target group and secondary target groups) and it might aim to achieve different objectives for each target group. Thus, a conference can primarily be aimed at serving an educational or instructive purpose, but secondarily provide a place for participants to meet. A performance can also be both entertaining and instructive or educational.

In addition to a central objective, events often have desirable or undesirable side effects (spin-off), for instance a festival can have an economic spin-off for hotels, bars and restaurants in a city. Furthermore, events can often provide important tourist-recreational advantages. Think of:

–extension of the traditional tourist season

–dispersal of the tourist demand over a region

–attraction of outside visitors

–creation of a positive image for a particular destination (city marketing)

Only when it has become clear what a project seeks to achieve (mission of a project), alternative solutions can be surveyed.

3.2.2   *Difference between a Public and a Business Event*

If you look at the great variety of events in literature, newspapers, journals, etcetera, a striking distinction can be made between *business events* and *public events*. The first are aimed at achieving a company objective, whereas the second is aimed at more general or idealistic objectives. Increasingly events are seen as an alternative medium to communicate with target groups and relations, especially in the business world. In this context, events, conferences and fairs are sometimes referred to as *three-dimensional communication tools*. In addition to the distinction based on the objective of an event, a certain type of character can also be attributed to an event. Thus, there are group trips for relations with a sports or educational character, parties for employees with a cultural character, or shows with a festive character. The subject of concern in these cases, is the atmosphere, or the 'dressing' that has been poured over the event.

The following are the central characteristics of public and business events:

Public Event	*Business Event*
– focused on the public or general interest	– set up in the company's interest
– usually little influence on who visits	– influence on who visits (through invitation)
– proceeds within the leisure/tourist domain	– proceeds within the business domain
– often originates from an idea	– often originates from a problem or need
– often has an idealistic goal	– often has a direct/indirect commercial goal
– funding often a challenge	– a budget is available

3.2.3 The Consumer Event

In the last years, a hybrid form has developed which is addressed to the general public, but which is nevertheless set up with a business objective in mind. This form is sometimes called the *consumer event*. For instance, a company decides to organise a party for the general public as (potential) clients. Businesses often do this in cooperation with, for example, a broadcasting company. The interested public can buy tickets to such an event, or save bottle caps, or send in a coupon from the newspaper. By staging these events, companies are very interested in the basic data of visitors, such as their names, addresses, email addresses and professions, in order to use it in their own marketing communications.

3.2.4 Choice of Different Types of Events

As mentioned before, there are many different types of events, all with their own atmosphere and character. In each case, there is a temporary and unique occurrence and interaction between organisers and visitors focused on a concrete objective. Another characteristic of an event is that it always occurs in a certain place or in a certain region and at a certain moment, and that it, therefore, demands a temporary organisation tied to a particular area. Sometimes, there is a periodical repetition. Within the framework of this book, stage, film, and television productions are also treated as events. As it happens, these are also focused on the design and development of an idea, followed by its production and resulting in the presentation of a concrete product. Below a more detailed description of different types of events from these two categories can be found. In practice new names for events are frequently coined.

3.2.5 Some Types of Business Events

Business Events – Companies organise events, for instance, to introduce a new product, to start an advertising campaign, to improve the relationship with specific target groups and to pamper regular customers. Often this is a form of relationship marketing. A business event can also start an innovation process within the organisation or celebrate a landmark or an occasion together with the staff and/or regular clients. Some examples of business events are: a business anniversary, a party for the employees, press conference, work conference, stockholders' meeting, incentive, company sports day, product launch, building or company opening, open day, and reception. A business event can also consist of a combination of some of these types of events and it can last for one or more days. Companies can arrange the organisation of an event themselves, but what they usually do is hire an external organisation or production company to carry out the event. Increasingly, production companies in the creative industry take on these types of activities.

Fairs/exhibitions – A fair/exhibition is more or less a static presentation. These are permanent, temporary, or travelling exhibitions, demonstrations and fairs focused on providing information, whether or not it pertains to the use of objects and/or is focused on products. The familiar division is:
- *object-oriented exhibition*: objects are at the centre of attention, with texts that relate only to those objects; an example is an art exhibition
- *concept-oriented exhibition*: the focus is on information, objects are only a means to tell the story, to convey the message, or to highlight a development; an example of this would be an exhibition at a museum of cultural history
- *product-oriented exhibition or fair*: the products/services of one or more companies or institutions are exhibited, often with a commercial goal (sales or promotion); for instance a holiday fair, a gallery or an art fair.

With respect to a product-oriented exhibition or fair a distinction can be made between:
- *trade fair*: this is primarily aimed at professionals, for instance the Prague Quadrennial, an exhibition held every four years on scenography for stage managers in Prague. Within the category of trade fairs another distinction can be made between a *horizontal trade fair* (specialised theme for a broad target group, for instance a fair on professional lighting equipment for institutions and companies, including stage technicians) and a *vertical trade fair* (broad theme and a specialised target group). Exhibitions that accompany a conference are often of the vertical-tradefair type: the theme is often related to the theme of the conference and the visitors are all specialised professionals.
- *public fair*: this can be aimed at the *general public* (for example a holiday fair or an antiques fair), or at a specific public (for instance an art fair for collectors or a phone card fair).

Conferences – The term 'conference' is used generically for gatherings that are presented under different names. Gatherings ranging from small to very large groups of people who, for one or more days, participate in a programme prepared in advance aimed at one or more objectives. A conference is a medium for the exchange of information and for the interaction between providers and consumers of information. Different types of conferences, or names for conferences, are:
- *congress* (gathering for joint deliberation, often on an international level)

- *workshop* (laboratory aimed at learning activities of participants)
- *seminar* (group of initiated people who study a certain topic under supervision)
- *symposium* (academic gathering (usually lasting a day) for the discussion of a certain topic)
- *theme or contact day*

Within conferences a range of other activities can often be distinguished such as lectures, discussions (panel, forum, plenary), work groups, competitions and social activities.

3.2.6   Some Types of Public Events

Cultural programmes – Cultural programmes include activities such as cultural excursions, town walks, boat trips through the city canals, trips to monuments or cities and guided tours through a museum. These kinds of programmes are organised by cultural institutions, but also by regular tour operators or cultural organisation companies. Sometimes these programmes have open registration, but they are often organised especially by commission, for example, on behalf of a company. Sometimes, these types of programmes are also linked to an (international) conference.

Markets – With respect to markets one might think of touristic markets, art markets, folkloric markets, cheese markets or flea markets, fairs and pasar malams.

Attractions – Temporary attractions are often part of an event. The purpose of attractions is generally to entertain people, but they can also be educational. More and more often, museums and visitor's centres are developing educational or cultural attractions. In these cases, the educational objective is the main concern, for instance events such as historical enactments in a museum, an historic fair, an oriental market, or a midnight mass on Christmas Eve. Just like exhibitions, attractions can also be permanent (for example in a theme park).

Performances – The performance as a type of event is characterised by images and appearances of people and groups. Examples are:
- dance and stage productions
- concerts
- film and television productions
- mixed performances

Festivals and folklore – A festival consists of a series of performances, for instance a jazz festival, a street theatre festival, the International Theatre School Festival or a Summer Festival. Folklore refers to, for instance, a naval pageant or folkloristic festivals and sports.

Happenings – A happening is characterised by a mix of different types of events, for instance an exhibition with demonstrations, combined with workshops and performances.

Commemorations – Commemorations refer to such things as centennials and other celebrations of historic significance, such as Liberation Day or the Memorial Service for the 9/11 Fallen NYC Firefighters.

Sports Events – In the field of sports there are also a number of events, such as a tournament, boxing gala, cup final, grand prix and concours hippique. Sometimes the consumer is present as a spectator and in other cases he can even participate himself.

Supporting projects – It happens quite regularly that one event is supported by another event, for instance a lunch concert at a conference, a conference linked to a fair or exhibition, or a press conference at the opening of an exhibition. More and more often exhibitions in a museum are accompanied by supporting projects such as special tours, educational programmes, appraisal days, demonstrations or fashion shows. There are museums where 'special events' are no longer solely used in a supporting capacity, but have become an integrated part of the management policy. This is primarily the case for large institutions with more than just a museological objective, for instance the Centre Pompidou in Paris or the Kunst- und Ausstellungshalle in Bonn.

Moreover, many events are supported by a publication, such as a programme for an exhibition, a catalogue for an art show or a syllabus, a book or reader for a conference.

3.2.7 *An Overview*

To refine the distinctions even further, a more elaborate breakdown of public and business events is provided below.

Public and Business Events	
Public Event	**Business Event**
Cultural Events	Relationship-Enhancing Events
Examples:	*Examples: (customers, employees,*
– Theatre festival	*etcetera)*
– Art exhibition (in a museum)	– Golf clinic
– Music festival (Jazz or Pop Festival)	– Company presentation
– Cultural travel programme	– Skidding course
– Historical tour	– Dinner show
– Tour of a band	– Diving safari
	– Visit to a musical
Sports Events	– Balloon trip
Examples:	– Organised tours for relations
– Sports tournaments (World Cup Foot-ball)	– Party for employees
– Marathon (New York)	Image-Enhancing Event
	Example
Leisure Events	– World Harbour Festival (Rotterdam, The Netherlands)
Examples:	– The Olympics
– Fair	
– Dog show	Conferences
– Boat show (Sail)	*Examples:*
– Dance event	– Conference (one or more days)
– Carnival parade	– Seminar (study and discussion, practical)
– Parade	– Symposium (academic character)
– Dinner show	– Congress (information from experts)
– Happening	– Work conference (as transformation instrument)
Religious Events	
Examples:	Fairs and Exhibitions
– Religious gathering	*Examples:*
– Open-air church service	– Trade fair (events fair)
	– Public fair (holiday fair)
Political Events	– General fair (for business and public)
Examples:	– Road show (travelling fair)
– Demonstration	
– Political happening	
– Meeting of world leaders	

Frame 3.2

Frame 3.2 Continuation

Chance Events

Examples:

- (Royal) burial
- Commemorations (Liberation Day Festival)
- Anniversary celebration

3.3 The Parties Involved

Events are occasions at which an interaction occurs at a certain location between people or groups. For instance, they could be held in a hall or at a square, where amusement, information or products are offered and exchanged for money or a return service.

3.3.1 Primary Parties Involved

The primary parties that are directly involved in an event have been listed in the blue text box below.

Parties involved in an event

The Supplier (of content)

- *An individual or single organisation*, for instance a company, an artist, a speaker, an orchestra (possibly through an intermediary, for instance an agency representing an artist or orchestra)
- *A collective*, for instance a group of manufacturers or importers, a number of cooperating museums for a joint exhibition, or several theatre companies for a co-production

The Consumer/Target Group

- *The primary target group* for instance, the general public, tourists, companies, business guests, school classes, experts, individual visitors, classical music enthusiasts
- *The secondary target group.* Often supporting projects are set up for sub target groups, such as a treasure hunt for children at an exhibition, or a press conference at a happening

Often it is also important to distinguish target groups according to their motivation. Some visitors have a strictly business motive, such as companies, whereas others have an intrinsic motive

Frame 3.3

and still others have a geographical motive, because they live nearby.

The Manager of the Site

For instance the manager of:

- A museum, visitor's centre, convention centre (for an exhibition or happening)
- A stadium, a sports complex or centre (for sports events)
- A theatre, cultural centre, jazz bar, concert hall (for a performance)
- An auditorium or conference centre (for a conference)
- City hall in its capacity of manager of public spaces (for a street theatre festival)

The Client

For instance the management or administration of a museum, a theatre company, sports organisation, cultural centre, company, shopkeepers' association, school. There can be an internal as well as an external client. At events which are the product of the organiser's own initiative the initiator or group of initiators play the role of the client.

The Financier

For instance, the subsidiser, the sponsor, the financial institution, funding. With respect to internal projects a department can be the internal financer.

The Suppliers

This includes everyone who is engaged, in the broadest sense, with the supply of products and/or services for the set-up, development and execution of an event. These are the designers, rental companies, volunteers, etc.

The Stewards on the Ground

The people who are involved in keeping the result of the project functioning and operational, for instance attendants that guard and maintain an exhibition once it has been opened. Often these stewards belong to the organisation of the site manager or the client.

The Indirectly Affected/Interested

For instance the people in the neighbourhood who might possibly be inconvenienced and the press interested in publicising information about the event.

In the real world many of these parties overlap, for instance the financier can also be the client. Or the consumer is sometimes also the future steward.

3.3.2 Who Takes the Initiative?

Events can be initiated and organised by one of the parties listed above, but also by an independent party. Several examples of these initiators follow below:

Initiators

The Directly Interested Parties
- *An individual or single organisation* that has a direct interest in the event, for instance a company or institution, a pressure group, an artist, a theatre company takes the initiative to organise an event all by itself
- *A collective*; for instance a trade organisation or a shopkeepers' association takes the initiative to organise an exhibition, a show or a fair

The party directly interested in an event is not always the party providing it. A small business association can take the initiative to organise a street-theatre festival, for instance, to promote their own shopping centre. In this case the artists are the providers.

The Manager of the Location
- For the administration of its primary task; for instance, a theatre puts on a stage production or a museum organises a temporary exhibition
- To support its own primary task; for instance a nightclub hires an artist to give a performance or a library takes the initiative to organise an exhibition on the art of printing

The Independent Organiser of Events
- *An intermediary*; for instance an agency, booking office or manager of an artist takes the initiative to organise performances by an artist, band or theatre troupe
- *An organisation company for events*; a company that organises conferences or concerts such as LiveNation concerts
- *A production company*; for instance, Endemol also produces television programmes and other events on their own initiative

Frame 3.4

Sometimes it cannot unequivocally be determined in which category the initiator or organiser belongs. It is also possible that the initiative has been taken by a party that is directly interested, while the organisation itself has been contracted to an independent organiser. Some examples are:
- A company wants to organise festivities to accompany the opening of a new branch, and contracts the organisation to a production company for events.
- A pop group wants to give a concert or go on tour, but leaves the organisation to an agent or a concert organiser.
- A broadcasting company wants to produce a documentary, but contracts the project to a production company.

Evidently, for an event to be successful, effective communication between the parties mentioned above is of paramount importance. The independent organiser of events will have to communicate intensely with all the parties involved. If the client or the location manager organises the event himself, the external communication will be limited to the two other parties. But then there will often be internal communication with supporters and colleagues, instead. Not only the content, but also the tone and form of the communication will be different depending on the particular target group addressed.

3.3.3   The Events Chart

The complete scope of an event is difficult to define, because so many parties from different trades participate in an event. For instance, artists from the cultural and/or the entertainment industry can arrange a performance on the occasion of an international conference for doctors (medical industry). This all takes place on a ship of a shipping company (transport industry), while the dinner is prepared by a catering company (catering industry). In Figure 3.1 the events chart is depicted. All the possible parties surrounding the independent events organiser, within the scope of an event, are represented in this chart.

3.4   An Event as a Project

As stated before, at the moment events are receiving a great deal of attention. In museums this can vary from taxation days, fashion shows, workshops and concerts to complete festivals. In the summer months it is hard to keep up with all the happenings and festivals in cities of any great size. And, in a endless flow of brochures and advertisements it is suggested that those who do not attend educational conferences, congresses, seminars and workshops, will be at a disadvantage. More and more people are being confronted with the setting-up and organising events.

As previously mentioned, all the events that have been referred to before can be viewed as projects, because they are restricted to a certain time span and place and because they lead to a concrete result. In principle, any event can be handled with a project approach. The *project-management concept*, as it will be presented in Chapter 4, will offer something to hold on to. Just like any project, when organising events it is of utmost importance to formulate very clearly and from the start what the basic assumptions and conditions are for the particular event. These form the foundation for the management of the whole process.

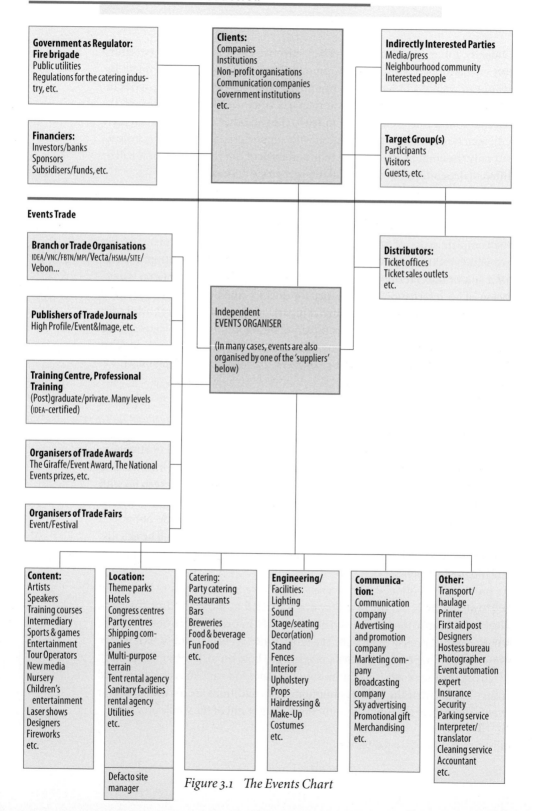

Government as Regulator:
Fire brigade
Public utilities
Regulations for the catering indus-
try, etc.

Clients:
Companies
Institutions
Non-profit organisations
Communication companies
Government institutions
etc.

Indirectly Interested Parties
Media/press
Neighbourhood community
Interested people

Financiers:
Investors/banks
Sponsors
Subsidisers/funds, etc.

Target Group(s)
Participants
Visitors
Guests, etc.

Events Trade

Branch or Trade Organisations
IDEA/VNC/FBTN/MPI/Vecta/HSMA/SITE/
Vebon...

Distributors:
Ticket offices
Ticket sales outlets
etc.

Publishers of Trade Journals
High Profile/Event&Image, etc.

Independent
EVENTS ORGANISER

(In many cases, events are also
organised by one of the 'suppliers'
below)

Training Centre, Professional
Training
(Post)graduate/private. Many levels
(IDEA-certified)

Organisers of Trade Awards
The Giraffe/Event Award, The National
Events prizes, etc.

Organisers of Trade Fairs
Event/Festival

Content:
Artists
Speakers
Training courses
Intermediary
Sports & games
Entertainment
Tour Operators
New media
Nursery
Children's
   entertainment
Laser shows
Designers
Fireworks
etc.

Location:
Theme parks
Hotels
Congress centres
Party centres
Shipping com-
panies
Multi-purpose
terrain
Tent rental agency
Sanitary facilities
rental agency
Utilities
etc.

Catering:
Party catering
Restaurants
Bars
Breweries
Food & beverage
Fun Food
etc.

Engineering/
Facilities:
Lighting
Sound
Stage/seating
Decor(ation)
Stand
Fences
Interior
Upholstery
Props
Hairdressing &
Make-Up
Costumes
etc.

Communica-
tion:
Communication
company
Advertising
and promotion
company
Marketing com-
pany
Broadcasting
company
Sky advertising
Promotional gift
Merchandising
etc.

Other:
Transport/
haulage
Printer
First aid post
Designers
Hostess bureau
Photographer
Event automation
expert
Insurance
Security
Parking service
Interpreter/
translator
Cleaning service
Accountant
etc.

Defacto site
manager

Figure 3.1   The Events Chart

That is why it is advisable to write an initiative report (also known as a project proposal) for every project, whether or not the project is to be managed professionally or not. The *general step-by-step plan for the initial phase* in Chapter 5.1 can serve as an important tool to accomplishing this.

3.4.1   When Do You Use a Project to Manage an Event?

As stated in the quotation by Kandinsky in Chapter 2, the creative process can take two paths, namely the path of improvisation and the path of composition. The project approach highlighted in this book is a tool for event projects that are achieved through composition, hence through consciously planned creation.

To call something a project is not the same as handling something as a project. For, once the decision has been made to tackle a certain job by setting up a project, this entails that a temporary organisation will have to be set up especially for this purpose. Before something is treated as a project, one has to consider the question whether the job needs to be handled as a project, and whether the job cannot be dealt with in another way, for instance by improvisation. See also the considerations in Section 2.2 on this topic. With respect to the grounds for handling a job as an actual project, the following characteristics of a project play an important role:

- It has a definable beginning and end.
- It is unique, i.e. it contains many new elements.
- It is a once-only occurrence.
- It is result-oriented.
- It is multi-disciplinary (often also involving people from outside one's own company).
- It is organisationally complex.
- It is uncertain.
- It can be managed centrally (management).
- There is one client, internally (usually management board) or externally.

When an initiative or idea conforms to most of these characteristics, it is expedient to consider actually handling the project as a professional project. This is, among other things, due to the risk of a transgression of preconditions (budget, deadline) or a failure of the project.

3.4.2   The Project Category

To what degree an event can be handled as a professional project is also determined by the category it falls into.

Besides being distinguished by their objective, for instance commercial or charitable projects (and thus including events) can be distinguished according to their degree of uniqueness. Is it truly a new design or is it an arrangement of existing, or previously designed components? Event organisers often provide made-to-measure solutions, but that does not always mean that it involves an entirely new concept. A bespoke weekend outing for employees, for instance, can consist of a treasure hunt, a survival course, a balloon ride, a dinner and/or a big party. The overall concept is made to measure, but the components often already exist and have been bought.

Finally, a distinction should be made between projects that are developed on commission for a third party and projects that are developed for the market.

Each category of project demands its own approach. Sometimes the emphasis is on developing the intrinsic concept, while with another project the emphasis is on developing a product that generates profits. In yet another project, commissioned by a client, the fine-tuning with the client can demand a lot of attention. When setting up an (event) project the person responsible for the project should always be aware of this distinction and of the implications of a certain

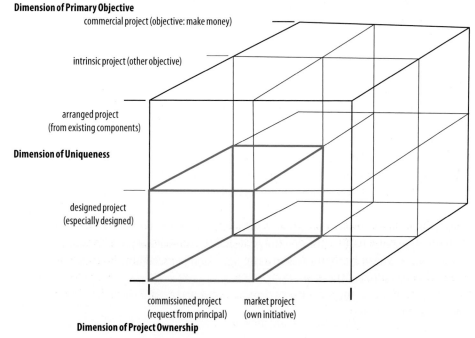

Figure 3.2   Project Categories in the Cube of Verhaar

type of project might have in regard to the terms and conditions that have been recorded in the project proposal or initiative report.

The project categories mentioned above have been represented schematically in the Cube of Verhaar, as represented in Figure 3.2.

An event which is organised to celebrate the three-hundred-year anniversary of a university, for instance, is a combination of: intrinsic project, designed project and commissioned project. Rather than a day for the employees that can be assembled from existing elements, such a project demands a thorough project approach because of its intrinsic objective, its uniqueness and its organisation on commission.

3.4.3 *The Advantages and Disadvantages of the Use of Projects*

With respect to the use of projects a number of advantages and disadvantages can be listed.

Advantages:
- Flexibility (as opposed to the routine approach; the routine approach is characterised by rigidity/unwieldiness/little innovative capacity)
- Decisiveness
- Purpose (as opposed to an improvised approach)
- Innovative

Disadvantages:
- Many things have to be developed and set up especially for the project; hence, this sometimes makes the project approach inefficient and, consequently more expensive
- There are fewer learning effects within project organisations
- It is more difficult for people to work on a focused career track
- Working in projects is complex and relatively risky

Often there is no choice. These disadvantages primarily concern the, by definition one-off character of a project. A building, film production or festival simply is a one-time-only affair. When there is a choice, moreover, the environment often forces the organisation to conduct its regular activities in the form of a project; because the advantages mentioned above are very beneficial in a turbulent environment.

In the next chapter the frame of thought which can help structure and manage the project development process will be elaborated.

Excercise   In preparation for the next chapter we recommend that you answer the following questions.

1   Imagine that you will be graduating this year from college and that you and a number of college friends have decided not to let this occasion pass unnoticed, but to celebrate it in grand fashion.

Brainstorm the possibilities that are open to you to do something on this occasion.

2   Subsequently, map what that would involve, again by brainstorming.
3   Try to structure the unstructured package of activities into clusters of similar activities.
4   Which phases can you distinguish from now until the moment when it is all over?
5   What are the characteristics of each phase?
6   What are some of the points that you need to keep in check so that the 'project' does not get out of control?

The Concept of Project Management

In general, management relates to controlling processes within organisations. This could involve production and sales processes, but also financial, communication and personnel processes.

Besides directing the collaborative process between all the parties involved, the manager or leader of a project also controls the functional processes within the project. Thus, he guides the development process from idea to result, but he is also responsible for making this happen within the terms set in regard to time, money, etc. Moreover, he also gives shape to the decision-making process.

In other words, project management is meant to guide the creative process completely, from the first formation of ideas up to the realisation of the final product, including possible aftercare. Because projects often involve complex processes, in which several parties are involved and in which many aspects interact, we have to look for a way to make this complexity manageable for the project leader. This is what is known as the structuring of the project process.

As a first step in structuring the project, it is often wise to look which, more or less natural, milestones can be distinguished during the process. By using these milestones the process can be divided into phases. This makes interim adjustment possible on the basis of the results obtained from each phase.

As a second step in the structuring of the project process, it is recommended that the different tracks and aspects within the process are distinguished which will play a role from the beginning to the end. This applies, for instance, to the aspects of 'money' and 'communication.' In this chapter a concept is developed on the foundation of the structuring of an (event) project according to these two steps. In short: if you visualise the project process as a thick arrow leading from the idea to the result, you can structure the process by cutting the arrow into both horizontal and vertical sections. In other words, you can distinguish phases (at right angles with the arrow) and tracks (lengthways with the arrow). The concept that has been developed here should be regarded as an aid and not as a straitjacket. The user of this book will always have to take his own practical situation as the point of departure. Sometimes the nature of the project, or the specific situation in which the project is realised, demands other ways of structuring.

4.1   The Basic Shape of the Concept

Within the project process, first of all, four functional tracks or sub-processes are distinguished.

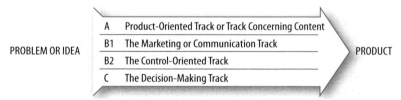

PROBLEM OR IDEA	A	Product-Oriented Track or Track Concerning Content	PRODUCT
	B1	The Marketing or Communication Track	
	B2	The Control-Oriented Track	
	C	The Decision-Making Track	

Figure 4.1   The four functional tracks of the project

A   *The Product Track or Content Track* – embraces all those activities that have to be performed in order to realise the concrete product, for instance an exhibition. Hence, it is concerned with aspects, relating to content, with respect to the collection as well as the production of the exhibition. Whenever cultural projects are involved, such as a theatre or film production, in which the artistic aspect is of central importance, this process is divided into an artistic track and a production track (for technical and organisational activities).

Within the product track, sub-projects can sometimes be distinguished that result in more or less independent sub-results that form an integral part of the end result of the project. Here, one might think of, for instance, an exhibition, performance, workshop or closing festivity as part of a larger cultural event. Furthermore, there could be supporting projects. These are not an integral part of the main result of the project. Here, one might imagine, for instance, a video recording of a theatre production, a catalogue for an exhibition, or a making-of video of a film production.

B1 *The Marketing or Communication Track* – When an exhibition is involved, all of the activities should be focused on the fine-tuning of the project to the environment.The communicative process is concerned with the marketing and promotional activities, polls reflecting the public opinion, fundraising and sponsoring activities, but also the acquisition of the necessary permits.

B2 *The Control Track* – The control track is concerned with the control of six aspects within the project approach, namely Quality, Organisation, Facilities, Time, Information, Money, which can be abbreviated as QOFTIM.

C *The Decision-Making Track* – The decision-making process ensures that in each phase decisions are made concerning the possible options and consequences.

4.2   Foundation of the project management concept

The tracks or processes described above make up the concept of project management. This forms the foundation of the project approach. One of the characteristics of a systematic approach used with a project is its organisation into phases. All the activities within the processes mentioned above are carried out more or less in a phased way, depending on the situation, for the purpose of control (management). Another characteristic of the project approach is that during the transition from each phase to the next a decision moment is included. This is the moment when permission is granted by a higher authority (for instance the client) to move on to the next phase on the basis of the phase results that have been obtained (frequently presented in the form of a report, also known as a decision document).

The listed processes form 'the four tracks' of the main activities of the project approach, which are carried out in a phased manner.

The basic model of the systematic or project approach is schematically represented in Figure 4.2. Below the four main activities that correspond to the concept of project management will be elaborated upon. The stages in the model (formation of ideas, formation of a plan, formation of results and performance) refer to the corresponding stages of the process represented in Figure 4.1.

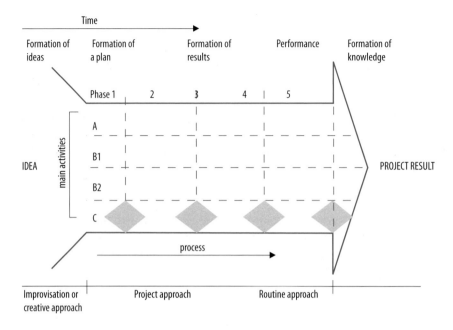

Figure 4.2   The Basic Shape of the Project Management Concept

4.3   The Product Track

We have seen that 'project' can mean many different things, for instance the design and construction of a house or the development of a conference, the organisation of an exhibition or the setting up of a public event or festival.

The Phased Management of the Product Track
In order to be able to control (manage) a project well, the route that leads to the result of the project is phased. This means that all product activities, i.e. activities that are necessary to achieve the result, are divided into logical steps. In each phase, the product activities will result in an interim phase result that can be checked against the terms and conditions that have been established in the previous phase (for instance by the client). These evaluations of the result in each phase make it possible to make intermediate adjustments. Each approved phase (by the means of a decision document) is the point of departure for the next phase.

In Figure 4.3 the project track is represented as a cyclical process. The project track is divided into a number of phases. The rational thought process, discussed earlier, forms the foundation for the process of a project. The phases of the project process, however, are not completely synchronous with the stages of the rational thought process. If the project track is followed to the end, then, after the evaluation phase, we will have gained some new experiences, on which we can develop new ideas. Hence, the project track can be seen as a development or learning process and can be represented as a spiral-shaped snail's shell.

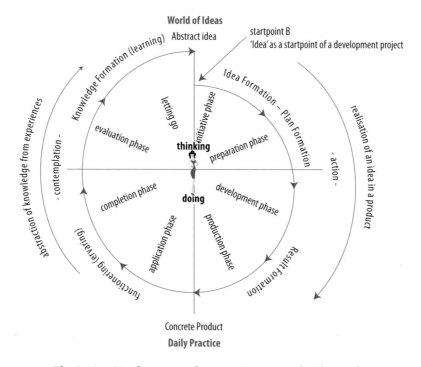

Figure 4.3   *The Project Track as a Development Process in the Shape of a Snail's Shell*

The project phases will be explained below, including a description of the phase result with which the phase can be concluded. The names used in the different phases of the project are general, and, therefore, apply as much as possible to different types of projects. Naturally, for specific projects, one can deviate from this. In some cases it might also be sensible to merge certain phases together or, indeed, to split up a phase even further. In the B-Appendices different phase models for different events projects have been included, as a type of checklist.

4.3.1   Initiative Phase

The initiative phase consists of the start-up of the project and establishes the basic assumptions and preconditions. The foundations are laid for a possible project approach. The intention is that at the end of the initiative phase all the participants will have a similar image of the project's end result and approach, and these will have been assessed by the client. This means that, among other things, it has been determined what significance the result of the project should have and for whom. The *objectives with regard to content* have to be formulated, the *target group* of the project has to be determined, and the *image* that the target group should have of the project has to be determined in the project mission and the project image. A formulation which includes all these elements is, for instance: 'This project intends to disseminate information about drug use to young people between the age of twelve and eighteen in a light-hearted manner.' Moreover, we need to know which product must be realised in order to achieve this. Therefore, the *basic concept* should be developed in this phase. The different alternative solutions or forms of projects, that qualify for the achievement of the objective or solution of the problem, need to be evaluated. In the example above the transferral of information can take place in the form of a publication, a course, an exhibition, a public event, or a lecture. From these a reasoned choice must be made. If the desired form of the project is a public event, for instance, it can include an exhibition. The overall programme of the public event needs to take shape in this phase and, in this case, it constitutes the basic concept of the project.

What is also important is that one knows within which set of *preconditions* the project needs to be realised. Here, you might think of the budget, the time available, the demands with respect to the facilities (such as location, housing, means of production and other arrangements) or the set-up of the project's organisation. Finally, one has to determine for whom the communication should primarily be aimed at and for what purpose. For instance, is it aimed at the government to gain a project subsidy for the exhibition, at young people as the target group to excite them about the event, or at the media to lend publicity to the event. Subsequently, a determination can be made for each target group with which message it should be approached. Together, these descriptions are the *communication strategy*. The distinguishing project mission and project image become the foundation of the communication strategy. For this, see Chapter 11 *Project Marketing and Communication*.

To illustrate, what the initial phase leads to, a comparison will be made with a project everyone can relate to, namely the building of a house. For such a project, the consultant or architect must present a list of demands and a first sketch of the house to the client, at the end of the initiative phase. For an event this would be called the basic concept. This is the *product information*. Also, a first overall estimate of the expenses will be provided and an indication of the possible building time. Moreover the client will receive some information about the organisational set-up within which the project will be realised, then technical advisers will be hired and later a contractor, etc. This is the information about the *control aspects*. The architect will also indicate that there will have to be communication with the local government to secure building permits. And, possibly, advice is also given about who could help to finance everything. This is the information about the *communication aspects*.

The initiative phase can be seen as the most important phase in the process, the foundation of the project is laid. In this phase *conceptual thought* is central and basic assumptions and preconditions are set. Also, when a professional approach to projects, according to the described model is not chosen for the remainder of the project, it is, nevertheless, strongly advised to formulate an *initiative report* (sometimes also called a project proposal) in which the results of this phase are summed up (See model in Appendix C1). When a project has a client, then the definitive commission can be provided on the initiative report / project proposal. The requirements for an initiative report in this case are provided in Section 5.1. When a project does not have a client outside the project team, it is still necessary to formulate unequivocally what the basic assumptions and preconditions are for each of the parties involved.

For extensive projects it might be advisable to split up the initiative phase even further into two sub-phases, namely the orientation phase and the definition phase. For projects which, for example, still need to seek financial backing, an intermediate step follows the initiative phase in which the feasibility, or the financial possibilities are investigated. Sometimes the initiative report mentions other necessary preconditions, beside financing. The survival of the project might also depend on, for instance, whether or not a certain location is available, or a certain permit. All these aspects can be researched in this intermediate phase, also known as the finance or feasibility phase. When the financial backing has been secured to a reasonable degree and, if necessary, all the other 'critical' preconditions have been met, the preparation phase can begin. For the initiative phase an elaborate, general step-by-step plan has been provided in Appendix C1.

4.3.2   *Preparation Phase*

Once the project has been commissioned based on the initiative report, the preparation phase, and the project can really get on its way. The general, basic concept which was developed in the previous phase will be developed into a plan or design in this phase. For complicated projects, a *framework for analysis* could first possibly be drawn up, which shows how the different parts of the project's result are cohesive. The detailed table of contents of a publication is an example of such a framework for analysis; it is a refinement of the basic concept (comparable to a general table of contents). A framework for analysis can also provide an overview in which is shown how, for instance, the themes of an exhibition or a film production (the story line), or the components of a public event or a conference (the line-up) cohere. On the foundation of the framework for analysis, the content is developed into detail, i.e. a design or plan is made for the project result. Sometimes it can be put into words, in other cases it might be better to visualise the design. With this plan or design, it becomes clear how the project result will appear. Beside a detailed programme of, for instance, the public event, all the components of the programme or sub-projects are described extensively. What is important here, is that there is an elaboration of the 'rough outline' of the initial phase.

The results of the preparation phase are summarised in the *project plan* (See Section 5.2 and Appendix C2). Within the project plan, not only the plan or design, but also their consequences will be developed further and compared to the preconditions, which have been established at the end of the previous phase (for instance by the client). Within the preparation phase the communication strategy, which was formulated in the initiative phase, will have to be developed into a *communication plan*, including a possible *fundraising plan*, both of which are part of the project plan. In this there are indications of how, and by which means, the strategy will be executed, for instance by making the public aware of the project through posters and advertisements. For further information, see: Chapter 11, *Project Marketing and Communication*.

If we apply the same example of the building process here, then at the end of the preparation phase the list of demands and the first sketch from the initiative phase will have been transformed into a final design for the house, with exact measurements, etc. It is not yet clear how, and with what materials, the house will be built, however. That will be placed on the agenda in the development phase.

When very complex projects are involved, it is perhaps desirable to split the preparation phase into a number of sub-phases, for instance the research phase (for the benefit of, for example, historic research for an exhibition) and the planning and design phase.

4.3.3   Development Phase

The development phase is an intermediate phase, which is necessary to translate the plan or design developed in the preparation phase into practical instructions for the people that are responsible for its production or realisation. At the end of the development phase all the definitive choices have been made. The project plan from the previous phase has been translated, technically, and developed, in detail, to such a degree that it can be carried out right away, possibly by another team (implementation team). All the production data are recorded in the *production schedule* (See Section 5.3 and Appendix C3). In the production schedule of, for instance, a festival, or a conference, a plan will have to be included for the production phase and, possibly, also a first draft of the plan for the conference or festival itself (the performance phase) and sometimes even a plan for the completion and aftercare. Moreover, floor plans and other production data are also part of the production schedule.

Just as in the example regarding the building of a house, this phase concerns the specifications and the working drawings. In these, there are precise descriptions and plans showing the way the house designed in the previous phase will be built, and which materials and tools will be used. At the end of the development phase, the fundamental go/no-go decision is usually made. After this decision has been made, the plug of the project can no longer be pulled without suffering great financial consequences, a breach of contract and significant image damage. Sometimes this moment occurs even earlier. This phase, too, can be divided further into sub-phases, if the need arises, for instance into a kind of specification phase and a commission phase, just like in a building project.

4.3.4   Execution Phase

The Execution Phase of an events project consists out of three sub-phases:

* The Construction/ Building (Production phase)
* The Event itself (Operational phase)
* The Wrap-up/ Disassembly

The Construction
In the example of the house-building project, this phase is about the actual building of the house. In the case of a stage production, the repetitions take place in this phase and the set is built up; in the case of an exhibition project, the exhibition is really set up; in the case of a festival the location is prepared; and in the case of a conference project, the physical preparation of the confer-

ence takes place, such as the printing of the syllabus or the preparation of the hall for the reception of the participants. When the production phase is completed, the product or the result of the project has been realised. Everything is ready for use, ready to function, or ready to be presented (depending on the type of product). For the benefit of the performance or application phase an *operational programme* is drawn up. This programme includes instructions and guidelines for the use, the functioning or actual performance and the possible maintenance of the product during the period of use. The operational programme is therefore a user's manual. The operational programme for an exhibition, for instance, contains instructions for the guides, but also instructions for the control and maintenance of the exhibition during the opening period. In some cases, for instance at an exhibition, the production phase is divided into several sub-phases, i.e. the (pre-)construction phase and the set-up phase.

Performance Phase

At the end of the performance or application phase, when all goes well, the application or presentation of the product has proceeded as was originally planned. This is the phase of the actual festival, public event or conference. For exhibitions and fairs it is the opening phase and for a stage or film production it is the phase when the product runs. In the case referring to the building project from earlier examples this is the phase of use, which could last up to 50 years or even longer. With such highly durable products, naturally the performance phase is no longer included in the life-span of the project. Also in this phase, it might be advisable in some cases to distinguish smaller sub-phases, like the application phase, the play phase, or the conference itself and the disassembly phase (disassembling of the exhibition, cleaning up and aftercare at a fair or conference).

Disassembly phase

In the hours and days after the event everything has to be disassembled, broken down, transported back to suppliers or stored and the location has to be cleaned.

4.3.5   Completion Phase

When the event has taken place and everything is cleaned up, some issues still need to be addressed. Such as sending out thank-you notes to sponsors, volunteers or speakers, producing the definitive Financial statement and the evaluation of the project.

At the end of every stage an intermediate evaluation has taken place. On the foundation of the decision document, in the form of the phase results, adjustments were possible. Each project, however, should also be concluded with a final evaluation. Here, the items that are checked for are, among other things:

a The target group (has it been reached?)
b The result or product (does it function, or has it functioned as was intended, in other words, did the product deliver the desired effect?)
c The method used (did the approach meet the demands?)
d The control aspects (did the activities concerning control, such as planning, budgeting and organising, lead to a situation in which the budget was not overrun, the deadlines were met, and everyone fulfilled their tasks and responsibilities, did the quality of the project meet the criteria of the client?)
e the cooperation between the people involved.

The evaluation yields experiential data for the next projects. This last phase is concluded by an evaluation report. This is also the moment in which a *blueprint* can be made of the project process, which can possibly be used as a manual for the next occasions. In this way the cyclical path of the project through the snail's shell (See Figure 4.3) has been completed and the experiences gained can be used to start new projects.

4.4   The Marketing and Communication Track

After discussing the content aspects of a project and the organisation into the phases above, we now turn to a brief description of the marketing and communication track.
Every organisation, whether it is a permanent organisation or whether it works as a project organisation, satisfies the needs or solves the problems for other people or groups outside of the organisation. Every organisation's right to exist, therefore, is anchored in its environment. To become attuned to the environment, organisations make use of (marketing) communication.

4.4.1   *Communicate: Why, With Whom and About What?*

An organisation needs to secure public support in its environment. On the foundation of that fact, an organisation can formulate its own mission statement. Through its mission statement the organisation can indicate what it represents and for whom it is important. Through the mission statement the organisation positions itself in its environment, i.e. the permanent organisation distinguishes itself from other companies and institutions, or the project distinguishes itself from other projects.

The mission and core value (of a project or a company) is the most essential part, or the core, of every organisation.

Communicative activities arise from the necessary adjustment of any organisation, hence also a project organisation, to its environment (which could include one's own permanent organisation). It is therefore about *external* communication. Concerning this issue, there are great uncertainties at the start of a project. Is the project result indeed interesting enough and will it sell, what image will the environment have of the project and how will the environment respond to the project, what effect will the publicity have, etc.? In order to influence this, the communication will also have to be managed (guided).

After a company or project has positioned itself with respect to *content* through a mission statement, the question can be posed: 'Which perception or image do we want the environment and the client to have of our company or product (stressing the distinctive features and core values)?' In other words, what is our image or the character of the company or project and how can we bring this image across? This is sometimes also referred to as *image*-positioning.

For the communication function of a company or project the following questions are important: Do we know our client? What is the profile of the client or the target group, what does their purchasing and consumption behaviour look like? Is he satisfied with our product, with the pricing and with our service? Does our promotion of the company or product reach the potential client, and if not, which means can we put to use to improve this aspect? What is implicit in the communication function, moreover, is the need to take care of public relations (PR), and to be alert to opportunities and threats to one's own organisation and products as a result of external developments. This marketing and communication function, as mentioned before, applies to both the permanent and the project organisation.

4.4.2   *The Marketing and Communication Track at an Event*

Many events have to be introduced into the market, just like any other product. When this is necessary a systematic marketing approach can be applied. At public events, such as an exhibition, conference, or a stage production, several additional communicative activities will also take place.

When an event project is developed within an organisation or company, sometimes *market research* or *market exploration* has been done before the start of the project. A demand or need already exists, or one assumes that it exists. On the foundation of this a concept for the product is developed.

The project has to be positioned, as a first step in the development track of an event project. Three fundamental questions are central, namely:

1 *How do we want to position the content of the project?* In other words, what does this project seek to signify and to whom? We do this by formulating a mission statement for the project, with which the project distinguishes itself from other projects.

2 *How do social groups and the possible financier/subsidiser see the project?* The issue here is *legitimation*. In other words, to what extent does our project fit with the policy of the government and with social issues?

3 *What character do we choose for the project?* In other words, how do we want the client to perceive the product/project, how do we want to come across? We do this by describing the image of the event, as a result of which it will be distinguished in more detail. This is sometimes also referred to as *image positioning* or *stressing distinctive features*.

When, on the positioning of the project, a basic concept is developed, this will subsequently have to be tested by means of a SWOT-analysis.

The next step in the marketing and communication track is that a communication strategy will have to be set up. Two questions are important, namely:

1 *With whom (communication target group) do we communicate for what purpose/effect (communication objective)?* This is also referred to as the communication *field*.

2 *How do we want to communicate the product or project result?* In other words, which message will we come out with, to reach the communication objectives with the relevant communication target groups?

After ascertaining the communication *strategy,* a marketing plan (for market projects), communication *plan* and possibly a fundraising plan (including sponsoring) is developed.

The marketing plan indicates how the project result is going to be introduced onto the market. For this the Marketing Mix (5 or 7 P's) is used. Of course, when it concerns a party for employees this does not apply.

The communication plan is a further elaboration of the communication strategy. The important question here is: In what way, and with which communication instruments, do we want to execute our communication strategy, in other words communicate with the target groups? For this, we make use of the instruments from what is called the *communication mix* (consisting of: advertising, public relations, promotion, direct marketing, personal approach).

The fundraising plan states in how the fundraising/sponsoring is going to be tackled.

When the communication plan and the fundraising plan have been framed, then the communication *action* plan and the fundraising *action* plan need to be formulated and executed. In these plans, it will be indicated *who* will execute *which* concrete promotion, public relations and fundraising activities, *when* and *how* (means).

The last step in the communication track often involves taking an evaluative public poll. The purpose of such a poll is to find out, afterwards, what the customer thought of the product, price, etc.

The remaining activities related to the communication track (for which a separate action plan is usually produced) are the organisation of the opening ceremony, the opening night, press conferences, press releases, sponsor deals, media partners, service to the client/user/visitor (among other things, dealing with complaints).

With the integral project management concept, the steps discussed above are mainly integrated into the project phases.

In Chapter 11 *Project Marketing and Communication* the steps of the marketing and communication track mentioned above will be discussed in detail.

4.5   The Control-Oriented Track

The control-oriented track is concerned with the six control aspects, namely Quality, Organisation, Facilities, Time, Information and Money, which form the acronym QOFTIM, making it easy to remember.

Carrying out of projects is often accompanied by great uncertainties. Many questions cannot be answered at the start of a project. How much is the project going to cost? How much profit will we make? Is the project feasible? How will it be funded? Are the necessary people and means available (on time)? Will the project be completed on time? Is there a suitable venue? Will we be able to achieve the quality demanded?

4.5.1   *The control cycle*

The principle of controlling something, whether it involves money, time, or something else is simple. Just as in the development process, for example, of a building or an event, the control process is cyclical. A number of steps can be distinguished in this cyclical process, see Figure 4.4 below.

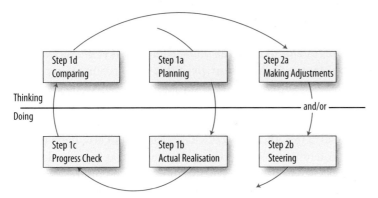

Figure 4.4   The control cycle, applicable to each control process

Below the steps in the figure above are described briefly.

Planning: this entails the points of departure or standards that are established *Step 1a* at the beginning of the control process, for each of the six control aspects mentioned, for example in the form of a control aspect budget, or a deadline (Control Aspect Time), all of this possibly including the necessary margins.

Actual Realisation: during the activities of the ongoing project, time is expend- *Step 1b* ed, money is spent, quality is achieved, teams are formed, etc.

Progress Check: in this case the measurable facts are monitored. This check pro- *Step 1c* ceeds with the use of the norms, points of departure and preconditions which were established earlier in Step 1. Planning which has been used as a gauge. When deviations are detected in regard to one or more of the control aspects an analysis will have to be made to find out what the cause is. On the basis of these conclusions, a decision will have to be made as to whether the execution needs to be adjusted or the planning needs to be adapted.

Comparing: that is that during and after the completion of each phase, the re- *Step 1d* sults that have been obtained up until now in regard to the control aspects are checked. In this way the progress of the work can be monitored (Control Aspect Time), but also the process of costs and profits should be closely checked (Control Aspect Finance) and the cooperation should regularly be evaluated (Control Aspect Organisation).

Making Adjustments: this involves adjusting the norms and preconditions *Step 2a* which were established during the first step Planning (Step 1). This could entail, for example, that cuts in the budget will have to be made, or that the deadline will have to be extended in the time schedule or the quality norms will need to be adjusted.

Steering: it might be decided to maintain the norms, but to steer how the pro- *Step 2b* ject is carried out. It might also be decided, for example, to hire more people in order to meet still the deadline that was originally set.

4.5.2 The six control aspects (QOFTIM)

At the beginning of the project, it should be agreed who will be authorised to adjust the standards and/or to make the actual adjustments at the various levels. In many cases, those who have been given this responsibility to report to the project leader.

It will have become clear that the six control aspects are linked very closely to one another and when monitoring and steering one of the control aspects, the consequences for all of the others aspects will need to be checked. If, for example a deadline threatens to not be met (Control Aspect Time), it can be decided to hire more people (Control Aspect Organisation), which however can have consequences on the budget (Control Aspect Money). In addition, it might also be decided to solve the timing problem by making a concession in regard to for instance, the level of performance (Control Aspect Quality).

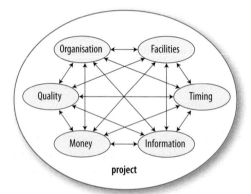

Figure 4.5   None of the six control aspects can stand alone (Remember them as QOFTIM).

Below the *control objective* is described for each controlling aspect.

Quality control is intended to make sure that:
– The quality level of the product or result being developed can be controlled intermediately, for instance by establishing quality norms or quality procedures, at the start of the project, for the assessment of the quality.
– All project activities are executed in accordance with the objective.
– The quality of the end product lives up to the quality standards set by the customer/client, possibly through intermediate adjustment.
– The necessary manpower and means are available.

Organisational Control is intended to make sure that:

- Everyone knows in each phase what his or her tasks, responsibilities and powers are, for instance by establishing the organisational set-up of the project. Often it is necessary to adjust the set-up of the project organisation for each phase, because new disciplines are constantly added or dropped; especially when many volunteers are used, and there is a high turnover (See Chapter 7 for the project organisation).
- The communication and cooperation between the people connected with the project runs smoothly, for instance by setting up a proper structure for consultation.
- The product of the project can be turned over to the initiator, user, or client; this refers to for instance the organisation of the premiere of a stage or film production, the opening of a fair or exhibition, or the completion of a (building) project.
- The personal leadership of the project leader is effective.

Control of facilities is intended to make sure that:

- The standards for the facilities are clearly formulated.
- There will be a venue or location available on time, which lives up to the standards formulated, including the necessary connections, permits, insurances, etc.
- All the other facilities necessary for the realisation of the project result are available on time, for instance technical equipment, catering, surveillance, cleaning, transport and waste collection. For this necessary inventories are made, quotes are requested, and contracts are looked into.
- The relevant legal preconditions are charted (think, for instance, of copyright etc.).
- The necessary permits are available on time and all the legal conditions have been met (take, for example, a licence to sell spirits, a licence that complies to Safety Measures, etc.).
- All the necessary financial means and manpower is available.

Time control is intended to make sure that:

- The progress of project activities are monitored, for instance by time planning, scripts and 'to do' lists and by regularly holding meetings about the progress. In Chapter 10 there is a description of how a time planning can be set up; this chapter provides an example of a script.
- The project result can be delivered on time or can function on time, possibly through intermediate adjustment.
- The necessary capabilities (people, money, space, and means) are available.

Information control is intended to make sure that:
- The correct project information is at the right place, at the right time.
- The project activities are executed in an unambiguous manner and the project result is always formulated unambiguously.
- Guidelines are formulated for internal project information. Among other things, these serve to record the intermediate results of the project coherently in reports and to approve of decision documents according to previously made arrangements.
- The decisive documents, reports of meetings and other carriers of information are available at the right time and at the place and that it is always clear which ones are most up to date.
- The distribution of the information carriers has been arranged. The internet provides possibilities to streamline the internal dissemination of information.
- It is clear by whom and in which way documents can be changed.
- The necessary legal documents (think of contracts/terms of delivery/legal procedures and regulations etc.) are drawn up.

Information control applies particularly to projects of a more complex nature with extensive flows of information. Complex projects generate enormous quantities of information. The need for (central) distribution of, among other things, reports, guidelines, frameworks, norms, procedures, checklists and plans, is often expressed by a cluttered pile of paperwork.

Financial control is intended to make sure that:
- An estimate of the expenses of the project is transformed into a budget. In Section 8.1 there are descriptions of how estimates and budgets can be set up.
- The development of the expenses during the process can be monitored, by making a new budget after every phase and by setting up budgetary control systems. In Section 8.3 budget control is discussed (See also Appendix A2).
- The expenses of the project will remain within the budget and/or supplementary financing is organised, possibly through intermediate adjustment.
- The planned revenue/financing for the covering of the expenses of the project are reached (See Chapter 9).
- The planned level of output of the end product is reached (if so desired).

4.6 The Decision-Making Track

The end of each phase of a project is marked by a *moment of decision*. At every moment of decision, depending on the situation, a decision document can be drawn up as the result of the phase in question. It should be clear that when the decision to proceed to the next phase can be taken by the project team itself, less attention has to be paid to the writing of a decision document, than when the decision has to be made by the board or an external client.

4.6.1 *For each decisive moment a decision document*

The three real decision documents are respectively, the initiative report (also referred to as the project proposal), the project plan, the production programme (also referred to as the performance programme). At the end of the production phase, there is still the operationalisation programme to be set up and then to wrap up the project an evaluation report is also made, including the financial closing statement.

Each decision document consists of five parts
Part one contains the core data of the project. Part two provides a description of the product of the project, as far as it has been developed at that moment (project content). As the project draws near to completion, the description will become more concrete. The third part is a description of the project trajectory and the project approach, which includes all the activities that still need to be undertaken to realise the product. For the next phase the description is detailed, but for later phases it is more general. In the production phase of for instance a festival, this description can take the form of a scenario (See the example in Section 10.2). In the fourth part, this is followed by a description of the communicative plans as they have developed up to that point and of the communicative activities that still needs to be completed. These are also detailed for the next phase, but they are more general in the next phases. It involves not only all of the the public-oriented and client-oriented activities, but also the activities aimed at sponsors, funds and subsidisers. In the fifth and last part, the control plans are presented for each of the control aspects Quality, Organisation, Facilities, Time, Information and Money (QOFTIM). In these control plans, for each control aspect a standard is provided for the next phase. For instance, for the aspect of time a time schedule is given, for the aspect of money an approved estimate or budget is included, and for the aspect of organisation, the organisation chart or the assignment of tasks is shown. Here, also, everything is worked out in detail for the next phase, and more general descriptions follow

for the next phases. Next to the standard for each controlling aspect, the control activities are described that still need to be undertaken in the control plans. Thus, it will have to be made clear who (in what way, with which frequency, and with what means) is responsible for checking the progress and who is entitled to make the actual adjustments.

In Appendix C extensive models have been included for the project proposal, the project plan and the production programme. In the step-by-step plans for an event and a conference, which are described in Chapters 5 and 6, the purpose and content of the first three decision documents are examined. Often, after each phase, the interim phase result is sent to the client.

This is often the board of directors of one's own company, but it can also be an external client. Sometimes, the client delegates the authority to the project leader to make the decision himself, at the end of a phase and within agreed upon parameters, on whether or not to proceed. The arrangement could be, for instance, that feedback will only be submitted when the set margins are exceeded, or only just before the production phase sets in. This is sometimes referred to as the 'go/no-go' moment, because it is the last moment that the project can be stopped without major consequences. These are agreements that have to be explicitly stated in the briefing of the project to avoid misunderstandings. If the project leader himself determines whether or not the project will proceed to the next phase, there will be less of a decision moment during the transition to the next phase. In that case the phases will succeed each other more naturally.

4.7 The Detailed Project Management Concept

In Section 4.2 the basics of the project management concept was presented. This shows that the project result is realised by a process which consists out of four tracks or constituent processes. For the intermediate control of these processes, it was organised into phases. In the succeeding sections the four tracks of the project process, the four main activities, were elaborated upon. If we integrate these elaborations in the previous pages into the basic form of the project management concept, as represented in Figure 4.2, then we arrive at the detailed model in Figure 4.6.

The project management concept represented here forms the core of this book. In the chapters that follow, different parts will be elaborated upon and explained. The phase models included in the B-Appendices of this book are also based on the structure of this project management concept and can be used as checklists for concrete projects.

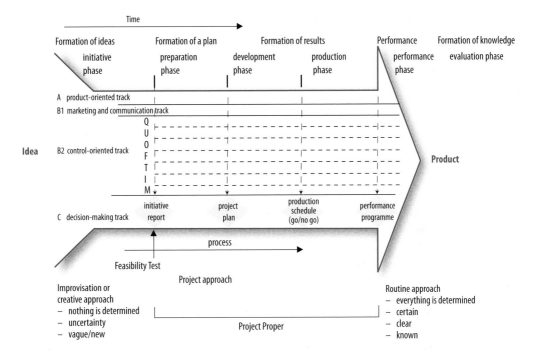

Figure 4.6   The Detailed Project Management Concept for an Events Project

Here, we want to repeat my warning from the introduction to this chapter one more time.

Use the project management concept presented here as something to hold on to, but not as a straitjacket. Have the courage to adjust it to your specific practical situation when necessary.

Part II
Getting started

The Application

The Wrong Table

Organising is planning in detail, but sometimes the effect is lost, because the guests do not always let themselves be controlled. P.A: 'That was the case during an award show, a few years ago. Fireworks were still very popular then, and immediately after the announcement of the winner, the spotlights would zoom in on the winning table, where a pyrotechnic tour de force would put the winner in the limelight. Everything was carefully directed and timed, only the winner did not cooperate. Just like some other people he moved tables just before the Grande Finale, as a result the fireworks were completely ineffective!'

Sprinkler System

We will stay with the fire theme a little longer. 'During a gala occasion a managing director would be presented in spectacular fashion: he would walk through a row of flaming torches,' says H.K. 'After a few rehearsals the producer decided that everything could be done more spectacularly. She wanted more fire. During the gala presentation that led to such heavy smoke that the sprinkler system was activated and everybody got their suits wet.'

Not Everything Can be Rehearsed

Some things are difficult to rehearse. 'During the presentation of the eight-colour press of Sens our hostesses were supposed to go around with champagne,' says G. V. 'However, the introductory magician's act was concluded with such a bang, that our hostesses dropped all their trays with champagne glasses. When the curtain came up, there stood the new colour press with around it a ring of pieces of glass and a pool of champagne.'

The Limit of 45 Minutes

Machinery that is acting up can often give rise to exciting moments during an event. P.A.: 'We once experienced that the tank installation with 5000 litres of beer broke down just before the reception! To play for time we had the band play some music already, while we speedily got some beer barrels from the building next door. We managed to solve the problem in 45 minutes and that was right on time. The limit is 45 minutes, any longer and the guests will notice.' R.S. confirms this. 'As long as you stay polite and explain the guests in a friendly way, you can hold out for 45 minutes; after that it has to be solved.'

It is Better to Rehearse

However, final rehearsals can also prevent bloopers. D.L.: 'For the presentation of a new accommodation with cold stores for a supplier to supermarkets, we had imagined our hostesses would appear from one of the cold stores on the supreme moment. It was, of course, important that they did not stay there for too long and, therefore, we checked the length of the speech. On the day of the opening things threatened to go wrong, anyway, because it turned out that the ladies' glasses fogged up as they left the cold store, as a result of which they could not see anything. We solved this by only using ladies who did not wear glasses for this component.'

(From *High Profile Events*, revised by the author)

5

Step-by-step plan for an event project

This chapter can be used as a practical guideline for the thematic development of an event. As described in Chapters 3 and 4, the transition from one phase to the next is marked by a decision *moment*. Each decision *moment* requires a decision *document*. This document should discuss all of the results from the previous phase.

An events project usually involves decision documents such as the *project proposal* which presents the basic concept, the *project plan* which presents a *detailed intrinsic plan* or design, and a production programme which presents the production data and the scenarios for its implementation. These three documents are drawn up upon completion of, respectively, *the initiative phase, the preparation phase, and the implementation phase.*

This chapter contains step-by-step plans for drawing up the decision documents of an events project. The step-by-step plan provides a format for each of the three decision documents. Use these documents in a flexible way and always gear the content, form and tone of each decision document to its purpose. For instance, a bank may place entirely different demands on your project proposal than a client, sponsor, or co-producer.

The step-by-step plan for an events project described below is based on the project management concept found in Chapter 4. The basic pattern of the arrow in

Figure 4.3 has been placed into phase models depicting the various production phases (See Appendix B). The step-by-step plan of this chapter elaborates the *Festival and Public Event Phase Model (See Appendix B3)*. *The* step-by-step plan for the developmental process of an events project includes five phases:

1 the initiative phase
2 the preparatory phase
3 the development phase
4 the execution phase, consisting of:
   – the build-up (production phase);
   – the event itself (working phase);
   – the disassembly
5 the completion phase.

The step-by-step plan described below lists the activities required per phase thematically to develop the event from the initial concept to the actual product.

If your study programme requires that you develop an event, then the step-by-step plan found in this chapter will be ideal for carrying out such an assignment. This step-by-step plan can be used as a guideline for setting up an events project. A step-by-step plan is a model; it portrays a neat linear course through the process. In reality, it will be much more capricious and the steps will not always be consecutive. Still, experience has taught us that a step-by-step plan can serve as a sound foundation (especially if one has little experience), provided that the plan is not adhered to too rigidly. First read the step-by-step plan before using it.

In order to help you get into the right mindset, each phase has been preceded by a short case related to that phase. A fairly traditional event is used as an example for the cases in this chapter. In order to show the many new possibilities the media has at its disposal, Chapter 6 describes a less traditional project, namely, a teleconference.

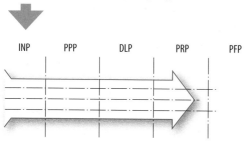

5.1 Step-by-step plan for the initiative phase (including project proposal)

The Application

'Last year in September I started my Higher Vocational Training programme Media & Entertainment Management. The entire first year I had been looking forward to my second-year traineeship. Three weeks ago it was time to start. We could sign up for a trainee assignment. I joined a group of five students who had accepted an assignment involving the development of an event for a medium-sized municipality in the *Randstad*[1]. In various housing estates within this municipality tension has erupted between immigrant youth and Dutch youths. The municipality believes that an event geared towards young people might work to ease the tension between the various groups. In the first week, an intake was held with the head of the Communication Department who will be our client and who is also the councillor for Sports and Youth Affairs. During this intake, we tried to find out what might be the main objective of the event and what the scope of the project was. The councillor proposed using *discrimination* as a central theme. It was clear that the event was to be aimed at youth from the age of 16 to 25 years old and that there is a budget of 28,000 euros available from funding for youth works. The intake was very elucidating and immediately after the meeting we set out all intrinsic starting points and preconditions. The next day, we did some brainstorming about the mission of the project. *Playfully, the event aims to make people aged between 16 and 25 years of different backgrounds aware that the differences between people contribute to the cultural wealth of a community.* Of course, this mission had to be expanded, for instance by dividing the target group into various subgroups, because it is useful to offer each subgroup a different programme. After this, the best part came for me: brainstorming

---

1   A densely populated Dutch urban area in the west of the country

with each other about ideas for the event. We came up with a whole list of options, but we had to be critical and select only ideas that contributed to the objective. Eventually, we were very satisfied with the basic concept. It is a mix of concerts to be held on two open-air podiums, workshops, forum discussions, and a quiz. For now, the event is planned to take place during the weekend of 16 and 17 May. We defined requirements for the venue and both the *Noorderpark* and the recreational park just outside the built-up area meet these requirements. The working title is: '1World'. We are now drawing up all the ideas in a project proposal, which has to be presented to the client in a week's time. The cost estimate and its accompanying financing scheme are almost ready. It is assumed that a sum of approximately 10,000 euros will be received from subsidies and sponsors. A bit high, but we have to meet our cost estimate. Today, I formulated the communication strategy which includes the fundraising strategy. Furthermore, we have to make an overall time planning for the course of the project and a plan of approach should make clear that the event is going to be tackled thematically. This will make it clear to the client that the interim results will be presented in a decision document after each phase so that he can give the 'green light' for the next phase. The project proposal must be presented orally. According to the client, the councillor and two other officials will be attending the meeting. It will be very exciting for us to present the proposal. We are hoping they will accept our cost estimate, but they should definitely be enthusiastic about the basic concept.'

The more fundamental decisions for the events project are made during the initiative phase. At the end of this first phase, everyone knows what the outline or basic concept of the event will be, for whom it is intended (the target groups) and *which effect* or *purpose* it is supposed to have (intrinsic goal). It is also clear what the channels of communication are and what should be discussed. The *commercial consequences* such as the budget, available time, requirements of the facilities (such as location, accommodation, production means, and other provisions), or the setup for a project organisation, are also clear. Finally, everything is put into a *project proposal* (or initiative report). This first *decision document* contains all of the *starting points and preconditions* to monitor the progress that has been made. On the foundation of the project proposal, the client can decide whether they wish to proceed with the project. If this is the case, it can function as the foundation for a project assignment. Even if the project proposal is not adapted, it can still prove useful when applying for a subsidy or a sponsor. Therefore, project programmes at institutes of higher education sometimes call the project proposal a *starting document*.

In practice, the project proposal is often drawn up by an initiator who acts as the project manager in a later stage, but sometimes the preliminaries are carried out by an initiator *group*. In higher education, a starting document is often drawn up by the student team, which then further develops (and possibly even implements) the project.

When an events project is being developed on someone's 'own initiative' or when it is a relatively simple project, it is useful to draw up a project proposal. It is always important to record all of the starting points and preconditions in advance so that they are clear to all parties involved.

First reread the general description of the initiative phase in Section 4.3.1. The initiative phase is of such a general nature that this step-by-step plan can be used as a guideline for all kinds of projects.

During the initiating phase of an events project, the following steps can be distinguished which all lead to a project proposal (see Appendix B3):
– Step 0: Project-Start-Up (PSU)
– Step 1: exploring the assignment or the idea
– Step 2: formulating the central question
– Step 3: defining the intrinsic starting points
– Step 4: developing a basic concept
– Step 5: drawing up a plan of approach
– Step 6: gearing to the market and surroundings
– Step 7: reflection on the business preconditions
– Step 8: drawing up the project proposal.

The step-by-step plan described in this section can serve as a checklist when creating a solid foundation for an events project.

Step 0
5.1.1   Project Start-Up

When dealing with large developmental projects involving several disciplines (including events projects), it is recommended to delineate the start of the project with a Project Start-Up (PSU). The PSU is a meeting during which members of the project team and other interested parties discuss their insights, expectations, and interests related to the project. Moreover, a PSU meeting can be used to create support for the project when external participants and stakeholders are involved, such as future clients and users, or (political) decision makers. In practice, a PSU meeting is often organised when the project has actually started. This does not take place until the project proposal has been approved of by the client at the start of the preparation phase, which is when the project team often meets for the first time.

When dealing with very large projects, a PSU meeting is organised at the start of each phase, when other people and parties become involved whose commitment is necessary.

When educational projects are to be carried out by a student team, it is advisable to set up a first meeting with the team as a PSU meeting. This usually takes place at the start of the initiative phase, immediately after the assignment has been given. During this first meeting, a discussion can be held about how to interpret the assignment. Moreover, you can exchange expectations relating to the project and the mutual cooperation, and you can also put agreements into writing (See Frame 5.1). In addition, the tasks can be divided up among the project team. A learning project, for instance, would consist of roles such as project manager, project secretary, financial expert, marketing manager, editor-in-chief, team builder, etc.

Example list of cooperation agreements

- The communication is open and honest
- We listen to each other's opinions
- The more quiet people are also given space to talk
- We respect each other's experience
- Irritations are openly discussed through honest feedback
- Everyone is on time for appointments
- Cancellations are relayed in time
- Meetings end on time
- Everyone participates in the meetings
- Consensus is strived for in the decision-making process
- We take turns taking the minutes
- Mobile telephones are switched off during meetings
- Contact with the client takes place via the project manager
- There is sufficient opportunity for informal contacts
- After each phase, the functioning of the team is evaluated and honest feedback is exchanged among team members
- Everyone is personally responsible for adhering to these cooperation agreements
- Each team member explicitly commits him or herself to the project assignment and the cooperation agreements
- Each team member addresses another team member if he or she shows insufficient *commitment*
- A team can warn a team member or remove someone from the team altogether.

Frame 5.1

Step 1   5.1.2   *Exploring the assignment or the idea*

Usually, an events project starts with a *question* or a vague *idea* that requires further exploration. An initiator may have the following idea: to organise an event that playfully introduces immigrant youth and Dutch youth to each other's way of life and their own cultural environment, or an initiator might organise a regional sporting tournament. A client may also provide a question or assignment, such as to propose an event for the launch of a new product. Or he or she might develop a proposal for a demonstration to introduce the public at large to the possibilities of new media.

Whether it is your own idea or the client's idea, the first step involves the project manager or the initiator group starting the assignment or project idea.

Step 1a Starting situation

Exercise Define the state of affairs. What kind of project is this?

First check whether this is a *development project.* In other words, did it start with an idea or suggestion which you and your client wish to accomplish? After all, this step-by-step plan only applies to these kinds of projects. If it is not an idea, but a problem or a symptom of a problem, then that should provide the foundation for the project. There often is a phase prior to the development project. This is the phase of a *survey/advice project. Working thematically* also describes a step-by-step plan for this category.

Then look to see which category this events project falls under (See Figure 3.2):
– Is it a *design project* (an exclusive design for this specific project) or is it a *composition project* (composed of existing components you can buy)?
– Is it a *commercial project* (primarily meant to make a profit) or an *idealistic project* (with a non-commercial, but intrinsic goal)?
– Is it an *assignment* project (for instance, for a learning project from an educational programme or a trainee company) or a project of your *own initiative?*

The starting situation of a project determines its approach. It is advised to first read Section 2.2 before proceeding. Look at the starting situation listed in Figure 2.6: how would you define your events project?
– Market-oriented creation question (A1)
– Product-oriented creation question (A2)
– Market-oriented design question (B1)
– Product-oriented design question (B2)

Situation analysis   *Step 1b*

Analyse the starting situation of the events project and become acquainted with   **Exercise**
the background of the project and the assignment or the project idea.

This step largely boils down to conducting research and describing the direct
reason for this project and carrying out a situation or question analysis. The
following assignment might be for you to develop an event to mark the opening of a new head office. This means you will have to learn about what is being
opened. What is the history of the company? What is its mission and what kind
of image does the company have? What are its main PMCs (product/market
combinations), etc.?

The questions below may help you to analyse the starting situation for your
events project:
- What is the reason for or the preamble to the project?
- What does the client wish to achieve through the events project?
- What is the idea or question?
- Who will benefit from the project being carried out (known users, an anon-
  ymous target group, or other stakeholders)?
- If the events project must solve an existing problem, is it a matter known to
  anyone else?
- Are there or have there been any other parties dealing with the matter?
- Does the problem or matter call for decision-making?
- Is the problem important enough to tackle?
- Is there any relationship with other upcoming issues/problems? What is the
  cause of the problem?
- Are we capable of tackling the problem/issue ourselves?
- Are there any main issues and/or partial issues or questions to be distin-
  guished?
- Does everyone see the same problem/issue?
- Are any of the parties involved '(company) blind'?
- How does the organisational setting of the project look, what department/
  company/branch are we dealing with?
- What is the relationship, if any, with the company mission or policy?
- Are there any cooperation partners?
- Does the project relate to other projects?
- Should the project (possibly as part of other projects) contribute to a higher
  cause?
- Who is going to be the contact person for the project manager?

– Is this contact person authorised as a client?
– How unique, large, or risky is the project? This question is also relevant in determining the degree in which the project must be tackled professionally (See Section 3.4).

Other methods that can be applied in a *situation analysis, or problem exploration,* are for instance:

- *First analysis on the basis of the six questions by Kipling (what, where, when, why, who, and how) It should be observed that these questions must pertain to the assignment or the idea, not the end product (i.e., the event itself).*
- The *mindmap technique*: this is a creative technique for mapping out all of the factors that may have to do with achieving the idea.
- The *preliminary survey*: for instance, when it is a creation question (See Section 2.6), when no decision has been made about the form, it may be necessary to conduct an *intrinsic* preliminary survey. Think about the question or the idea, talk to others about it and start reading about it.

If the above analysis leaves any questions unanswered, it is often advisable to obtain supplementary information via an *intake* with the client.

When you have enough information, you have to ask yourself one last question at this stage: is this question suitable for me (us) or should someone else resolve this matter? If the answer to this question is yes, you can proceed with the following steps so as to conclude this phase with a sound project proposal.

Step 2

5.1.3 Formulating the central question

The previous step has clarified the situation in which the question or the idea presented by the client or you as an initiator plays a role. Step 2 involves 'formulating the central question' and consists of two parts. First, define what you or the client wish to achieve by carrying out the project (*objective* or the 'why' of the project). Then, formulate how the *starting question* or the *assignment* to the project team or client will be defined (*central question* or assignment, the 'what' of the project).

Step 2a Objective of the client or initiator

Exercise Concisely and clearly define what the client (or you as an initiator) wishes to achieve by holding the event or which problem should be solved.

Suppose that the government finds that young people below the age of sixteen are drinking more and more alcohol and that this can seriously damage their health and they feel something should be done about it. Or suppose that the figures showing how many participants attended an event held every other year have dropped, and that the organisers would like to raise these figures to what they were before. Or suppose that a producer of mildly alcoholic drinks wishes to launch a new product for the target group 'youths'. Or suppose that you are a student who is enthusiastic about parapsychology and New Age ideas and who regularly muses: "Wouldn't it be great if the public at large could learn more about these exciting subjects?"

In these kinds of situations, it is clear which problem should be solved (objective) or what the client or initiator really wishes to accomplish by holding the events project.

Central question (or assignment) for provider or project team	*Step 2b*
Concisely and clearly define the starting question of the events project.	Exercise

Assuming the objective has been defined in Step 2a, what might the assignment be or what might be the starting question of the events project? The starting question or assignment is the actual starting point for the provider or the project team.

In addition to an assignment for an event, the client may also seek other means for accomplishing their objective. For instance, in addition to an event for making youths aware of the harmful effects of alcohol at a young age, the government could set up a media campaign, publish a booklet, or organise a conference.

Below are a few examples of a starting question or assignment for an events project, including an indication of the question type from Figure 2.4:

- Develop a proposal for an event during which the public at large can be introduced to the possibilities of new media (*creation question*);
- To what extent does the existing concept of the Prague Quadrennial *(PQ)* match the new situation (*innovation issue*)?
- How can a playful event be organised to bring to the youth's attention the hazards of alcohol intake (*design issue*)?
- Is it possible to organise an event that contributes to reducing in the increasing problem of burn-out among young people (*design issue*)?
- Present a proposal for an event launching our new mildly alcoholic drink among the target group 'youth' (*design issue*).

With projects that are developed for a particular *anonymous* target group, it is not enough to just know the client's objective because you are dealing with idealistic and commercial *public events*, such as setting up a street theatre festival, developing a musical production or organising a contractor's fair. In this case, it is also important to consider what the target group or any subsidising parties or sponsors might like to see or experience. In the case of public events, therefore, there are some intermediary steps that need to be taken (See Steps 3a, 3b and 3c).

Step 3

5.1.4 Defining the intrinsic starting points

The previous steps have made it clear why the event is being set up and how the assignment or *central question* has been defined by the provider or the project team.

In Step 3, you are going to translate the assignment or central question into the *intrinsic starting points* for the events project: goals and target group, but also the ambiance, the delineation of the project and any supplemental criteria.

Step 3a Project mission (for public events only)

Exercise On the basis of the starting question or assignment, define the *project mission:* what is the events project supposed to signify and for whom is it intended (project positioning)?

As mentioned before, in the case of public events, not only does the client's objective determine the project result, but the target group's objectives also determine the project result, possibly even more so.

The project mission is about what people expect from the event in relationship to the central question. In other words, how will this project answer the starting question? By defining the mission, the event is positioned (intrinsic positioning). The mission answers the question: for whom will the project (result) be meaningful and how? In addition, the first parameters of the project will be set accordingly, i.e., determining what the project will be and what it will not be. As a result, everyone will know what can be expected from the project. The project mission must be defined concisely.

Examples of missions related to the central questions from Step 2:

– A large-scale event, in which the leading media companies are to participate, thus introducing the public at large to the latest developments in new media.

- The project is going to perform an integrated screening and provide advice on the concept of the event for the management of the Prague Quadrennial.
- The project is going to develop and implement the idea of a street theatre festival, aimed at the city centre's residents and the shopping public.
- The conference project will make managers from large companies aware of the social consequences of an ever-increasing work load.

Project image (public events in particular)   *Step 3b*

Define the project image: what image should the event have (project profile)?   **Exercise**

Something can be added to each mission; the project image (the *profile* of the project). In other words, what do we want the event to come across as: is it going to be an event for the elite or for ordinary people? In order to illuminate the above mission statements, here are a few options for creating such an image:
- For instance, during an event about new media, you can opt for a very accessible or a specialist and technical feel.
- The PQ advice could be quick, amicable, or very thorough.
- For the street theatre festival, an image can be chosen that is fun, entertaining, and of high-quality, or one that is attractive to the entire family.
- For the manager of a conference project, a traditional conference can be opted for, in plush red velvet style or a playful one held in a factory hall.

The *project mission* and the *project image* make clear what you have promised the visitors/participants.

Project legitimisation (only for non-commercial public events)   *Step 3c*

Legitimise the events project: why should the event be held in the first place?   **Exercise**

By defining the project mission, a foundation has been laid for developing the event and the project is then *socially* legitimised. Subsidised public events, such as a festival or exposition, must be formally legitimised. This is done by testing the mission against the policy of the subsidising agency (See also Section 4.3).

By defining the *project mission,* the *project image,* and the *project legitimisation,* the actual essence of what can be expected from the event has been made clear to everyone.

The components 'what' and 'for whom' that correspond to the project mission of a public event can then be further detailed into *target group(s)* and their *intrinsic goal (s)* (See Steps 3d and 3e).

Step 3d   Target groups

Exercise   Based on the project mission and the project image, determine the target group(s) for the events project: who is the event aimed at?

In other words, it is about further specifying 'who' is mentioned in the mission, in target group(s), or market segment(s). This step can only be made in relation to the *intrinsic goal* of the event (Step 3e). When determining the target groups, do not forget:
- to make a distinction between main and sub-target groups, for instance:
  - general public
  - families with children
  - local residents
  - people interested in culture
  - tourists
  - experts
  - children under the age of ten
  - young people
  - senior citizens
  - pupils
- a description of the profile of the target group(s), with such aspects as:
  - the reference framework
  - the (educational) level, etc.
- an estimation of how large the target group(s) will be
- and specifically for conference projects:
  - a preliminary list of participants (main and sub-target groups)
  - a further analysis of this list (probable motives, expectations and interests, expected/desired numbers, origin, accompanying partners, colleagues)
  - which non-participating *influentials* are important?

Step 3e   Intrinsic goal

Exercise   Per target group, define the intrinsic goal(s) of the events project: what should be achieved at the end of the event for the various target groups or what purpose must it serve for them?

When events, fairs, and conferences are organised for certain user or consumer groups, the intrinsic goal can be determined rather easily. In many cases, it has already been described by the client or initiator. Whenever events projects are held for an anonymous target group (public events), the goal should be mulled over more thoroughly. For commercial events, such as fairs for entrepreneurs, conferences for managers, or musical productions, the client or initiator's goal is primarily to *generate profit*. In addition to their own goal, the aims and expectations of the participants, audience, or visitors should be considered. For instance, a company may decide to participate in a fair so as to sell their product directly to the fairgoers, to launch a new product or to create brand awareness (See also Frame 3.1).

In other words, what is the event supposed to achieve per target group? Several intrinsic goals can be defined for each of the various groups to be distinguished. This is a further specification of the 'what' described in the mission which is aimed at concrete target groups.

The intrinsic goal gives information about two aspects which are connected, i.e., the *desired effect* that the project result should have on the target group(s) and the *purpose* that the event is to fulfill so as to achieve that effect.

An intrinsic goal, for instance, of a non-profit information project may read as follows: 'To promote an understanding amongst pupils at a secondary school regarding people from other cultures (desired effect), these pupils will have to be given information about these cultures (purpose).'

It is important to render the objectives measurable as much as possible (see the SMART criteria listed in Step 4d).

Often, the intrinsic goal of an events project comes from the policy of the organisation or from the place or industry where the project is being set up. A few examples:

- In order to improve the company's image with a younger audience (the desired effect of the project in a certain target group); younger visitors attending the event will have to be informed about new company activities (the purpose of the project for that target group)
- In order to promote an understanding amongst pupils at a secondary school regarding people from other cultures (desired effect), the event will have to give pupils information about these cultures (purpose).
- In order to have administrators of care institutions consider participating in the broad-based school (desired effect), these administrators will have to receive information about the possibilities within such a system (purpose).

First reflection on spin-off   *Step 3f*

Anticipate any desirable or undesirable (side) effects that the events project **Exercise** might have (the spin-off).

For instance, a fair might have an economic spin-off for the merchants of the town and a museum organising a festival might have a spin-off in the form of additional turnover in the museum café, or it might have a social or cultural spin-off. Of course, as much positive spin-off as possible should be generated and any unwanted, negative spin-off should be countered (such as a high noise level for the local residents, or any negative impact on the environment). However, in most cases, spin-off cannot be anticipated until the form of the event has been more established. Therefore, the spin-off question will return in Step 4c.

Step 3g Project delineation

Exercise Describe how the events project has been delineated.

By defining the project mission in Step 3a, the event has been roughly delineated. This step further clarifies the parameters of the project. This concerns which phases (delineation of length) and which parts (delineation of breadth) no longer belong to the project?

For instance, is it only about making a plan (for instance, a plan for a trade show or a festival), or does it also concern the details in a production programme. Is the execution of the detailed plan also part of the project? Sometimes a project entails even more. For instance, a blueprint for the next edition of the events project can also be included in the project. Then it involves what the project is geared towards and where it exactly ends. In other words, what belongs to the project and what does not? A clear delineation of the project is very important, especially for projects that are carried out during a traineeship or when someone is to graduate from an institute of higher education.

Types of criteria for projects

Step 3h

Draw up an inventory and describe the criteria (both intrinsic and business)
Exercise which the event, and possibly the developmental process of the event, should unconditionally meet.

The criteria can be set by the client, or it can arise from the target group selected and its intrinsic goal, or from the specific circumstances (it is not about the consequences and preconditions you can come up with yourself, such as how much the project will cost and when it must be ready; these will be dealt with later).

Examples of *business requirements and criteria:*
- The events project cannot cost more than…
- It must be financed by the budget from the department of…
- It must break even
- It must be developed and/or accomplished by our own staff
- Only volunteers can be recruited
- It must take place on our own site or in our own building
- Is the conference (inter)national? Which language(s) will be spoken?
- Have a certain duration, place, and required accommodation been established for the conference?
- Has the client stated any preconditions for the way the conference is to be run?

There are three types of *intrinsic criteria:*
- *Functional criteria:* Which criteria can be defined in relation to the end product? Usually, functional criteria are set by the client. For instance, the criterion which states that the event can only be held at a certain venue or that new media be used for the event.
- *Operational criteria:* Which criteria are there in regard to the project result? Operational criteria usually come from future users or from the expectations from the target group or they are related to the circumstances. For instance, a fireworks show automatically implies that the event will have to be planned later in the evening, whereas a liberation festival will be restricted to a certain date. And a street theatre festival is usually organised in summer.
- *Design criteria:* Which criteria can be defined in regard to accomplishing the project? Usually, design criteria are set by the client or the developers and designers of the events project. For instance, the client might state that inclement weather conditions should be taken into account. Or the client might stipulate that the festival can only take place at a square which is difficult to access in the city centre. This places demands on the size of the facilities to be used and the transport.

It should be observed that in some cases it will be necessary to elaborate on certain criteria. When more complicated technical events projects (e.g., pop concerts, larger theater productions, and large sporting events) are held, then the specific technical requirements will have to be worked out in detail. This can best be done during a separate *defining phase* which should take place in between the initiative phase and the preparation phase.

Step 4   5.1.5   *Developing a basic concept*

The intrinsic starting points from the previous step have been translated into a number of sub-steps and a *basic concept* for the events project. When there is no creation question involved, in other words, if the form of the event has already been established (you already have determined that it should be a conference, a festival, an exposition, or a concert), Steps 4a, 4b and 4c can be skipped. If anything, these steps can be used to check which event form should be chosen and a discussion can be held if you would like to propose a different form. Otherwise, the intrinsic goal has been defined prior to the start of the initiative phase but it is not yet clear how this can be achieved. For instance, if the initiative group is told to assume an intrinsic goal about transferring information, this can be done in various ways such as holding a series of lectures, staging an exhibition, or showing a video presentation. Thus, Steps 4a and 4b must be followed.

Step 4a   Possible (event) forms for products or solutions

Exercise   Draw up an inventory of possible products or solutions that can be used to accomplish the intrinsic goal(s).

The question is as follows: Which event forms, products, or solutions match the intrinsic goal while, at the same time, they comply with the project criteria (See Section 3.1)? For instance, does an exhibition, a publication, a conference, an event, a video production, or any other form or product match the intrinsic goal which is aimed at discussing and exchanging information between colleagues from different countries?

Developing alternative products or solutions is a creative process that calls for sound information and communication, a creative attitude, an open ambiance, and a free exchange of views. Creative techniques for generating new ideas are: verbalisation (brainstorming, free writing), visualisation, free association, synectics and morphologic analysis. In particular, projects with different intrinsic goals will consist of a number of partial projects or programme parts which can benefit from using such a morphological analysis. This technique can map out the various variants of form that can be used during the event.
Finally, it should be clear that this step could indicate that an event might not be the most suitable form for fulfilling the particular intrinsic goal of a particular target group.

The most suitable event form

Step 4b

Make a well-argued choice from the inventory of alternative event forms or so-   **Exercise**
lutions. Do this on the basis of the intrinsic goal and the project criteria.

The question is which event form would be the most appropriate for fulfilling a certain intrinsic goal for a particular target group and for achieving the desired effect with the main target group? To determine this, it is necessary that:
– the desirable and undesirable consequences for each alternative have been investigated
– alternatives have been arranged according to quality
– a critical attitude has been maintained
– the ambiance for discussion is open and stimulating
– the decision-makers know what they are doing.

Among other things, the decision can be based on or tested in regard to:
– project criteria (See Step 3h)
– relevant information
– experience
– feasibility
– risk (uncertainty)
– time available, means, and possibilities.

Consequences of having chosen an (event) form

Step 4c

Draw up an inventory of intrinsic, technical and other consequences which are   **Exercise**
inextricably linked to the event form. It is not about how much the event will cost or how long it will last. These control aspects are dealt with later. Think as well about the spin-off.

The issue at hand concerns what will happen as a result of having chosen a certain event form or having thought of a particular solution (corresponding critical success factors for the form chosen).
Look at the consequences in the broadest sense of the word. For instance, if in the previous step it was decided to achieve the intrinsic goal by making a video production by using existing music or film fragments, or if it was decided to organise a photography exhibition, then as a consequence copyright expenses will have to be paid. You might think of such critical success factors, as *financing, expertise, accommodation, permits,* and *ownership* which are perhaps required for carrying out the project. If the critical success factors cannot be met, this will immediately influence the feasibility of the project.

Step 3b considered the spin-off of projects. In most cases, it is not until the current step that any spin-off can really be thought through, as more becomes known about the form of the event. As mentioned before, as much positive spin-off as possible should be generated and any undesirable, negative spin-off should be countered (such as the high noise levels experienced by the local population or any negative impact the event might have on the environment).

Step 4d   Definition of partial products

Exercise   Define the preliminary package of separate product-market combinations (PMCs), check which programme or project parts should be part of the event so as to achieve the various intrinsic goals for the different target groups (coherence between parts is to be achieved later).

To work out the details for the (events) form that has been selected the parts or partial products can be defined and linked to the target group(s). Ensure that the definition of each solution meets the SMART criteria:

s   = Specific
m   = Measurable
a   = Achievable
r   = Realistic
t   = Time bound.

An example of a non-SMART objective is to *develop a study packet for young people on Moroccan women.*
An example of a SMART objective is: *writing a two-page hand-out for young people in the age group between eight and twelve years old, with the objective of playfully informing 75 per cent of this visitor category about the position of Moroccan women in Dutch society when they visit the exhibition.*

In addition, it will need to be verified whether any supporting activities/products can or should be linked to the project (See Section 4.1 for the distinction between *partial projects* and *supporting projects*). Perhaps Step 4a provided the preliminary work necessary for taking this step. Consider as well the possibility of applying the brainstorming technique and that of making a morphological analysis.
The entire package of separate PMCs (product-market combinations) ensures that the intrinsic goal for each target group can be achieved. Step 4e fuses the individual parts together. The package of PMCs can be presented in a product-market matrix or table such as that presented below in Figure 5.1.

(sub)target group	part or product	desired purpose/effect
for the main target group	an exhibition	for information transfer
for school groups	a hand-out	for education
for business groups	lectures	for more background
for younger children	a puzzle hunt	for education and entertainment

Figure 5.1   Example of a PMC package for an exhibition project

Figure 5.1 states that each partial product should fulfil a purpose for and/or should have an effect (intrinsic goal) on one or more (sub) target groups.

The basic concept of the event   *Step 4e*

Place the various programme parts or partial products into one coherent basic   **Exercise**
concept for the event. This will clearly define the project result for everyone.

The basic concept is the intrinsic result of the initiative phase (See also Section 4.2). This concept makes clear how the event will look. This means that all the parts or partial products form a whole, both intrinsically and in external design. This step concerns the creation of a logical coherence between the separate parts of the event. The whole of the project result is expressed in the basic concept, which gives significance to each part of the event. Via the project mission, the event as a whole, promises to be of significance to the target group(s). Everything has a 'purpose'. The basic concept also makes it possible to distinguish the event from other products. This is because of the project mission having positioned the event. After all, the basic concept is supposed to give the event some lasting value In other words, visitors' or participants' commitment should not be fleeting. People should want to stick around, and they should look forward to the event being held again.
Below, the starting points are listed for developing coherence between the parts of the basic concept:

- Look for a *theme* for the events project that matches the contents of the event.
- Use a metaphor, a central idea or image that supports the contents of the event.
- See if the nature and form of the event's venue offers starting points for coherence within the basic concept.
- Look for a logical coherence in time.
- Search for binding elements in the type of event or in the image of the event.

The starting points described are often expressed in a statement, a short concise sentence, comparable to an advertising slogan which presents the essence of the event to a tee. Two examples of slogans which use this technique are 'Fifty years later we give colour to liberation' and 'With a historic festival back to the future'. Internally, the statement can serve as a beacon. During the developmental and production process, it could provide an unequivocal representation for all those involved of the mood to be evoked in the end result. The statement often plays an important role in communicating to those living in the immediate area, particularly when establishing the image for the event. The starting points are used to obtain a general programme depicting the end result (the basic concept).

Here the basic concept of a relatively traditional conference can be given as an example. This example has been based on the following starting points:
– four days, including the evenings
– clear start, middle, and finish
– goal-oriented self-activation of participants with intermediary extrinsic stimuli
– following the natural dynamics of the day, i.e., actively introverted agenda in the morning, extroverted agenda in the afternoon, and passively receptive agenda in the evening.

The general programme or basic concept for a conference project could resemble that found below in Figure 5.2. The basic concept as a whole and each separate part is explained in the project proposal. Describe this in such a way that the reader can obtain a clear picture of the event, and can even visualise it. In the following phase, the preparation phase, this basic concept has been further refined into a detailed programme or plan. Each part is then described in detail. Altogether, this forms the core of the following decision document, namely the *project plan*.

morning		1st workshop	2nd workshop	final workshop
		(A wing)	(A wing)	(A wing)
afternoon	official opening	plenary meeting	plenary meeting	plenary meeting
	(blue hall)	(large auditioriuml)	(large auditorium)	(blue hall)
evening	lectures 1+2	lectures 3+4	lecture 5	
	(large auditiorium)	(large auditorium)	(large auditoriuml)	
	Sunday 14/9	*Monday 15/9*	*Tuesday 16/9*	*Wednesday 17/9*

Figure 5.2   *Example of a programme (basic concept) for a conference project*

This step outlines how the event and each of the separate parts will look. It is not a clear plan with exact specifications such as times, numbers, and names (of artists or speakers, for instance). This is detailed later, in the next phase (preparation phase).

The value of an event is not only determined by the initiator's intentions, but also, and particularly so, by how the visitors/participants have experienced it. It is therefore of great importance that the concept is revived at a later stage. It must obtain an *entertainment value*. It depends on whether the event is capable of enticing the target group to show up, become involved, and enjoy their visit.

It should be observed that the project proposal may be needed for a detailed proposal, or that the client would like to give the green light to the intrinsic starting points before the basic concept has been developed. If this is the case, it means that the basic concept is not part of the trimmed down project proposal. In other words, Step 4 (developing the basic concept) is not carried out in the initiative phase, but in the definition phase, where it is inserted between the initiative phase and the preparation phase.

A description of the ambiance   *Step 4f*

Describe the mood to be evoked during the event you have detailed in the basic   **Exercise**
concept.

In the project proposal the basic concept must be presented by justifying the choices that have been made. It is recommended that a description of the ambiance be added to the basic concept. This is a vivid description of what the developers of the event think the project result will mean to future visitors/participants. Such a description is absolutely essential in order to obtain an accurate idea of live products such as events.

5.1.6   *Drawing up a plan of approach*   *Step 5*

This step concerns the plan of approach that is used for the events project. The project process will have to be phased and clarity will have to be given to the phased decision-making.

The approach of the events project   *Step 5a*

Describe how you plan to tackle the events project. Are you using a thematic   **Exercise**
approach or another approach?

The result of the events project has generally been established in Step 4e (the basic concept) and now you need to determine how to achieve this. One option would be to choose a *thematic approach*. You could also decide to carry out the event by improvising or by trial and error, in which case there is more freedom during the process, but there are subsequently more risks involved as well. In this step, a final decision will need to be made in regard to the approach used and this must be accounted for. You should also read Sections 2.2 and 3.4 once more. The latter section lists a number of project features that advocate using a sound *thematic approach*. If your events project adheres to the majority of these features, then it is recommended that you use the thematic approach. This section also mentioned various project categories in Verhaar's cube (See Figure 3.2). The degree to which a project can actually be approached thematically partially depends on the project category. In the initiative report, which is presented as a recommendation to the client, you provide an explanation for why you have chosen a certain approach and why you think it is the most suitable approach to use for your events project. In order to determine whether the events project should be tackled thematically, the following questions must also be considered:

– Which tasks must be carried out?
– What are the critical success factors for the events project? In other words, what are the minimum requirements for achieving the basic concept?
– Who would be the most suitable person(s) for developing/carrying out the event?
– Is there any relationship between the developmental process of this event and other developmental processes or projects being conducted in addition to this event?

Step 5b   The phasing of the events project

Exercise   Using the breakdown analysis (See Section 10.5), describe how you would like to phase the project process. Finally, indicate how you plan to organise the decision-making during the developmental and execution process.

If the professional thematic approach was decided on in the previous step, then the process will have to be analysed. Subsequently, the process can be structured. The *breakdown method* can be used for this. As a result of this structuring, the following will become clear:

– the order of the tasks to be carried out
– the phasing of the tasks (possibly change the (names of the) phases to match the type of project)

- the distinguished partial projects and/or supporting projects (See also Section 4.1)
- how you think the decision-making process should go, in other words, will you ask the client for feedback after each phase, or only when the execution phase has begun?

Finally, the purpose of the decision documents should be considered. For instance, is the project proposal only meant to fine-tune the expectations and ideas of the team members, or is it also supposed to support the client's decision-making process? Or, is it also supposed to fulfil an external purpose for the subsidising agency or sponsor? What demands does this place on the decision documents? See also Section 5.1.9 (Step 8).

5.1.7   *Gearing towards the market and surroundings*   *Step 6*

This step tests the end product of the project (the event) on the foundation of the basic concept as applied to the market. Such a test can provide an indication of the market-technical feasibility of the event. The external communication should also be considered at this point: with whom should communication take place and about which subject and what should the purpose be in order to carry out the event (communication strategy) successfully?

The SWOT analysis and the strategical issues (including market test)   *Step 6a*

Map out the strengths and weaknesses of the event (project result) and of the   **Exercise** (project) organisation (internal analysis). Then, map out the opportunities and threats for the market and greater surroundings (external analysis). Draw conclusions, or decide which *strategic issues* should be taken into account? What are you going to do?

For a SWOT analysis, see the steps listed in Section 11.2, Step 2.

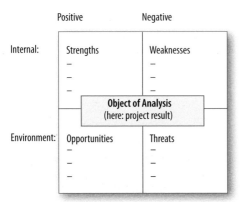

Figure 5.3   Basic shape of the SWOT *analysis*

When dealing with internal projects, at first it does not seem obvious that the project should be tested in regard to the market, even though there is an internal client. Often this may be the client, although it can also be a different department. The client (internal or external) can legitimise a project. If the basic concept and the preliminary product-market combinations (PMCs) weather the market test well, the basic concept can be determined. This will help to establish how the event should generally look.

Step 6b   (Marketing) communication strategy

Exercise   Describe the (marketing) communication strategy (See Section 11.2, Step 3), i.e., draw up an inventory of the parties that should be kept informed and describe the goal and the message that will accomplish this.

The communication strategy revolves around the question 'What message should be given to whom to achieve which purpose?'
After all, the communication strategy is aimed at achieving the following three goals:
- *product promotion*: to make the target groups aware of the event, and to interest them in visiting or participating. An event meant for the market, for instance, involves a marketing communication strategy.
- *fundraising: to encourage government* agencies to *subsidise the event*, receive private funding, and stimulate the business community to give money, goods, services, and lend support to the project (See also Chapter 9).
- *communication conducted with other parties: to foster communication with regulating governments, media, local residents, etc.*

Firstly, this is about creating the necessary support for the events project. This requires insight into both the collaborating and opposing forces at play, which can be mapped out by analysing the field of force (See Figure 5.4 and Section 8.1).

Figure 5.4   An example of a field of force analysis

The foundation for the communication strategy was established in Steps 3a and 3b of this step-by-step plan, by defining the project mission and the project image. The project mission determines which position the event should assume in relation to competitive products (intrinsic positioning). If, for instance, a large festival is already being organised in town during the same weekend, it would not be wise to open an exhibition at the same time unless the two initiatives might enhance one another. Then, it would be advisable to gear them towards each other. The project image should help you determine how you would like the event to be perceived by the potential visitor (image positioning).

A communication strategy is not yet meant to determine how and by which means (posters, flyers, advertisements) you should communicate because this will be done later in the communication plan.

During the course of the project, there may be reasons for informing the media even at this early stage. This is often done by means of a press release, one of the instruments from the communication mix.

Think as well about whether a public survey should be taken during the event (See Section 11.2.1 for an approach to using such a survey).

It should be observed that because fundraising often expenses a great deal of time, the fundraising plan (preparation phase) and the fundraising action plan (development phase) must be given priority. Therefore, read the remarks found in Step 10b.

Step 7   5.1.8   *Reflection on the business preconditions*

In this step you are to deal with the six control aspects (quality, organisation, facilities, time, information, and fundraising). For each control aspect, you should establish a standard for which they can be tested during the process. For the fundraising plan, the budget is the standard that you will use to test expenditures. For the other control aspects, you should now establish comparable testing criteria. Finally, you should draw up an inventory of the risks involved in the events project.

Step 7a Quality control aspect

Exercise Describe how you plan to guarantee the quality of the event and the developmental process. First define the quality criteria the project result must meet by answering the following questions:
– How good should the project result be when it is ready?
– How can you guarantee the quality of the event and the developmental process?

For a general description of the quality control aspect, first see Section 4.4. The notion of quality is much less concrete than the other control aspects. Particularly within the cultural industry, we tend to claim that the quality must be the highest, but what is the highest and who should decide what the highest standard is? Maximum or optimal quality is not a standard that can be controlled. Moreover, why should each events project be of maximum quality. Often projects have the starting point of: 'Good is good enough'. When achieving quality, the 80/20 rule often applies. This means that 80 per cent of the quality is obtained by 20 per cent of effort/investment. If 100 per cent quality is to be obtained, the extra 20 per cent will cost four times as much extra effort/investment. It remains to be seen whether or not this would be a wise decision.

In a number of cases, it is possible to draw up quality criteria in advance. In many cases, particularly in the cultural industry, this is a very subtle, and an often subjective issue, making it therefore very difficult to define. When an indication of the eventual quality is requested at the start of an events project, then this standard should be formulated as concretely as possible. The quality criteria should meet the SMART criteria listed in Step 4d. If no criteria can be defined, then a similar project that was held before could be used as a standard. Each interim result will be checked to see if it meets this standard. In addition, the decision-making concerning the intrinsic quality could be placed with an expert team member or the project manager. When a theatre or film production is concerned, then this will involve the director. It is also possible to assign an (committee of) expert(s) that/who can judge(s) whether the product is of sufficient quality. In this case, no quality criteria are defined in advance, but the committee itself is the 'standard' and a procedure is described for the quality testing to be carried out by this committee.

Organisational control aspect   *Step 7b*

Draw up a general setup for the project organisation and the discussion struc-   **Exercise**
ture.

Before an events project can actually begin after the initiative phase, the following question must be considered: 'Who will do what and who will be responsible (initiator, client, project manager, project team member, planning group, support group, conference committee, etc.)?' This is described in the setup for the project organisation, which is part of the project proposal. This setup should give insight into the official relationships between all of the parties involved in the project. To obtain an idea of how such parties might look, study Figure 3.1 for an events project and see also Appendix A11 for a conference project.

For a general introduction to the organisational control aspect first see Section 4.4. Setting up the project organisation may consist of a number of tasks, but it usually results in a flow chart of the organisation.

First, the relationship between the project organisation and the parent organisation must be structured (when it involves independent projects, this relationship naturally does not exist). The model of the project matrix organisation can be used (See Section 7.2). Then the temporary project organisation itself is structured, which clarifies who does what (task delegation), who is responsible for what (responsibility delegation), and who will have authority over what (authority delegation). This first requires an inventory of all the disciplines, people, groups, and organisations involved in the project and their responsibilities and authority (this may differ according to the phase). Choosing the person responsible for the project (or the project manager) and determining who will fill the role of client (and sometimes the role of the agent) is very important here (See Section 7.3).

For setting up the project organisation various models and tools can be used, for instance:

- *the steering committee work group model (See* Section 7.2): this model structures the authority relations between policy-makers/decision-makers, the project management, and the executors. If several projects are developed within one programme, these can be structured according to the programme structure.
- *the allocation of tasks* (See Appendix A3): this shows how easily it can be indicated who does what, etc.
- *the job description* (See Appendix A4): this tool defines the tasks, responsibilities, and the authorities of each project team member and their place in the organisation.

Depending on what needs to be organised, these tools can be used together.
Among other things, the plan for the project organisation must be arranged:
- the formal internal communication channels and discussion structures: who holds consultations with whom, how often and why?
- the decision-making processes: who decides on what basis, when and about what?
- third-party contracting: should an external designer be involved and if so, do they belong in the project team?
- the position and the status of any external experts or external project team members (volunteers, trainees, students, etc.)
- the possible cooperation with other organisations, for instance co-producers.
- the staff input and degree of expertise from the client/parent organisation.

In some cases, for instance with a large-scale festival or a large exhibition with several participants, it is advisable to establish an independent legal entity (such as a foundation) especially for the event. Not just for the sake of the personal liability of the initiator, but it can also be helpful, or even necessary, for obtaining funding or money from sponsors. In this way, the liability of, for instance, the parent organisation or the initiator can be covered during risky projects (See also Section 8.5).
In many cases the basic structure for setting up a project will remain the same throughout the course of the entire project. However, for each phase it will have to be evaluated whether any of the disciplines have been added and/or withdrawn as they may have already made their contribution to the project. As a consequence, the project organisation will then need to be adjusted.
The setup of the project organisation serves as the starting point for cooperation within the project. If there is any uncertainty, then this setup can always be referred to. Maintaining a close cooperation requires more than the struc-

turing of tasks and the making of official agreements. Other aspects also play an important role, such as the organisational culture, team building, leadership, dealing with conflicts and stress, and meeting and negotiation skills. *In addition to the organisational* culture, the meeting culture must also be given thought. Which meeting forms are relevant within this events project, what is being discussed during the meetings, who attends, who chairs the meeting and how often are the meetings held? This information can also be summarised (See Figure 7.7).

Facility control aspect   *Step 7c*

Draw up a first inventory of the facilitating criteria, i.e., the criteria that the   Exercise
venue and other facilities must meet. Then, draw up an inventory of the legal
aspects of the events project.

When drawing up an inventory of the *venue criteria, take the following into account:*
– the size of the venue.
– the preparation of the venue, furnishings, and decoration.
– the type of venue, dimensions, special designs or any adjacent rooms such as office space or dressing rooms, and the width of the passages for parts of the set.
– the presence of wall sockets or other connections for lighting, sound, or other equipment; the presence of high voltage power current (Will you need a generator?).
– connections for the utilities such as gas, electricity, water, sewage, telephone, cables, and the internet and communications, etc.
– accessibility from public roads, signposting, parking, parking assistance.
– the first impression of the climatological conditions, especially important for exhibition:
  – relative humidity.
  – incidence of artificial and natural light.
  – amount of dust.
  – temperature and its adjustability (does the event require heating?).
  – presence of any vermin (e.g., woodworm).
– options and criteria for security and surveillance in view of fire, burglary and theft.
– suitability for the public, such as the number of seats or the standing room, accessibility for wheelchairs.
– possibly taking into account another audience than that for the project

alone, for instance in the case of an exhibition held in a public building such as a city hall or a library.
– the location of the venue.
– the ambiance and the feel of the venue (also test this in regard to the project image).
– other features.

When drawing up an inventory of other facilities, take the following into account:
– sound and lighting equipment.
– stage facilities, crush barriers.
– waste disposal.
– toilet and cloakroom facilities (including the cleaning of toilets).
– catering and bar facilities.
– transport options, copying facilities, especially at conferences
– internet, telephone and fax facilities, and other provisions regarding telecommunication.
– computers and other facilities for data communication.
– presentation facilities, such as an overhead projector with sheets, a flip-over with felt-tips, colour television, video players, video cameras.
– optional borrowing or hiring of various facilities.

When drawing up an inventory of the legal aspects, do not forget:
– permits
– contracts
– copyrights, etc.

This is a first inventory. Only the main criteria and expected bottlenecks are listed in the project proposal. More details are dealt with in the preparation phase.

Step 7d   Time control aspect

Exercise   Using the task overview, draw up a time sheet for the entire process.

The time sheet is the foundation for monitoring the time control aspect during the process. For a general description of this control aspect, first see Section 4.4. When drawing up a time sheet a bar chart can be used (See Figure 5.5), which will present the run time of the tasks as horizontal bars. This way, the tasks and their order and coherence in time is rendered visually. The run time of a task is the entire time required to carry out the task (from start to finish). For a conference or an event, the preparation time can take as long as six months to three years. In addition, remember to allow for the decision-making time required by the client (based on the decision documents) at the end of each phase. Chapter 10 describes a step-by-step plan for making a bar chart.

An overall time sheet such as the one shown below in Figure 5.5 cannot be omitted from a project proposal. It should be clear that the initiative phase is no longer included as this phase will have been completed by the time the project proposal is presented.

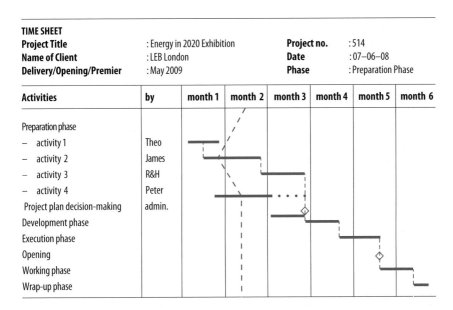

TIME SHEET								
Project Title	: Energy in 2020 Exhibition				**Project no.**	:514		
Name of Client	: LEB London				**Date**	:07–06–08		
Delivery/Opening/Premier	: May 2009				**Phase**	: Preparation Phase		

Activities	**by**	**month 1**	**month 2**	**month 3**	**month 4**	**month 5**	**month 6**
Preparation phase							
— activity 1	Theo						
— activity 2	James						
— activity 3	R&H						
— activity 4	Peter						
Project plan decision-making	admin.						
Development phase							
Execution phase							
Opening							
Working phase							
Wrap-up phase							

Figure 5.5   Example of an overall time sheet for an exhibition project

Information control aspect   *Step 7e*

Develop a monitoring system for the internal information, i.e., a registration   **Exercise**
system for the project information and a description of the procedure for the
distribution and filing of the information. Make use of the internet. This step is
especially important when large complicated projects are organised, involving
a great deal of information flows.

For this control aspect it is important to have access to the right information at the right time. See Section 4.4 for a general description of the information control aspect. Project team members are producing information that has to be communicated to others, but they also depend on information from third parties. However, systematic information control and good communication are absolutely essential in many cases (See Section 12.3.3 concerning the systematic control of information in multi-project organisations).

In addition, a system of time registration should be considered for the hours put in by the project team members. Finally, agreements or procedures should be recorded in writing concerning who is allowed to change or approve certain information or who should be authorised to do so (authorisation).

The internet offers a vast opportunity for streamlining internal information flows. In the past, those who possessed information were responsible for its distribution. Nowadays, such information is simply put on the intranet and the responsibility of the intake of relevant information lies much more with the user. This should be made clear to those involved in the early stages of an events project.

Step 7f   Fundraising plan

Exercise   Draw up a general estimate of the project expenses and earnings (a financial plan).

In an *estimate of the project expenses,* all (direct and indirect) expenses and earnings (such as participator contributions, entrance fees, subsidies, sponsor funds, and warranties) are included that are related to the preparation and execution of the events project. See also Section 4.4 for a general description of the fundraising plan and see Section 8.1 for drawing up an estimate of the project expenses. In this phase it is still an estimate, which is much more of an outline than a budget. This is also the reason why it has any 'miscellaneous items' in this estimate to a percentage from 8 to 18 per cent or more, depending on the degree of uncertainty. For the setting up of this estimate the standard cost type division as presented in Figure 5.6 can be used (See also Section 8.2). Sometimes the nature of the events project might require that this division be deviated from, as it should serve only as a guideline. For some projects, the subsidiser sets the criteria for drawing up estimates.

For each estimate or budget, indicate whether the amounts are including or excluding VAT. Each item on a budget should always be explained, including the premises. You should also start an events administration.

PROJECT COST ESTIMATE

Stage project title	: 'Energy in 2020* Exhibition	**Project no.** : 514
Name of Client	: LEB London	**Date** : 07-06-09
Date of Premier	: May 2010	**Phase** : preparation phase

Cost description	Expenses	total	
Type	materials and third party	wages expenses	
1000 Venue expenses	–	–	–*)
2000 Direct production expenses	22,500	30,000	52,500
2100 – panelling	4,500	21,000	
2200 – showcases and sockets	18,000	9,000	
3000 Direct production expenses (software)	45,500	–	45,500
4000 Design, advice and support	42,925	–	42,925
5000 Additional expenses	–	–	–*)
6000 Supporting sub-projects	7,000	–	7,000
6100 – lectures	6,000		
6200 – puzzle hunt	1,000	–	
7000 Promotion, publicity and PR	–	–	–*)
8000 Organisation expenses and miscellaneous expenses			7,075
Project cost estimate (excluding VAT)			155,000
VAT		(all incl.)	
Project cost estimate (including VAT)			155,000
9000 Earnings (financial plan)			123,000
9100 – entrance fees			68,000
9200 – project subsidies			40,000
9300 – funds and sponsoring			15,000
Positive/negative project result in euros			-/-32,000

*) directly at the client's expense

Figure 5.6   Example of a project cost estimate of an exhibition project

Risk analysis   *Step 7g*

Carry out a risk analysis and describe the measures for reducing or eliminating   **Exercise**
the risks found.

As a final step in the initiative phase, it is advisable to carry out a risk analysis. This is done by following these four steps:

1 Take stock by brainstorming, for instance, about the risks that could threaten the events project from being successfully carried out:
    – *financial risks* (insufficient funds or tardy security regarding funding)
    – *commercial risks* (ticket sales lagging behind prognoses)
    – *legal risks* (required permits have not been granted or necessary property rights have not been obtained)
    – *organisational risks* (for instance, parties pull out)
    – *practical risks* (for instance, inclement weather)
    – *technical risks* (for instance, a power failure).
2 Make a selection of the main risks (critical failure factors).
3 Brainstorm per critical risk factor about the possible measures to eliminate it.
4 Finally, choose per critical risk factor a solution strategy and describe the measures that should be taken.

As a supplement to this analysis, the risk analysis tool given in Appendix A16 can be used. It can also be used as a checklist to draw up an inventory of the risks within the framework of Step 1 above. The risk analysis tool should be applied with due care. Always let common sense prevail over the results calculated by using the risk analysis tool.

The risks listed in the risk analysis tool are of a general nature. For specific fields of expertise, other risks can be added. In addition, risks can be removed if they do not apply to your events project. The 'weight' of the risks can also be adjusted. Of course, this will change the total number of 'points' that can be awarded. The result of the analysis must first be interpreted. At the end of the analysis, an indication of the risk is given. The main conclusions of the risk analysis and the proposed measures should also be included in the project proposal.

Step 8   *5.1.9   Drawing up the project proposal*

As mentioned before, all of the starting points and preconditions of the events project which were defined during the initiative phase are recorded in the project proposal (or initiative report). The results obtained from all of the previous steps taken serve as the building blocks for the project proposal.

The project proposal is the *starting document* for the events project and it serves as a criterion for guiding the entire project. When a project has been commissioned, the project proposal is the first decision document presented to the client.

For the decision-making process, the project proposal must contain enough information for the client to be able to receive an impression of the *project result*, in other words, how the event will roughly look, but also what it might signify and for whom this might be important. What image will the event evoke (project positioning and profiling). In addition, the client should gain insight into the main tasks that must be carried out to develop the event further for its actual execution. Moreover, the project proposal must give insight into the *marketing and communication of the project*. Finally, this decision should clearly state the agreements that have been made concerning such aspects as organisation, time, money, and facilities. Then, the funding of the event can be arranged, or subsidy can be applied for.

By having a project proposal the client is able to take a decision about whether or not the project can go ahead and he can give the green light for the following phase (preparation phase).

Most fundamental decisions (intrinsic and business starting points and preconditions) to be made concerning the project will be based on the project proposal. This is often done by senior managers, who are used to doing their jobs on the basis of very *concise* information! Once the project proposal has been approved by the client, it will become what is called the *project contract.*

Format for the project proposal	*Step 8a*

Process the information that was collected during the previous steps, in the format for the project proposal (Appendix C1 contains an extensive format that can be applied to a project proposal for an events project).	**Exercise**

The answers to the questions from all of the previous steps can be seen as building blocks for writing the various chapters and sections of the project proposal.

Warning 1: It is not simply a matter of listing the results obtained from the previous assignments and placing them into one report. New (concise) text should be provided, which has been based on the assignments.

A project proposal can be drawn up as follows:
- Table of contents
- Introduction (Steps 1 and 2)
- Intrinsic starting points (Step 3)
- Project contents (Step 4)
- Plan of approach (Step 5)
- Project marketing and communication (Step 6)
- Business preconditions (Step 7)
- Appendices.

See Appendix C1 for the detailed contents of the project proposal.

Warning 2: When writing the project proposal, keep the goal of this first decision document in mind. The project proposal should describe the starting
points and preconditions of the events project (both intrinsic and business). It
can, for instance, aid the client in his decision making. This first document is
not meant to contain all of the information gathered thus far. Remember that
managers have a great preference for very concise information when making
their decisions!

Step 8b Supplementing the project proposal

Exercise Draw up the project proposal into a complete report.

When the intrinsic texts for the project proposal have been written, they must
be completed and given a cover, a summary of the core data on the page following the cover, a table of contents, and appendices.
A project proposal for an average events project consists of approximately 1,000
to 1,500 words, the core of which is formed by the *intrinsic starting points*, the
basic concept and the *plan of approach*. When choosing the tone of the project
proposal, it must be decided which purpose it must serve and for whom. For
instance, if the events project is being carried out for an (external) client, the
project proposal may have the status of an offer or quotation. In addition, the
project proposal may be included as an appendix to an application for a subsidy
or it can be used as a foundation for obtaining a permit.

Step 8c Completing the project contract

Exercise Discuss the project proposal with the client (and possibly other parties involved)
and then finalise it. The final version can be seen as the project contract, which
can be used to check all of the subsequent decisions.

If the client agrees with the starting points and preconditions stemming from
the project proposal, this means that an agreement has been reached between
the client and the *agent* (project manager/project team). The assignment becomes tangible and the events project can begin.
In educational settings, it is also important to conclude a written contract on
the basis of an approved *starting document* before the project develops further
and its execution begins.
If it is decided to apply a *professional thematic approach,* the project team

(which may have changed) will start the next phase under the leadership of the project manager. In some cases, there is an intermediary phase after the initiative phase, i.e., the definition phase, but usually the preparation phase is the very next phase, in which the project plan has been worked out on the foundation of the starting points (possibly amended by the client) from the project proposal. After the preparation phase, there is the development phase, in which the *production programme* including all of the production data is drawn up. This programme is then carried out in the production phase.

5.2 Step-by-step plan for the preparation phase (including project plan)

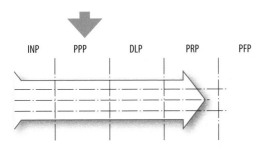

INP   PPP   DLP   PRP   PFP

The Application

'Our knees were knocking. There we were, with our nice PowerPoint presentation that showed a video clip of one of the bands we had in mind and provided an idea of how the event would transpire. We were surprised when eight people showed up in the conference room at city hall, but everything went smoothly because we had prepared it so professionally. The attendees responded with enthusiasm to the basic concept and fortunately they only asked the questions that we had anticipated. The client had a few objections regarding the fact that there was too much focus on entertainment and the estimated expenses were thought to be too high. The client thought we were aiming too high by assuming that we would receive 10000 Euros in subsidies and sponsoring, which was more than 25 per cent of the total estimated expenses. The client thought a sum of 5,000 Euros was more realistic. Eventually, the client set the total budget at 33,000 Euros, of which the municipality would fund 28,000 Euros. The recreation park was decided upon as the venue. We are now working out the basic concept into a detailed plan for the event. Of course, the client's comments are being taken into account. We have changed the Sunday programme and we have allowed more room for discussion. Last week, we learned that the band we had wanted to book for the main act was not available. We are now negotiating with a fairly well-known DJ who is far less expensive than the original band that we had planned to have. The line-up is nearly finished and because we found two other bands who will perform for free for the charity, it looks like we will stay within the budget. We also worked the communication strategy into a communication plan. To receive attention from the local and regional media, we are planning to carry out a real stunt a week before the actual event. We are not saying what it is going to be, but it will be spectacular. At the start of next week, everything we have worked out will be put in a project plan; the second decision document. In two-and-a-half weeks, the project plan will be discussed with the head of the Communication department.'

When an agreement has been reached concerning the project proposal, (which means there is an agreement about all of the starting points and preconditions of the events project), the *preparation phase* can start. This phase focuses on the planning or development of a design or solution. It is advisable to read the general description of the preparation phase in Section 4.2 first.

The results of the preparation phase are summarised in the *project plan, in which the* consequences have been further elaborated on and compared to the preconditions set at the end of the previous phase, in addition to the intrinsic plan or design.

During the preparation phase of an events project the following steps can be distinguished:
– Step 9: developing a detailed plan or design
– Step 10: developing plans for marketing/communication
– Step 11: reconsidering the business preconditions (control aspects)
– Step 12: writing the project plan.

Step 9   ### 5.2.1   *Developing a detailed plan or design*

The core task during this preparation phase is to work out the basic concept developed in the previous phase.

If we look at a festival, the basic concept is converted into a detailed plan with the exact dimensions of the venue, the exact times of shows and other activities, a final list of artists who are going to perform, etc. How the production is going to be organised is not yet known, but that will be worked out during the development phase.

Structure plan	*step 9a*

Draw up a structure plan.	Exercise

Where complicated events projects are involved, it is always useful to draw up a structure plan first. Such a plan indicates how the various parts of the event are related. Think of, for instance, an exhibition project or a video production which shows the themes in a logical order. The structure plan for an exhibition, for instance, results in a *story-line*. Such a structure plan is also important at a festival where the order of artists must be presented in a line-up. The general contents of a book could be used as a metaphor for the *basic concept*, and a detailed table of contents of a book could be used as a metaphor for the *structure plan*.

Detailed plan or design	*Step 9b*

Work out the basic concept (optionally including a *structure plan*) in a detailed plan or design for the events project.	Exercise

This step further defines the contents of the events project. In some cases, such a plan can be described by texts, but sometimes it is better to use diagrams or some other kind of visualisation. When it involves an events project, it usually is a combination of text, plans and diagrams. This makes it clear how the project result is going to look. For instance, when an event is to be held, the programme parts are described in detail, with the exact times, programme, names, dimensions, venues, etc. Where necessary, these descriptions will be illustrated by designs with legends. Descriptions and/or designs should be provided for each programme item. At the end of the preparation phase, the festival programme, the scenario of the video production and the story line of the exhibition are defined in detail and all of the parts are filled in and described in detail. These are put into an overview or a drawing.

It should be observed that a detailed technical and organisational elaboration of the event belongs to the next phase (the development phase).

Step 9c   A description of the ambiance

Exercise   During the initiative phase you can adapt how the mood to be evoked during the events project is described.

A short description of this ambiance was probably included in the project proposal as a vivid description of the way the event is going to be experienced by future attendees (Step 3g), and it must be adapted in this phase to suit the detailed design or plan.

Remember that the project plan is usually presented on a broad scale (often orally) so as to obtain support for the project. That is why the description of the mood to be evoked during the event must really enliven the project.

Step 9d   Production method

Exercise   Start thinking in general about possible production methods.

If it is thought to be relevant, a general description can be made of production methods and execution tools. For an exhibition project, it might be decided to not make the panelling, showcases, and pedestals on location, but instead to have them made elsewhere because of the limited space. When a festival is to be held, it can be decided during this phase to make a stage of previously used sections or to rent stage trailers. This pertains to the main decisions related to the production, not the details. More detailed information about the production or execution can be described later during the development phase, in the *production programme*.

Step 10   **5.2.2   *Developing plans for the marketing/communication***

During the preparation phase, the (marketing) communication *strategy* from the initiative phase must be worked out into a marketing plan, a fundraising plan, and a communication plan. These plans usually form an integrated part of the project plan, but they can also be presented separately. They state how the communication strategy will be carried out. For instance, public awareness can be raised by using posters, having a website, or placing advertisements, and showing commercials. In some cases, for instance when an extensive fundraising plan is part of the events project, these plans will be drawn up during the initiative phase. Such a plan always expenses a great deal of time. In addition, further elaboration of the project will not always make sense if, for example, there is no prospect of a closing budget. Further instructions for drawing up these plans are given in Section 11.2, Steps 4-6.

Marketing plan *Step 10a*

Develop a marketing plan for the events project (only for marketing projects). **Exercise**

A marketing plan (See Figure 11.4 for a format) is of course only relevant for projects with an end product for the market (market projects). When it involves a company party, a symposium by invitation, or a product presentation, this does not apply (a product presentation is not a marketing project, but is used as a *communication tool* for putting another product on the market.)

A marketing plan clarifies how the event is going to be marketed. When making such a plan, usually the marketing mix (the five Ps) is used. The five Ps are aspects that when combined should satisfy the needs and wishes of the target group of the event. It concerns choices related to:

– **P**roduct, which (part) product per target group (product market combination, or PMC)
– **P**rice, price level, price differentiation
– **P**lace, where on offer, distributed how
– **P**romotion, how is attention drawn
– **P**ersonnel, attitude, mood, etc.

Fundraising plan *Step 10b*

Develop a fundraising plan for the events project. **Exercise**

During the initiative phase the fundraising target groups, when applicable, were included in the communication strategy. These are subsidising agencies, funds, companies, and potential collaboration partners.

The fundraising plan (See Figure 11.5 for a format) must detail the approach for the fundraising/sponsoring.

It should be observed that the fundraising plan is worked out in a fundraising plan of action. Fundraising is often time-consuming. Therefore, it is not wise to wait until the development phase before drawing up and carrying out the fundraising plan. In such cases, the fundraising plan must be drawn up in the preparation phase, or perhaps even right after the initiative phase!

Communication plan *Step 10c*

Develop a communication plan for the events project. **Exercise**

The communication plan (See Figure 11.6 for a format and Section 11.2, Step 6) is also a further elaboration of the communication strategy found in the project proposal.

If the communication plan is an integrated part of the project plan, it usually consists of the following two parts:
– a communication matrix
– a communication plan (plan of the communication tasks, for instance in the form of a separate GANNT chart (bar chart).

Step 11

5.2.3   *Reconsidering the business preconditions*

By the end of the initiative phase, the preconditions will have been set for each control aspect. This then takes you to the next phase. The basic concept has been elaborated into a detailed plan for the event. This means that each control aspect must be re-examined. Record, in advance, for each control aspect, which starting points have been changed in regard to the approved project proposal.

Step 11a   Quality control aspect (Q)

Exercise   Describe how to monitor the quality of the events project that is being developed.

This is in answer to the question, 'How does the process of monitoring quality proceed based on the quality criteria set in the project proposal?' Should an adjustment be made in order to proceed further to the next phase (development phase)?

Step 11b   Organisational control aspect (O)

Exercise   Adjust the organisational setup

This step focuses on the question regarding to what extent the earlier setup for the project organisation (the organisation flow chart) should be adjusted before proceeding to the next phase? It should be observed that the production staff will be more involved in this phase (development phase) and in some cases, the staff will have to be included in the organisation flow chart.

Facility control aspect (F)

Step 11c

Draw up a facility plan.

Exercise

This step (if applicable) falls into the following three parts:
- *Venue plan*: which venue has been chosen and why? How will the venue be set up and furbished? Can all practical matters in relation to the venue be described (for instance, fire safety requirements)? It is important that the provisional booking of the venue be changed now into a definite booking. This also means that the final facilitary requirements in regard to the venue will also have to be set.
- *Facilitary plan*: Can the necessary facilities be described and how can these be obtained (draw up an acquisition list with prices and conditions)?
- *Legal plan or permit plan*: Which permits/approvals/rights (also copyrights) and other legal issues are necessary and how will these be obtained?

Time control aspect (T)

Step 11d

Draw up an adjusted time sheet.

Exercise

The central question is how does the new overall time sheet look when it is depicted as a bar chart, from the end of the preparation phase up to and including the completion and evaluation of the event? In order to use the time sheet for monitoring the next phase (development phase), the planning for that phase must contain a detailed task overview. The following phases can be described more generally. Sometimes, it is useful to draw up a separate time sheet for the development phase.

Information control aspect (I)

Step 11e

Consider the project information system.

Exercise

The question is, does the control and monitoring system for the information supply have to be adjusted, and if so, how?

Fundraising plan (M)

Step 11f

Draw up a cost estimate of the various parts (components of the event) and provide the financial figures.

Exercise

This concerns the following questions. How does the budget look for each part of the project (See Section 8.1.2)? How does the financial scheme look? What can currently be said about the state of the budget (See also Section 8.3)? And:

– Keep an events administration
– Arrange contracts and financial agreements
– Set entrance fees, participants' contributions and other earnings
– Set the financial remuneration for artists, speakers, etc.

Step 12

5.2.4 *Drawing up the project plan*

For detailed decision-forming, the project plan for the client must contain sufficient information in order to provide an exact idea of the events project. In addition, it must provide insight into the tasks that are still to be carried out in order to achieve this result. For marketing projects, the project plan must also contain a marketing plan. It must also be described how, with what means, and which channels will be used to communicate (communication plan) and which funds or sponsors are going to be approached (fundraising plan). Furthermore, the client should be able to read about the *consequences* regarding the progress, the budget, etc. in the project plan.

If the project plan provides insight into the above, then the client will be able to visualise how the project is coming along and to decide whether the plan should be turned into a production programme during the development phase (either for the execution or production).

Step 12a Format for the project plan

Exercise Process the information collected in the preparation phase in the format for the project plan.

The answers to the questions from the previous steps will serve as the building blocks for the texts in the different chapters and sections of the project plan. The core of the project plan is formed by the detailed *intrinsic* plan or design. The chapters of a project plan could appear as follows:

– Table of contents
– Introduction
– Project contents (Step 9)
– Project marketing and communication (Step 10)
– Business preconditions (Step 11)
– Appendices.

See Appendix C2 for an extensive format of the project plan for an events project. Just like the previously presented format for a project proposal (in Appendix C1) this, too, must be seen as a model or checklist, and not as an inhibiting straightjacket.

After having received the client's approval of the project plan, the decisions made in the preparation phase and the correlating consequences will provide a new foundation for the project team during the next phase (development phase). It is difficult to predict the size of a project plan because it greatly depends on the type and size of the events project itself and on the purpose for which the project plan has been written. A careful balance will always have to be found between the effort required to describe and draw up all of the conclusions from this phase into a sound plan or design on the one hand, and the purpose that is served as such, on the other hand. In addition, it should also be remembered that not every client wants to see and read everything in detail as they may simply lack the time.

It should be possible to read the project plan separately from the project proposal, but it should also be clear that it is one in a series of decision documents. Furthermore, the tone of the project plan depends on the purpose the plan is supposed to fulfill and for whom. Because a project plan often entails making people enthusiastic about the project, its design and its tone are particularly important.

If the project assignment entails that a plan be developed for an event or an exhibition, for example, then the project plan should be considered as the end product of the project. The actual manifestation of the plan in this case falls outside the framework of the project. This is true of many learning projects within higher education. This should have become clear from the project delineation described earlier in the project proposal.

Supplementing the project plan   *Step 12b*

Finish the project plan and provide a complete report.   Exercise

Once the contents of the project plan have been written, then it should still be completed by providing a cover, a summary of the core data on the title page (the page after the cover page), possibly a preface, an executive summary, a table of contents and the appendices.

5.3 **Step-by-step plan for the development phase (including production programme)**

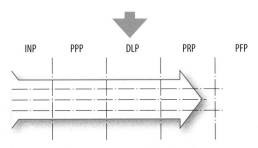

INP   PPP   DLP   PRP   PFP

The Application

'Discussing the project plan with the client went well. The head of the Communication Department was pleased with the adjustments we made to the basic concept and he was satisfied that the set budget had not been exceeded. After making just a few small changes, we got the green light to prepare the plan for execution. It is starting to become a very practical matter, which is something I am not very good at. I prefer the first phase, in which you can be more creative. Fortunately, everybody is different. Two of my team members prefer much more the practical side of things now that they can organise the scenarios and draw up all kinds of order lists. They are putting together a script for the days when everything will have to be set up, a script for the Saturday and Sunday of the event, and a script for Sunday night and the Monday when everything will be taken down again. I am currently writing a second press release and drawing up a setup for the survey. During the event, the client would like to gauge whether the target group is being reached and whether the objectives are being achieved. In the meantime, I am also thinking about the organisation of the execution phase, when many volunteers and production staff will be coming on board. During the execution, each member of our project team is responsible for part of the event. I will do the overall coordination myself. One of the team members is currently drawing up an action plan for the communication and she will also carry this out. This means that she will also be responsible for whether the stunt succeeds or not. In addition, she will put up posters, speak to the press, and distribute flyers together with a group of volunteers. According to the time sheet, all of the execution information must be put together in the production programme within a month's time. The educational programme refers to this as the third decision document, but in all actuality, the client cannot call off the event after having approved the project plan. The event has been announced in the media and the artists and other parties involved have been contracted, including the caterer. Strange that it is all going to happen soon, after having worked so hard for so many weeks.'

Section 4.2 provides a short introduction to the development phase, in which the plans drawn up during the preparation phase are prepared for execution and attention is paid to the tasks still to be carried out once the event is over. This means that some final decisions must be made in this phase, concerning for instance how to execute the event, which materials to use, which dimensions, and in regard to the project team members' schedules. In addition, an inventory should be drawn up of the information required (work plans, production lists, rental lists, order lists), when what must be done by whom (scripts), and what is going where (floor plans). The plan or design stated what should be accomplished, whereas now it is all about *when, where, how, what with,* and *by whom* this should be done. This is predominantly practical information. The results of the development phase are put together in the production programme, which could contain the following: scripts, production lists with possible work plans, floor plans, volunteer plans, time sheets, and rehearsal schedules.

During the development phase of an events project the following steps can be distinguished:
– Step 13: translating the plan into production information
– Step 14: drawing up and executing the action plans for marketing/communication
– Step 15: guarding the business preconditions
– Step 16: drawing up the production programme.

5.3.1 *Converting the plan into production information* Step 13

The core task of the development phase is formed by working out the plan or design for the execution team. Using the building process as a metaphor to illustrate our point, we could say that this is the phase which transforms the house design developed during the previous phase into a set of specifications with work plans. These specifications contain all of the production data, including the exact specifications and description of the organisational provisions, and they are meant for those who are actually involved in building the house.

Step 13a   Production information

Exercise   Translate the plan or design of the event from the project plan into production information (intrinsic, technical and organisational).

The question here concerns which intrinsic and production-technical information should be described or drawn up in order to implement the events project? In other words, an inventory will be drawn up showing the information that those who are going to put the event together will need. It should be very practical! Describe the production data, such as any production methods, implementation aids, material applications, etc. This information can be recorded in floor plans (outside/inside), work plans, technical descriptions, and detailed plans, or in artist lists, players lists, speaker lists containing all of the relevant information, routes (to the venue, and within the venue), volunteer overviews, call sheets, rehearsal schedules, etc.

step 13b   Pilot-testing

Exercise   Consider whether it is useful and feasible to test certain parts of the event on a small scale.

Live projects such as events have to go smoothly right from the very start. There are no second chances. If the risk of carrying out the event in one go is too great, perhaps it is possible to test certain parts first. This is not always possible, but when it involves a stage production, it is very common to hold a dress rehearsal. When it involves a conference project, you could hold a preliminary conference or coach and train the panel chairs, speakers, monitors, and the conference chair.

Step 13c   Drawing up a working programme

Exercise   Draw up an instruction manual (working programme) for 'using' during the event. A *calamity plan* must also be included!

A working programme describes how the event 'works' and what is needed to have it work as planned. This programme is meant for those who are responsible for the inner workings of the event when it is up and running. It resembles a kind of user manual or maintenance instruction guide.
The working programme for an exhibition, for instance, contains the instructions for the attendants, so that they can manage the atmospheric humidity in

the exhibition rooms or it might describe how they should handle the aggressive behaviour displayed by a visitor, answer media questions, or deal with calamities. Put your heads together about possible calamities that might occur during the event and detail how potential threats to the event should be handled.

Often the script for the event itself, dealt with in Step 15d, suffices as a working programme for short events. However, it is always advisable to draw up a (separate) emergency plan.

Drawing up the aftercare programme	*Step 13d*

Draw up an inventory of the post-event tasks that should be carried out during the completion phase.	**Exercise**

The aftercare programme describes all of the tasks required to be carried out during the completion phase of the events project. Think of matters such as:
– setting up a plan for and communication about possible follow-up tasks
– sending thank-you notes to parties involved, for instance speakers, volunteers, and sponsors
– creating an album with photographs/clippings
– updating the website and press releases
– writing a general report about the workings of the project, or specific reports
– reporting back to participants, target groups or other parties involved (for instance concerning results, answers to questions and any follow-up tasks).

5.3.2	*Drawing up and executing action plans for marketing-/ communication*	*Step 14*

This concerns plans of action that (if applicable) are an implementation of the marketing plan, the fundraising plan, and the communication plan, all of which have been developed in the previous phase (the preparation phase).

Drawing up and executing the action plans	*Step 14a*

If this was not done in the previous phase, then draw up a set of concrete plans of action for marketing, fundraising, and communication and execute them.	**Exercise**

Such plans of action must contain all relevant tasks in a script. For an example, see the format for a communication action plan presented in Section 11.2, Step 7/8.

When projects have a longer preparation time, the plans of action do not have to be executed until the development phase. However, in practice an events project is often under pressure, which is why these plans are often already being drawn up and executed in the preparation phase (especially the fundraising action plan). Their execution continues into the development phase. The plans of action concern how to reach visitors, buyers, users, participants, viewers (marketing action plan), how to obtain subsidies, funds, and sponsors (fundraising action plan) and how to create goodwill and receive media attention (communication action plan).

It is recommended that you keep the sponsors that you have already contracted informed of the developments during the event. In addition, the development phase often also involves publishing a press release (See model in Appendix 5).

Step 14b   Setup for a public survey (only for public projects)

Exercise   Draw up a proposal for a public survey.

If it has been decided to carry out a public survey for a public project, it should then be set up in this phase. Section 11.2.1 contains a separate step-by-step plan for setting up and carrying out an evaluation public survey. Follow Steps 1-7 from this separate plan to set up a survey proposal. Steps 8-13, which concern the actual preparation of the survey, can also be carried out in this phase.

For certain small-scale events, a concise evaluation form can be drawn up for the visitors/participants and possibly a separate evaluation form for the speakers/artists.

Step 15   5.3.3   *Guarding business preconditions*

During this phase, the events project is worked out in detail and put into writing. The only step that must be taken is to execute the plan. This means that almost all of the business consequences for the project can be foreseen. For a final go/no-go this overview of all the consequences is crucial. Furthermore, it is important that you have considered how to monitor the various control aspects during the execution phase.

Quality control aspect (Q)   *Step 15a*

Explain the decisions made during the development phase in relation to the   **Exercise**
quality criteria set for the event.

The production programme, including the production methods and facilities,
is now measured according to the quality standards previously established. The
desired 'feel' of the event should also be monitored. In addition, any remarks or
guidelines should be described in the working programme in relation to monitoring the aspect of quality during the execution phase.

Organisational control aspect (O)   *Step 15b*

Drawing up a design for organising the execution of the project   **Exercise**

This step is about organising the execution of the project. This means that production roles must now be put into the organisation flowchart included in the
project plan during the previous phase. In addition, it must be considered what
to do yourself and what to contract out. When it involves an events project, for
instance, the executors, contractors, freelancers, and volunteers participating
in the execution phase will have to be included in the flowchart. In this way,
their official position within the project organisation will become clear to the
other project partners (such as the project manager, the coordinators for the
various parts of the event, the publicity coordinator, the designers, the advisers, and the client).
When organisationally complicated events are involved, it is sometimes necessary to provide a separate description of the organisation during the construction phase, for the event itself, and during the wrap-up phase.
In addition, all kinds of contracts will have to be drawn up in this phase, such
as employment contracts, artist contracts, contracts for volunteers, trainees,
and freelancers, etc. (See the models in Appendices A6, A7, and A8). Furthermore, working schedules will have to be drawn up for the next phase(s).
All of the schedules which have been drawn up for clarifying the organisation of the execution are included in the *production programme,* under *project
organisation.*
See Chapter 7 for more detailed information on this control aspect.

Step 15c   Facility control aspect (F)

Exercise   Translate the facility plan from the previous phase into a concrete *facility action plan*.

Everything must be prepared during the development phase so as to ensure that the venue and the facilities required are available in the execution phase. In many cases, this means that many different action plans and lists must be drawn up. Furthermore, the preliminary layout of the venue and the decoration must be elaborated in detailed floor plans. Moreover, the preliminary acquisition list for other facilities must be elaborated into action lists (order lists, rental lists, supplier lists, etc., for buy/rental/lease of required technical tools, such as computers, audiovisual equipment, sound installation and view data equipment, and for other materials required such as tables, chairs, rostrum, decorations, etc.). The action plans for sign-posting and parking supervision must also be drawn up. Finally, any legal matters should be finalised at this time.

Step 15d   Time control aspect (T)

Exercise   Draw up the execution planning in the form of scripts for the three sub-phases of the execution phase. This involves a script for the construction phase, one for the event itself, and one for the wrap-up phase. Draw up additional time sheets as well.

This step is mainly about setting up the execution plan for the people who are going to set up the event (the production team). In such a plan, all tasks that must be carried out during the execution phase (with three sub-phases) are listed. Depending on the course, the plan will have the form of a bar chart or a script. As you will learn in Section 10.2, a script is a planning technique that is usually used when the tasks are concrete and when details are paramount. Time may have to be monitored during the weeks or days prior to the opening of a festival, or during the festival itself and of course for the days after the event, when everything is taken down and the venue cleared.

Script

Name of the project	: 65 Years of Liberation		Project no.	: 02
Name of Client	: VBN Amsterdam		Date	: 1 March 2010
Completion/Opening/Premier	: 5 May 2010		Phase	: Production Phase

No.	Day/date	Time	By	Activity	Component	Place	Materials/Remarks
01	Mon 03-05	10.00	VHR	Retrieving costumes	Performance	Square	At theatre society
02		11.15	SDS	Picking up keys	General		At administration
03		13.30	ALL	Cleaning	Reception	Hall	Material from supervisor
04	Tue 04-05	09.00	SRT	Preparing drinks	Reception	Kitchen	Crates in supply room
05							
06							

Figure 5.7   Example of a Script for a Public-Event Project

Sometimes it is necessary to include explanatory information in the appendices to the script, such as schedules, time sheets, maps, floor plans, inventory lists of necessities and a description of implementation methods and tools.

When the scripts are large, it is better to add them as appendices to the production programme. It is advisable to include the floor plan of the venue in the script.

When drawing up a bar chart or script, sufficient space must be allowed for miscellaneous circumstances during the execution phase. Two examples of risky projects are an international sporting event and a meeting held with high-profile politicians attending. For projects such as these, a separate calamity script is should be included.

A script for the execution phase of a conference, for instance, can be subdivided into three parts, which correspond to the three sub-phases of the execution phase:

1 The build-up script (production phase) concerns preparing the venue, the catering, and the accommodation of the guests, etc.

2 The event script (working phase) contains all the details per programme item or per day, the direction of the event itself.

3 The wrap-up script concerns the supervision of any guests when they are leaving, taking down/disassembling/removing the facilities and clearing up the venue.

An execution plan can be supplemented with a *capacity plan*, which details the use of manpower, space, machines, equipment, etc.

Step 15e   Information control aspect (I)

Exercise   Consider the project information system.

This step is about taking the necessary measures for further detailing and streamlining the control and monitoring system for the project information (including the information records and distribution) for the execution phase.

Step 15f   Fundraising plan (M)

Exercise   Draw up a detailed working budget of the expenses and income (including a financial plan for any deficit). Then, state how the budget will be monitored during the execution phase.

In many cases, a detailed execution or working budget will be drawn up at the end of the development phase, when the events project has been detailed completely. For the decision-making (the final go/no-go), this budget will provide a rather accurate insight into the eventual expenses and income.

Furthermore, this working budget will provide a detailed cost budget for monitoring the fundraising plan during the execution phase. A budgetary control system must be set up for this, including a clear procedure describing who is authorised to enter into obligations and to make payments and how this should be administrated. Among other things, this means that:

– an execution administration must be set up for the events project.
– financial agreements must be made and any contracts should be arranged.
– a system must be thought of to collect, process, and safely store any participants' contributions, earnings from ticket sales, and other earnings.
– the liability and copyrights must be monitored.

The drawing up of a working budget is described in detail in Section 8.1.3 of Chapter 8 and monitoring the budget is described in Section 8.3 of that same chapter.

Step 16   5.3.4   *Drawing up the production programme*

As described above, all of the production information described and drawn up in the development phase is put together in the production programme. The production programme, therefore, is a collection of separate pieces of information which helps the execution team to carry out the project. In addition, the production programme is the final decision document on the basis of which the client can take the final go/no-go decision for the events project.

To foster the decision-making the production programme must contain sufficient information so that the client can form a detailed idea of the project result, that is, what the event will feel and look like. In addition, the client should gain insight into the main tasks that will have to be carried out during the execution phase. The production programme can also contain action plans (particularly in the case of public projects) that are related to the marketing and communication plan of the project.

Finally, the business consequences in regard to time, money, and facilities must be clear from this final decision document.

Format for the production programme   *Step 16a*

Process the information gathered during the development phase into the for- **Exercise**
mat for the production programme (See Appendix C3).

The answers to the questions defined in the step-by-step plan for the development phase are also the building blocks for the various chapters and sections of the production programme. The core of the production programme is formed by the *production information* and the *scripts*. It is difficult to provide a guideline for the size of a production programme, because it largely depends on the kind of events project and its size.

When the assignment is to develop a plan that is ready to be implemented, this means that the production programme is also the end product of the project. For learning situations within higher education, the production programme is often the end project.

Appendix C3 presents a detailed format for a production programme for an events project. In addition to the formats presented earlier for the project proposal, this format should also be viewed as a model or a checklist and not as a straightjacket. The production programme should be able to stand on its own as a separate report. This is an operational programme primarily intended for the implementers, which means that its tone and design should be practical, business-like, and concise. When drawing up this document, you should always focus on the people who will read it, i.e., the people who are going to carry out the (partial) project concerned. The production programme should contain all of the information required to produce the event. Given the limited function of the production programme, it is usually advisable to keep certain parts of it separate. For instance, this could include the *working budget* and the *communication action plan* because the information found in these two parts is not always relevant to everyone involved in the execution of the event.

Step 16b Supplementing the production programme

Exercise Draw up the production programme into a complete report.

When the intrinsic, technical, and organisational components (schedules, drawings, descriptions, lists, and scripts) have all been put into the production programme, this report should also be completed by giving it a cover, providing a summary of the core data on the title page (the page after the cover), a table of contents, an introduction and appendices. Contrary to the *project proposal* and the *project plan* drawn up earlier, the production programme will be less of a normal report and more of a varied collection of information on the production. Chapter 14 provides additional tips for the general parts of a report.

5.4 Step-by-step plan for the execution phase and completion phase

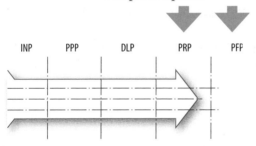

INP   PPP   DLP   PRP   PFP

The Application

'It is now one o'clock on Friday afternoon and we are sharing a sandwich with the team. Tomorrow is the big day. Last Wednesday evening we held a meeting with all of the volunteers and we explained all the plans. In addition, we assigned everyone one of the work groups under our individual supervision and discussed the relevant parts of the script. This morning, the production team started paving parts of the site and setting up the marquee. The caterer has also arrived. The script has already been discussed with them. The toilet vans have just been delivered and placed on the side of the road. It is not very busy on the site and everyone seems to know exactly what they need to do and when. This afternoon, two stage trailers and the lighting and sound equipment will arrive. As the coordinator, I did not assign myself any concrete tasks during the days of the event, which means I can walk about the site with the scripts under my arm and be available for anyone who may have questions and who might need me to solve a problem. Together with the team member who is responsible for the communication, I am going to visit the regional broadcasting company for a semi-live talk show to be broadcast tonight. The stunt has produced a great deal of publicity and the media is all ago. It is becoming very real now, very cool.'

With the delivery of the *production programme* as the final decision document, the *preparation* of the events project has now been completed and ready for execution. After the development phase these steps usually follow:
- Step 17: execution phase
- Step 18: completion phase.

During the above phases the scripts and the aftercare programme are carried out.
These phases of the events project are described below, including the individual steps (See also the general descriptions of these final phases in Section 4.3).

5.4.1   Execution phase   *Step 17*

This phase consists of three sub-phases which involve very practical tasks which for the most part will take place at the event venue:

Structure (production phase)   *Step 17a*

Build the event according to the *production programme* (script for the struc-   **Exercise**
ture).

If we continue using the metaphor of a building project, then this is the building phase. When it involves an event as a live project, it is called the construction phase. Now, everything will be made ready to receive the visitors or participants, naturally in accordance with the script for the construction (See the tasks listed in Step 18a of the step-by-step plan for a conference project in Chapter 6). At the end of the construction phase, the event is ready to be opened or started. There is a detailed programme, a script for the event and for the wrap-up. If we compare it to a building project, then the building will be ready to be inhabited at the end of this phase. At the end of the construction phase, the team will have a *working programme* (for instance, in the form of a user manual and a maintenance instruction) and an *aftercare programme consisting of all of the tasks to be carried out during the* completion phase. Often these programmes have been made during the development phase.

Step 17b   The event (working phase)

Exercise   Allow the event to take place as it was intended to.

During this phase, the event will take place according to the detailed working programme and the script for the event. When a building project is carried out, this working phase could take up to fifty years or longer, which means that this phase would fall outside the scope of the project.

The main difference between a film or video production and a live project is that the latter category does not involve a great deal of rehearsing and nothing can be redone. If something does go wrong and it cannot be remedied immediately, then this will always be a determining factor, regardless of how much work was done beforehand. The result is what the visitors experience and what they take home with them in this regard. It is therefore of utmost importance that the script for the event itself is carried out very precisely (See the tasks listed in Step 18b of the step-by-step plan for a conference project in Chapter 6).

In addition to the programme, the reception, supervision, and service provided to the visitors will be the main focus during the event. When technically more complicated events are involved, the project manager gives *cues* to start carrying out certain tasks from the script. In practice, there are often miscellaneous circumstances. It is therefore very important that the events project manager is always present during the event and that he or she is always available by mobile phone or other means of communication for technical details, for those responsible for the various parts of the event, etc. When event has reached an end, the evaluation form should be completed by the bands/artists/speakers/ etc.

Wrap-up	*Step 17c*

Dismantle the event according to the script for the wrap-up.	Exercise

During the hours and days immediately following the event, the event venue will be dismantled, cleared away, and tidied up. This is done according to the script for the wrap-up (See the tasks in Step 18c of the *step-by-step plan for a conference project* in Chapter 6).

Press and public services	*Step 17d*

Organise the press and public services.	Exercise

During the opening or at the start of the event, it is likely that a press release has been planned in the communication plan (including the distribution of the press folder upon production of the press pass and having reporters sign an attendance list). Make sure this reception goes flawlessly.

Whenever live projects are involved, the service provided to the visitors should be the main focus during the event. It is all about keeping the visitors satisfied and seeing to it that their questions are answered. Organise the public service as described in the action plan.

Public survey	*Step 17e*

Carry out the evaluation public survey now (in the case of public events).	Exercise

If it was previously decided to carry out an evaluation public survey, and Step 14b comprised a survey proposal, then this survey will be carried out during the event. Artists and other participants may also receive an evaluation form (See Step 14 in the step-by-step plan for such a survey in Section 11.2.1).

Business preconditions	*Step 17f*

Monitor the business preconditions during the execution phase.	Exercise

At the start of the execution phase a briefing should be organised for all those involved in the construction and working of the event, but also for suppliers (technicians, caterers, etc.)

During the execution phase, especially during the *construction,* large financial obligations are entered into and you will be faced with unexpected expenditures. It is therefore of vital importance that the execution budget be well-monitored. Also keep a financial project administration (for assignments and invoices, among other things. Often there is no time for this because everything is so busy, but you will pay the price later if you do not do this. In addition, be sure to monitor the quality of the event during this execution phase. Furthermore, the project information that is available during this phase will have to be coordinated. Finally, coordinate the execution of all tasks in this phase, on the basis of the scripts.

Step 18

5.4.2   Completion phase

At the end of the completion phase, the event will have been completed, the survey report will have been presented and the project will have been evaluated (evaluation report).

Step 18a   Aftercare

Exercise   Carry out the aftercare programme.

The speakers, volunteers, etc., receive a thank-you note. There may be a follow-up. All this will take place according to the aftercare programme which was previously set up.

Step 18b   Survey report

Exercise   Report the results of the public survey, if applicable.

Section 11.2.1 contains a step-by-step plan for such a survey. If it is held during the event, Steps 15 (processing and analysing survey) and 16 (reporting public survey results) are carried out during the completion phase.

Step 18c   Financial settlement

Exercise   Compose the financial settlement.

Upon completion of the event, the final payments are made and the financial settlement must be drawn up for the client. It is recommended that the format from Figure 8.3 be used again. When it involves an event that has been carried out by an external organiser, the final invoice of such an agency is settled with the client. Sometimes, for instance, a financial or intrinsic account is required by a subsidising agency.

Project records	*Step 18d*

Start project records.	Exercise

It is recommended that all of the relevant project information be recorded in an orderly fashion for the next edition of the event. This is often neglected because the project manager was too busy already organising the next project during this phase. At the start of the next edition, those involved are often confronted with a huge pile of former documents that have been poorly organised. Try to avoid this from happening.

Project evaluation	*Step 18e*

Evaluate the event with all its parts (project result) and the project process from idea to implementation and draw up an evaluation report.	Exercise

For the final evaluation of the event, the following questions can be posed: has the target group (when it concerns a public event) been reached and was it satisfied? Did the event work the way it was supposed to work? In other words, did the event achieve the desired effect? Were the methods used during the preparation and execution adequate? Did the control tasks, such as time planning, budgeting, and organising, ensure that the budget was met (or the targets were met), the deadlines were met, the tasks and responsibilities were carried out by all of those involved, etc? Was the cooperation among those involved to everyone's satisfaction? Has the project manager done a satisfactory job?

It is important that an evaluation report be concluded by providing a summary with points to focus on for the next time. Sometimes, even a blueprint can be made for the next edition of the event. The team can also evaluate how it functioned during the project.

6

Step-by-step plan for a conference project

We all eventually come into contact with conferences, whether we work for the government, are involved in health care, in the cultural sector or in the business community. Almost on a daily basis we are invited to sign up for seminars, symposiums or workshops via brochures, announcements and advertisements.

When designing a conference, however, there is hardly any room for experimentation. Usually a tried-and-true recipe is used: a number of prominent speakers address the conference goers, who then ask questions and meet in small groups for discussion, and afterwards report what was discussed at a plenary meeting. Subsequently, the chairperson will make an attempt to summarise and lend structure to what has been said. Why do those who organise conferences so often choose a traditional speaker-dominated conference design? One reason might be that such an approach - certainly in the case of large groups - is easy to manage. Participants, on the other hand, also feel the need to participate, and they would prefer to have less of a demand made on their intellectual capacity, but instead prefer a conference that is less geared towards achievement and one that contains a bit of humor. They expect, among other things, to acquire new knowledge and skills and to make acquaintances. A conference can also serve as a strategic tool for achieving goals. This requires a new approach by the organisers. The design of the conference will need to become more varied in shape and form and it will have to achieve a balance between freedom and constraint. The programme will have to offer active participation and two-way communication.

Programme makers will have to be open to spontaneous (out of the ordinary) ideas and ways of working. 'Conference tourists' will have to make way for more involved participants. Preferably a conference held in an empty factory building than one which is boring and set in between coffee and lunch, red velvet couches and dark mahogany furniture.

Conference as a collective noun

The term 'conference' is used here as a collective noun to designate meetings of a specific nature. A conference involves small to very large groups of people who participate in a programme planned to last one or more days. The conference serves as a medium for exchanging information and for promoting interaction between the providers and users of information and is aimed at achieving one or more goals. The various terms which are used to describe conferences are:

– congress (a meeting for joint deliberation, often at an international level)
– workshop (place for participants to share in activities)
– seminar (advanced group who studies a certain topic under supervision)
– symposium (an academic gathering at which a certain topic is discussed, usually lasting a day)
– theme day or get-together
– excursion.

The conference is often a multi-disciplinary project. The complexity of developing and organising such an event makes it necessary to tackle the project in a professional way and to assign the end responsibility to a conference coordinator or a conference project manager who will lead all those involved with the organisation, check the agreements made, and manage the preparations. During the conference he or she is in charge of the production. The conference project manager is a generalist. His or her main contribution is that, while preparing, carrying out and following up the conference he or she is able to unite otherwise, more or less, isolated experts. The conference project manager is particularly geared towards involving the participants and during the entire project he or is creating the opportunity for participants to engage actively. In practice, the preparation for a conference is usually done by a temporary group of non-professionals. The commitment is often greater than the expertise, especially when it involves the conference project manager's understanding of the task described above.

The phases of a conference project

In Appendix B1 a model is shown which depicts how a conference project is developed. This phase model is a variant of the basic form which is described in Chapter 4, and which is represented by the arrow shown in Figure 4.2. In this chapter, the phase model has been worked out into a step-by-step plan for the entire development process of the conference, from start to finish. The step-by-step plan is meant to help those who would professionally like to develop and organise a more extensive conference project. It consists of five phases, namely:

1 Initiative phase
2 Preparation phase
3 Development phase
4 Performance phase, consisting of:
    – The application (production phase)
    – The conference itself (performance phase)
    – The dismantlement
5 Evaluation phase

In the step-by-step plan which follows, the activities have been included which need to be professionally carried out in order to produce the product, the conference.

If during your study you are given the assignment to develop a conference, then you can apply the step-by-step plan for a conference project that is described in this chapter. However, even this step-by-step plan should be considered as a guideline. It is a model which gives a linear outline of the process. Reality will turn out to be much more capricious, and the steps will not necessarily follow perfectly one after the other in practice. Still, experience has shown that a step-by-step plan can offer some guidance (particularly when one has little experience), as long as it is not applied too strictly. First read through the step-by-step plan in its entirety before you start applying it. In order to get you into the right mindset, each phase has been preceded by a short case study, which is related to the phase concerned. The case that was presented in the previous chapter was somewhat traditional. In order to indicate how new media offers many new possibilities. A case has been presented in this chapter which portrays a less traditional project, namely, a teleconference. However, the steps described in the step-by-step plan are related to a more commonly used form for conferences in regard to place and time.

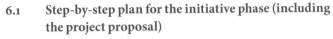

6.1 Step-by-step plan for the initiative phase (including the project proposal)

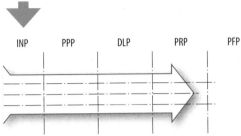

INP   PPP   DLP   PRP   PFP

The Application

I am currently enrolled in Communication Studies at a professional university and one day I would love to find a job in an international setting. At our study we were given the opportunity to go abroad for six months and together with my fellow student, Esmee, I am now attending lectures at a university in Jakarta. When we return to the Netherlands, we will be finishing our studies. Two weeks ago, we came up with the idea to do our final study project on organising a teleconference on cross-cultural communication. We would like to involve both our educational institute in the Netherlands and in Indonesia in such a project. First we discussed the idea with our senior lecturer here at the university in Indonesia and he was enthusiastic right from the start. Then we explained our idea in an e-mail message to our final project coordinator in Amsterdam. She also agreed provisionally to the idea and assigned us a project leader. We only could receive final consent once we had written a project proposal that was fully worked out. The senior lecturer here in Indonesia paired us together with two Indonesian students in their third year who were eager to gain experience in *teleconferencing*. When we have to go back to the Netherlands, they can arrange things on this side. During our study we learned about virtual meetings and teleconferencing, but in the last few weeks we have really delved deeper into the subject and seen a lot on the internet and had loads of discussions about the topic. We believe that there are wonderful possibilities, but our final project leader advised us not to make it too big of a project, since it is a new phenomenon. To begin with, we want to gear the project toward the students participating, but we would also like to involve the teachers from both institutes. We know now what the technical and functional possibilities are. For our project mission we have formulated the following: "The project is meant to make the third-year students as well as teachers from both institutes more aware of the cultural differences and to get them to think about the consequences that these differences can have on the business communication between the two cultures." Yesterday evening the four of us met again. The basic concept of the conference is beginning to take shape. We are thinking about holding four sessions, lasting from an hour and a half to two hours, during four consecutive Monday afternoons, sometime in April. We cannot hold the conferences in the evening, because of the time difference, Jakarta being 6 hours later than in the Netherlands. The working title for the conference will be "Understanding leads to Respect." The basic concept is as follows. The first session will be a try-out and will involve getting acquainted with one another and with the phenomenon of teleconferencing. A short introduction will also be presented about the theme of the conference. During the next two sessions the cultural differences will be outlined by giving presentations and holding discussions. The university in Jakarta will take responsibility for the content of one of these sessions. During the final session, the consequences on business communication in regard to the differences that have been signalled will be discussed. This session should result in five recommendations for business people from Indonesia and the Netherlands. Each session will be introduced and interspersed by short, stimulating presentations consisting of stances taken by experts from both institutes. During the evenings we have been developing the points of departure, the basic concept and the business and technical aspects that need to be put down on paper. We have also formulated criteria for the software to be used during the conference. Furthermore, we have developed a plan of action for the project in which we explain that the conference is to be seen as a project and how it will be carried out. We have come up with a time sheet and we have clearly described in an organisational plan how the tasks will be distributed in the following phases. The general budget plan includes a sum of 1,900 euros. We are going to ask our institute to contribute 1,000 euros since it is an experiment from which everyone can learn. To cover the difference of 900 euros, we will seek a sponsor. Furthermore, we have thought about the communication that will need to take place between the two institutes and about recruiting participants and developing a fundraising plan. By the end of next week, this should take the shape of a project proposal to be presented to the senior lecturer here and our final project leader in the Netherlands. Once they have agreed to the proposal, we will work it out further into a detailed project plan.'

In the initiative phase the most fundamental choices are made concerning the conference project. In this phase the preconditions and starting points are determined in order to steer the course of the project. First read again the general description of the initiative phase in Section 4.3.1.

The initiative phase is concluded by writing a project proposal in order to further the decision making which is sometimes called an initiative report. In project-oriented teaching at institutes for higher education, the project proposal is sometimes referred to as a starting document. The project proposal can be adjusted so that it can be used when applying for subsidies or when seeking sponsors.

During the initiative phase of a conference project, the following steps are distinguished (See Appendix B1 Phase Model Conferences):

Step 0: Project Start-Up (PSU)

Step 1: Exploring the assignment or the idea

Step 2: Formulating the central question

Step 3: Defining the intrinsic starting points

Step 4: Developing a basic concept

Step 5: Making a plan of action

Step 6: Gearing it to the market and surroundings

Step 7: Reflecting on the business preconditions

Step 8: Writing a project proposal

For the step-by-step plan for the initiative phase go back to Section 5.1

The step-by-step plan for the initiative phase of the project is of a general nature. That is why it can be also be used for the initiative phase of a conference project described in Section 5.1, which has been used to describe the initiative phase of an event project. After you have described all of the points of departure and preconditions for your conference project using Section 5.1.9 as a guide to write your project proposal, you will return to this page. Then you can follow the development phase of your conference by using the step-by-step plan intended for the preparation phase described below in Section 6.2.

6.2   Step-by-step plan for the preparation phase (including project plan)

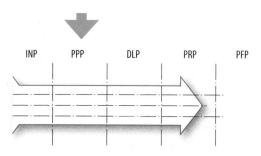

INP   PPP   DLP   PRP   PFP

The Application

'Two weeks ago we returned to the Netherlands. Both the senior lecturer in Jakarta and our final project leader agreed to our starting points and preconditions for the virtual conference as we had described them in the project proposal, a week before we left Jakarta. Before we left Indonesia, we had a brainstorming session with the two Indonesian team members about how to work out the basic concept into a detailed plan. At the moment we are staying in touch via e-mail. On the basis of the criteria regarding the software that we will use which was stated in the project proposal, we decided to facilitate this by using *Macromedia Breeze*. That is a communication system that makes teleconferencing possible. *Breeze* was implemented into the electronic learning environment *Blackboard* that is used at our institute. The university in Jakarta has also decided to install *Breeze* in the near future. It is not possible to install *Breeze* at home. The online meeting of the teleconference is planned to take place on 6, 13, 20 and 27 April from 1 p.m. to 3 p.m. (in Jakarta it is six hours later). With Breeze it is possible to work in three circles. On the inside circle we would like to place at the most two teachers and four students next to the chairperson (who will lead the discussion and stick to the script). They will appear on screen and communicate with one another, since they are the presenters. These participants will have a webcam and a headset. In the next circle we will seat a maximum of eight students, who can contribute to the discussion via a chat programme (these are the participants). Then at least a thousand students will be able to listen passively and watch the session or a filming of the sessions afterwards (these are the viewers). Esmee and I will act during the sessions as moderators (kind of like directors). The participants in the different circles will be a mixture of students and teachers from Jakarta and Amsterdam. Chatters can only ask questions at the end of the presentation, otherwise it will be very difficult for the chairperson to keep the thread of the discussion. As moderators we will direct this. For each session we will make a starting film of a few minutes. All of the teachers here and in Jakarta are prepared to give short presentations containing discussion points which students can respond to. These teachers will make up the first circle and act as experts. We understood that it is very important to organise everything exactly to the letter, and that is why we have drawn up a conference programme that resembles a detailed script for each session, to prevent everyone from talking at once. Questions have been included in the form of a poll in the script that will be asked of all the participants which can serve as starting points for the discussions. We found a teacher who is somewhat experienced with using *Breeze* and who will take on the role of chairperson during the sessions. The contact with the two students in Jakarta is going well. Although it is our final study project, we are keeping them informed almost daily and they are reporting back to their institute. We are working out the teleconference now into a detailed project plan. We also have included a budget and a time sheet in this plan. The budget appears to have been increased and now it amounts to a sum of 2,100 euros. It looks like our institute will indeed be contributing a sum of 1,000 euros. In addition, we are just getting ready to sign a sponsor agreement for the remaining sum. Companies apparently are eager to participate in this experiment. The communication strategy from the project proposal is now being adapted for use as a communication plan by Esmee. We also decided to record each session for later use, since the possibility is available in *Breeze*. We promised our final project leader and our senior lecturer in Jakarta that we would hand in a detailed project plan in two weeks' time. If they agree, then we will prepare for the teleconference to be carried out.'

When an agreement has been reached concerning the project proposal and subsequently over all of the starting points and the business preconditions pertaining to the conference project, then the preparation phase can begin. In this phase the main focus is on developing the conference theme. In order to comprehend this phase well, it would be advisable to first read the general description of the preparation phase found in Section 4.2. The results from the preparation phase will be summarised later in the project plan. In this plan, in addition to the conference theme, the consequences will further be elaborated on and compared with the business preconditions which were used as a gauge at the end of the previous phase.

During the preparation phase of the conference project the following steps can be distinguished:

- Step 9: Organising the information for the conference
- Step 10: Developing the conference theme
- Step 11: Developing plans for the marketing/communication track
- Step 12: Reflecting on the business preconditions (control aspects)
- Step 13: Writing a project plan.

Step 9

6.2.1   *Organising the information for the conference*

The core activity during this preparation phase is to work out the specific details of the basic concept that were developed during the previous phase into a detailed conference theme, including the group dynamics and didactical methods.

When planning a conference project, organising the information and further elaborating on the contents of the conference theme often make this task time consuming and one of the most difficult parts of the conference project.

The purpose of providing information during the conference can be varied:
- Knowledge transfer and exchange
- Stimulating discussion (for example by making propositions)
- Expanding existing knowledge
- Introducing thought and action alternatives
- Introduction to the conference theme (for example by using a role play or a video clip)
- Offering new topics for discussion.

At the end of the preparation phase, the basic concept is transformed into a detailed conference theme, including a programme consisting of exact times, a final list of speakers and leaders of workshops, featuring the exact details concerning the venue and the service facilities, etc. It does not state how the conference will be exactly organised for this will be done during the development phase. The organisation of the information can be achieved via several different channels. The following is only one possible approach.

Conference approach   *Step 9a*

Make a choice between the 'push' and the 'pull' approach.   Exercise

Should the information be presented to the participants by third parties (knowledgeable speakers) (push approach) or should it be produced by participants who exchange information (limited) amongst themselves (pull approach)? In the first case, the conference project leader will have to organise a more or less complete supply of information beforehand. In this case, satisfactory solutions will have to be sought in order to create interaction amongst the participants so that they can respond to the topic and the information supplied. In the second case, those who organise the conference will have to prepare the information beforehand so that it will encourage the participants themselves to start producing the information and exchanging it amongst themselves. Both approaches require conducting a similar amount of research on the conference theme and possessing empathy towards subject matter that will intrigue potential participants.

Conference theme   *Step 9b*

Study the conference theme in even greater detail.   Exercise

If everything has gone as planned, then you will have conducted preliminary research during the initiative phase on the conference theme. Now you should delve more deeply into the subject matter, and think about the following areas:
– brainstorming about the aspects that are linked to the theme and conduct extensive research in regard to these aspects
– developing the theme, for example, by inviting several experts on the subject or a few of the participants in order, among other things, to decide on a leitmotiv.

As you work on the conference contents, if all goes well, a kind of interplay with the other components of the conference will emerge, namely, the form with respect to content, the group dynamics and the didactical methods (See Step 10).

Structural outline   *Step 9c*

Make a structural outline of the content information.   Exercise

The leitmotiv that has been chosen can be turned into a structural outline by clustering it into (sub) themes. Provide brief descriptions of these themes. In the speaker-dominated approach (push), you can search for and select speakers on the basis of these descriptions. In consultation with the speakers, the supply of information is then further developed.

In the participatory approach (pull) the descriptions of the themes should be developed into concise, stimulating information, initial questions, propositions and discussion programmes.

Step 10

6.2.2   Developing the conference design

Content and form determine how the conference will look. What eventually happens during and after the conference to the supporting theme and programme depends, to a large extent, on the interaction amongst the participants, the speakers, the conference staff, experts and the like. How this interaction unfolds is the most difficult of all the points mentioned to gauge and to plan. That does not mean that you cannot do anything about it.

If contributing factors to this interaction process are not judged properly (such as possible problems and interests), then, instead of the desired value, damage can occur. Arguably, those who organise the conference would prefer to maintain the effectiveness criteria for this interaction process in order to achieve the desired results. This often implies an apparently rational-functional criterion for a usually rather irrational-emotional process between people. A good sense of empathy in regard to what intrigues (stimulates, inspires, irritates) the participants is of great importance.

Step 10a   Differences among participants

Exercise   Think about the differences that you might find amongst the participants attending the conference.

Participants at conferences might belong to different organisations or they might come from different countries with great differences in cultural behaviour. At a conference there may also be differences in interests, ideologies, history, traditions and customs, rules and agreements, ways of thinking and doing (norms and values) and leadership styles. As a consequence, discussions during the conference can often lead to irrational and ambivalent behaviour.

Participants' situation   *Step 10b*

Take the participants' (home) situation into account.   **Exercise**

It is a well-known fact that the contrast formed between the conference setting and the home situation is not always ideal. How can the conference project
manager create a conference community in which the participants receive support so that they can cope with this duality? The conference project manager
finds the task rather daunting when trying to design a conference that differs
from the participants' usual ways of thinking and doing and which provides
enough of a challenge for learning and initiating change. On the other hand,
the conference should not become such an isolated world that the participant
cannot link it to his own home situation. If the participant does not feel involved with the conference community, then it is quite likely that the conference will hardly have any lasting effect on him or her. Moreover, there is another difficulty in that participants who attend a conference have sometimes
received a specific mandate or have their own hidden agenda. As a result, they
will be less inclined to air their views, criticism and the like if they feel this
might entail obligations for the group or organisation that they represent. The
conference project manager is thus faced with the problem of how best to link
the participants' different targets, intentions and interests. That is why it is important to make a general analysis of the targets and interests, expectations and
limitations and peculiarities of the potential participants' 'situations at home'.
Gather and verify this information by conducting interviews and by holding
(telephone) surveys and response panels.

Criteria regarding form and design   *Step 10c*

Formulate the criteria and points of focus for the group dynamics and didacti-   **Exercise**
cal forms used at the conference.

Consider the factors that might influence the interaction, the communication
and the learning process of the participants. You might want to think about the
following factors:
– The diversity of the targets, the expectations and interests of the participants
   and 'stay-at-home participants' (This is what happened during a summit
   meeting when the contribution made by the Minister of Foreign Affairs was
   partially determined by the expectations of the parliament as upon his return he had to account for his actions), the same kind of influence that you
   find outside the conference, you will also within the conference community

– Resistance to change
– Different learning styles of the participants
– A normally one-sided appeal made to the intellectual and verbal capacities of the participants
– The presence or rather the lack of humor and possible diversions in the programme
– Continual effect of earlier events
– Mistakes in the programming (for example, too much one-way communication, too rigid
– Mistakes in the programme, not enough light in the conference room or a freezing cold temperature.

Determine which factors could influence the interaction during the conference and find out which role these might play by asking those concerned. On the basis of this knowledge, formulate the criteria and points of focus regarding the communication and interaction process. Afterwards, decide what implications these points will have on the programming.

Step 10e   Choosing a conference design

Exercise   Develop a design for group dynamic and didactical forms at the conference.

Design and set guidelines so as to avoid any difficulties which might preclude problems resulting from ruling interests and objectives. It is important to:
– use a plan that stimulates the participants to participate actively and assume responsibility for the way things go and the outcome of the conference
– use a plan that offers the participants the possibility to take the conference outcomes home with them
– instruct speakers/panel chairpersons to attune their talk to include possible problems/or to relate it to the situation at home.

Look for or design suitable methods and ways of lending form to the communication and interaction process and see if they comply with the criteria mentioned (See also Appendix A12). Consult any literature available on this subject.

Step 10f   Conference plan

Exercise   Develop a coherent, interesting and varied conference plan.

The main focus will be on scheduling the activities to take place during the conference. The organisers will design the conference as accurately as possible, step-by-step. While doing so, they will allow themselves to be guided by concerns regarding the desired end product, the conference theme, the possible objectives and the participants' expectations and responses. A good conference plan should not resemble a train timetable, but it should strike somewhat of a balance between an acceptable degree of freedom and constraint for the participants. The structure is only a tool. When developing a conference plan, take the previously designed basic concept as a starting point and develop a coherent and varied plan as far as contents (Step 9) and design (Step 10) are concerned. When developing a conference plan you must think about programming activities, the supporting sub-projects and activities, and possible follow-up activities after the conference. Make sure that the conference plan includes the steps and events which took place prior to the conference and work towards creating possible follow-up activities. A few examples of possible activities are:
– 'Warm-ups' or 'ice-breakers' (to introduce the theme)
– Lectures, introductions and the like
– Discussions, debates
– Forums, _hearings_, panels
– Drama workshops
– Information fairs
– Theme groups
– Audiovisual presentations
– Product displays
– Social and entertainment programmes
– Play acting (mime, theatre, radio play).

See Appendix A12 as well for _Supplementary group dynamic and didactical forms._

Supporting sub-projects activities could include:
– Conference book or paper, syllabus or documentation folder (which content, for whom, by whom?)
– Expositions, demonstrations and the like
– Performances (music, artists)
– Excursions, social events and opportunities for informal contacts
– Programmes for those accompanying participants (known also as _partner_ programmes and the like)
– Possible mobilisation of travel agencies for travel and transport arrange-

ments for participants
- Welcome package, conference souvenirs
- Photo shoot

Step 11

6.2.3 Developing plans for the Marketing and Communication Track

During the preparation phase, the marketing and communication *strategy* that you developed in the initiative phase will be worked out into a marketing *plan*, a fundraising *plan* and a communication *plan*. These plans are usually an integral part of the project plan for the conference, but they can also be presented separately. In the plans, it is stated how and by which means the marketing and communication strategy will be carried out, for example: the recruitment of participants will be done via posters, the website, advertisements and commercials. In some cases, for example when an extensive fundraising campaign is a part of the conference project, the fundraising plan will be drawn up in the initiative phase. This campaign actually costs quite a bit of time. In addition, it is not always worth spending more time on the project, if there is no prospect of receiving a closing budget. Further instructions for setting up these plans can be found in Section 11.2, Steps 4-6.

Step 11a Marketing plan

Exercise Develop a marketing plan for the conference project (only applies to market projects).

A *marketing plan* indeed only applies to conferences which are meant for the market (market projects/ selling entrance tickets). For a symposium by invitation, this is not the case.

The marketing plan clearly indicates how you plan the conference will be introduced into the market. When drawing up such a plan, the Marketing Mix (the 5 Ps) is usually used. In Section 11.2, Step 4, a description of how to make a marketing plan can be found. In Figure 11.4, a format is given for a marketing plan in which the renowned five Ps are used. These five aspects should combine together to satisfy the needs and wishes of the target group of the conference. It concerns such choices in regard to:

- **p**roduct (which (part) product per target group (product market combination, also known as PMC)

- **p**rice (price level, price differences)
- **p**lace (where it is sold, how it is distributed)
- **p**romotion (how attention will be drawn)
- **p**ersonnel (attitude, charisma, etc.)

Communication plan	*Step 11b*
Develop a communication plan for the conference project.	Exercise

The communication plan elaborates further on the communication strategy found in the project proposal. In other words, at this point it should be determined from a tactical perspective how communication will take place with external groups and which means (the website, brochures, posters, magazine articles, etc.) will be used. In Chapter 11, the entire marketing and communication track will be described.

When drawing up a communication action plan you should consider such questions as:
- What kind of information do I want to provide or which message to I want to convey?
- Which medium will I use for this purpose?
- Which form should I use to present the information?
- Who should receive the information?
- With what purpose should the information be distributed?
- Which method of distribution would be most suitable for this?

When the communication action plan forms an intrinsic part (chapter) of the project plan, then it usually consists of the following two parts:
- communication matrix (See the information provided in Section 11.2, Step 6)
- communication planning (planning of the communication activities, for example in the form of a separate GANNT chart (bar chart).

See further information on the communication action plan in Section 11.2, Step 6 and use the format for a communication action plan that is given in Figure 11.6.

For international conferences an inventory should be made of the border restrictions (the necessary customs documents and procedures) for the participants and possible goods.

When a conference project is placed under time constraints, a communication action plan can be made in this phase and the mailings, for example, can be sent to potential participants as well. In other cases, you should wait before making a communication *action* plan and carrying it out until the development phase. A model of a table of contents that can be used for a communication action plan can be found in Section 11.3. Guidelines for a possible press release have been placed in Appendix A10. For examples of information carriers, see Appendix A13.

Step 11c Fundraising plan

Exercise Develop a fundraising plan for the conference project.

During the initiative phase you will also have included, when applicable, the fundraising target groups in the communication strategy. This might include, among others, subsidisers, funds, companies, and potential partners for cooperation. In the fundraising plan you will describe how you intend to acquire sponsors and go about fund raising. In Figure 11.5, a model has been provided that can be used for a fundraising plan.

Attention: The fundraising plan will be worked out into a fundraising *action* plan. As the fundraising campaign often requires a great deal of time, it is therefore too late in most cases to draw up and to carry out the fundraising action plan during the development phase. In such cases, this action plan should also be drawn up in the preparation phase and be placed in production. Sometimes this should even be done right after the initiative phase!

Step 12a ### 6.2.4 *Reflecting on the business preconditions (QOFTIM)*

At the end of the initiative phase, the business preconditions will have been set for each control aspect in the project proposal. You have now reached the next phase. The basic concept has been worked out into a detailed plan for the conference. This means that each control aspect must be reexamined. Record, in advance, which starting points have to be readjusted for each control aspect in regard to the approved project proposal.

Quality control aspect (Q)   *Step 12a*

Describe how to monitor the quality of the conference project that is being de-   **Exercise**
veloped.

The following questions will need to be addressed: How does the process of
monitoring quality control progress according to the standards set for quality
criteria determined in the project proposal? Should an adjustment still be made
in order to proceed further to the next phase (development phase)?

Organisational control aspect (o)   *Step 12b*

Adjust the organisational setup for the conference.   **Exercise**

When taking this step the following question is of importance: To what extent should the plan, which was previously made for organising the conference
(organisation flow chart), be adjusted in order to proceed further to the next
phase (development phase)?
– Make a chart showing the distribution of tasks which have been assigned for
  the development phase.
– Draw up an internal communication plan. This should include a consultation and briefing with all of those internally involved and the mutual agreement of what everyone's role and contribution should be.

Here it should be mentioned that in the following phase the production crew
will be much more involved in the conference project and in some cases, it
should also be assigned a place within the organisation flow chart.

Facility control aspect (F)   *Step 12c*

Draw up a facility plan.   **Exercise**

This step can be separated into three parts, namely:
– *Venue plan*, including the following questions: Which venue has been chosen and why? How should the venue be set up and furbished? Can all of the
  practical matters in relation to the venue be described (take, for example, fire
  safety requirements, electrical wiring, Internet connections)? And should
  accommodation be reserved for the participants?

Attention: The option that was had on the venue should now be finalised. This means that the final facility criteria in regard to the venue will also have to be set.

- *Facility plan*: Can the necessary facilities be described (for example, audio-visual equipment and computers) and how can these be acquired (draw up an acquisition list including the prices and conditions)?
- *Legalities plan* or *permit plan*, including the question: Which permits/approval/rights of acquisition (consider copyrights) and other legal steps are necessary to obtain and how should these matters be approached?

Step 12d Time control aspect (T)

Exercise Draw up an adjusted time sheet.

The central question is how does the new general time sheet look when it is depicted as a bar chart, from the end of the preparation phase up to and including the completion and evaluation of the event? In order to use the time sheet for monitoring the next phase (development phase), the planning for that phase must contain a detailed task overview. The following phases can be described more generally. Sometimes, it is useful to draw up a separate time sheet for the development phase. Furthermore, it is often useful, to draw up a capacity plan (how many people/space available/means) as well, having consulted all of the participants first.

Step 12e Information control aspect (I)

Exercise Consider the project information system.

The question is, does the control and monitoring system for the information supply still need to be adjusted, and if so, how? (See the information carriers mentioned in Appendix A13.)

Step 12f Financial control/ Money aspect (M)

Exercise Draw up a cost estimate for the various parts (components of the conference) and provide the financial figures.

The following questions should be addressed: How does the budget look for each part of the project (See the components budget that is discussed in Section

8.1.2)? How does the financial scheme look? What can currently be said about the state of the budget (budget report)? (See also Section 8.3).

And:
– Set up and keep a conference administration.
– Organise contracts and financial agreements.
– Determine participants' contributions and other earnings.
– Determine the financial compensation for speakers, panel chairpersons, and the like.

6.2.5   Drawing up the project plan   *Step 13*

For detailed decision-forming, the project plan for the client must contain sufficient information in order to provide an exact idea of the conference project. The *conference project* forms the intrinsic core of this project plan.

For the steps that result in a project plan for the conference project, you are advised to refer to the step-by-step plan for an events project found in Section 5.2.4. An extensive model for a project plan can be found in Appendix C2.

6.3   Step-by-step plan for the development phase (including the production programme)

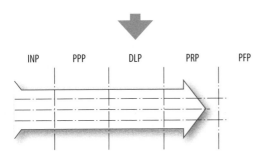

The Application

'Both our project supervisor as well as our senior lecturer in Jakarta were enthusiastic about the detailed project plan for the teleconference. We are now busy getting the project ready to carry it out. In the meantime, we have edited three of the four films and the fourth one will be ready by next week. We also asked our teachers from Amsterdam and Jakarta, who will be functioning as experts, to send us possibly *PowerPoint* presentations and other material. We are going to place all the contents in *Breeze* in advance. We are also in the process of making the scenarios, one for the preparation during the two weeks before the conference and the other for using during the weeks of the conference. We are also making an aftercare programme including a final evaluation. *Breeze* has different 'modi' in which you can work, such as preparing a session, uploading content and designing screen lay-out. Esmee has made a nice screen lay-out. The first e-mail message has also been sent to all of the potential participants in Jakarta and Amsterdam. Yesterday I was busy writing instructions for the different people involved on how to participate in the teleconference. A week before the first session starts, we are going to hold a technical test. All of the participants will be requested in advance during this trial session to test their connection, their equipment and the sound. In this way, the participants can become familiar with the interface and how it works. Esmee and I have appointed ourselves as hosts or moderators for the teleconference. Two weeks ago we took a basic training course in *Breeze*. As hosts, we have the most liberty and we can recognise small problems and solve them. For the three different types of participants, we have put instructions down on paper about how to access the teleconference. After they have requested an account, we will send them these instructions. In addition, I have to still develop a web form for the participants' survey, since such a survey was one of the preconditions of our study in order to receive financial funding for our project. Once we have put everything on paper, we will take this information about how to carry out the conference and put it into a performance programme (also known as a production programme). Just like the two earlier decision documents, we will also close the performance programme with, among other things, a time sheet (in the form of scenarios), a work budget and an organisational flow chart. The final budget has now been set at a sum of 2,200 euros. That is 100 euros more than the approved budget, but we will compensate for the difference. The graduation project supervisor and the senior lecturer in Jakarta will have to give the final green light based on the performance programme, before the production phase, but they cannot actually say 'no' anymore. According to plan, this last 'go' will be given within three weeks at the most.

In Section 4.2 a brief introduction was given about the development phase, so read this through once more. The conference project was given its content and form during the preparation phase. In the development phase, the design and plans will be made ready for the performance and thought will be given to what should take place once the conference has ended. Therefore in this phase final choices will have to be made in regard to how the conference is to be carried out, the way it will be set up, and possibly how the schedules of those employed should look, etc. In addition, consideration will have to be given as to which information is necessary (take, for example, drawings showing how the venue has been divided up, rental lists and order forms), when who does what (scenarios) and where things should be placed (maps).

In the project plan, including the conference design, it was rendered in detail *what* should be accomplished, but now it concerns more *when, where, how,* and *with what* and *by whom* it should be done - mainly practical information. The results obtained from the development phase are put together in the *production programme*. This might contain, among other things, the scenarios, technical plans, rental lists including possibly work drawings, maps, a volunteer plan, timetables and rehearsal schedules.

The following steps can be distinguished during the development phase of the conference project:
- Step 14: translate the conference design into product information
- Step 15: make and carry out the action plans for the marketing and communication track
- Step 16: safeguard the business preconditions
- Step 17: set up the production programme.

6.3.1 Translating the conference design into product information
Step 14

The core activity during the development phase is formed by working the conference design into product information in order to assist those who will be setting up and carrying out the conference.

Developing and conducting a pilot test
Step 14a

Work out the plans. Decide afterwards whether or not it would be useful and perhaps possible to test certain parts of the conference in advance.
Exercise

You might want to think about having the conference syllabus or a documentation folder printed and about developing supporting activities/sub-projects (See also Step 10e, under supporting sub-projects and activities).

Developing a live project such as a conference requires that all goes well in one go. Sometimes it is possible to test certain parts in advance, for instance, by using pilot testing, by holding a general rehearsal or pre-conferences, and by coaching and training speakers, panel chairpersons, observers and the conference chairperson.

Step 14b   Setting up the operational programme

Exercise   Take stock of which instructions should be given during the conference and to whom. Include these instructions in a user manual (operational programme). It is advisable to make a calamity plan, possibly as part of the operational programme.

In an operational programme a description is given of how the conference should 'operate' and what is necessary in order for everything to run as smoothly as planned. It is a user manual for those who are responsible for the daily routine during the conference once it has started.

In the operational programme for a conference the instructions can, for example, be found for those who are to receive the guests and who will give out badges and documentation folders, but also instructions are given for the sound technicians and for hostesses on what to do about aggressive behaviour, how to deal with the media and calamities.

Brainstorm with each other about the possible calamities that could occur during the conference and try to describe what could subsequently be done.

The script for the event can sometimes be used for a conference project, and the script that is described in Step 16d can serve as an operational programme.

Step 14c   Drawing up the aftercare programme

Exercise   Draw up a list of everything that will still need to be done after the conference, and do this during the completion phase.

The aftercare programme includes all of the activities that were described in the completion phase of the conference project. Think of such matters as:
– a plan for and communication regarding possible follow-up activities
– thank-you notes to be sent to, for example, speakers, volunteers and sponsors

- creating an album with photographs/clippings
- updating the website and press releases
- writing a general conference report about the workings of the project, or specific reports
- reporting back to participants, target groups or other parties involved (for instance concerning results, answers to questions and any follow-up tasks).

6.3.2	*Making and carrying out the action plans for the marketing and communication track*	*Step 15*

This concerns plans of action that (when applicable) implement the marketing plan, the fundraising plan, and the communication plan, all of which have been developed in the previous phase (the preparation phase).

Drawing up and carrying out the action plans   *Step 15a*

If this was not done in the previous phase, then draw up a set of concrete plans   **Exercise**
of action for marketing, fundraising, and communication and carry them out.

Such plans of action must contain all of the relevant tasks found in a script. For an example, see the model of a communication action plan presented in Section 11.2, Step 7/8.

When projects have a longer preparation time, the plans of action do not have to be carried out until the development phase. However, in practice a conference project is often placed under pressure, which is why these plans are often already being drawn up and carried out in the preparation phase (particularly the fundraising action plan). Their execution continues into the development phase. The plans of action concern how to reach visitors, buyers, users, participants, viewers (marketing action plan), how to obtain subsidies, funds, and sponsors (fundraising action plan) and how to create goodwill and receive media attention (communication action plan).

It is recommended that you keep the sponsors that you have already contracted informed of the developments. In addition, the development phase often also involves publishing a press release (See model in Appendix A10).

Setup for a public survey (only for public projects)   *Step 15b*

Draw up a proposal for a participant survey.   **Exercise**

If it has been decided to carry out a participant survey, then in this phase it should be set up.. Section 11.2.1 contains a separate step-by-step plan for setting up and carrying out an evaluation public survey for a public event. You can use this evaluation public survey for a conference as well. Follow Steps 1-7 from this separate plan to set up a research survey proposal. Steps 8-13, which concern the actual preparation of the survey, can also be carried out in this phase.

For certain small-scale conferences, a concise evaluation form can be drawn up for the visitors/participants and possibly a separate evaluation form for the speakers.

Step 16   6.3.3   *Safeguarding the business preconditions (QOFTIM)*

During this phase, the conference project is worked out in detail and put into writing. The only step that must be taken is to carry out the plan. This means that almost all of the business consequences for the project can be foreseen. For a final go/no-go this overview of all the consequences is crucial. Furthermore, it is important that you have considered how to monitor the various control aspects during the execution phase.

Step 16a   Quality control aspect (Q)

Exercise   Explain the decisions made during the development phase in relation to the quality criteria set for the conference.

The production programme, including the production methods and facilities, is now measured according to the quality standards previously established. The desired ambiance of the conference should also be monitored. In addition, any remarks or guidelines should be described in the operational programme in regard to monitoring the aspect of quality during the execution phase.

Step 16b   Organisational control aspect (O)

Exercise   Draw up a design for organising the execution of the project

This step is about organising the execution of the project. This means that production roles must now be put into the organisation flow chart which was included in the project plan during the previous phase. In addition, you will have to decide what you should do yourself and what you should contract out. In a conference project the following roles can be included in the organisational flow chart:

- technical staff
- transport authority
- guides, hostesses
- interpreters, translators, photographer
- conference editor
- webmaster
- secretarial staff, receptionists, registration desk for participants
- staff for creating the content of the conference (for example, chairpersons, observers, authors, minutes secretary, voting committees, interviewer and speakers)
- staff for implementing the internal communication plan.

When conferences are organisationally complicated, it is sometimes necessary to provide a separate description of the organisation during the *construction phase*, during the *conference itself*, and during the *wrap-up phase*.

In addition, all kinds of contracts will have to be drawn up in this phase, such as employment contracts, artist contracts, contracts for volunteers, trainees, and freelancers, etc. (See the models shown in Appendices A6 to A8). Furthermore, all of the working schedules that are drawn up in order to clarify the organisation of the execution phase have been included in the *production programme,* under the heading *project organisation.*

For more information concerning this control aspect see Chapter 7.

Facility control aspect (F)   *Step 16c*

Translate the facility plan from the previous phase into a concrete *facility action*   **Exercise**
plan.

Everything must be prepared during the development phase so as to ensure that the venue and the facilities required are available in the execution phase. In many cases, this entails that many different action plans and lists must be drawn up. Furthermore, the preliminary layout of the venue and the decoration must be elaborated in detailed floor plans. Moreover, the preliminary acquisition list for other facilities must be elaborated into action lists (order forms, rental lists, supplier lists, etc., for buying/renting/leasing required technical tools, such as computers, audiovisual equipment, sound installation and view data equipment, and for other materials required such as tables, chairs, rostrum, decorations, etc.). The action plans for signposting and parking supervision must also be drawn up. Finally, any legal matters should be finalised at this time.

Step 16d　Time control aspect (T)

Exercise　Draw up the execution planning in the form of scripts for the three sub-phases of the execution phase. This involves a script for the construction phase, one for the conference itself, and one for the wrap-up phase. Draw up additional time sheets as well.

This step is mainly about setting up the execution plan for those who are going to set up the conference. In such a plan, all tasks that must be carried out during the execution phase (with three sub-phases) are listed. Depending on the course, the plan will have the form of a *bar chart* or a *script*. As you will learn in Section 10.2, a script is a planning technique that is usually used when the tasks are concrete and when details are paramount. Time may have to be monitored during the weeks or days prior to the conference, or during the conference itself and naturally afterwards, when everything has been taken down and the venue has been cleared. In Figure 10.3, you can see a fragment of a script.

Sometimes, it is necessary to include explanatory information in the appendices to the script, such as schedules, time sheets, drawings, maps, inventory lists of necessities and a description of implementation methods and tools. When the scripts are long, it is better to add them as appendices to the production programme. It is advisable to include the floor plan of the conference venue in the script.

When drawing up a bar chart or script, sufficient space must be allowed for unforeseen circumstances during the execution phase. For risky projects such as a summit meeting of international political figures, a separate calamity script should be included.

A script for the execution phase of a conference, for instance, can be subdivided into three parts, which correspond to the three sub-phases of the execution phase:
1　The build-up script (production phase) concerns preparing the conference venue, the catering, and the accommodation of the guests, etc.
2　The conference script (working phase) contains all the details per programme item or per day, the direction of the conference itself.
3　The wrap-up script concerns supervising guests when they leave, taking down/disassembling/removing the facilities and clearing up the conference venue.

An execution plan can be supplemented by a *capacity plan*, which details the use of manpower, space, machines, equipment, etc.

Information control aspect (I)   *Step 16e*

Consider the project information system.   Exercise

In this step it must be decided whether the control and monitoring system for the project information (including the information records and distribution) used during the execution phase needs to be extended further and streamlined. Take the necessary measures based on this observation and pay attention to the information carriers that are mentioned in Appendix A13.

Financial/ Money control aspect (M)   *Step 16f*

Draw up a detailed working budget of the costs and income (including a finan- Exercise
cial plan for any deficit). Then, state how the budget will be monitored during
the execution phase.

In many cases, a detailed execution or working budget will be drawn up at the end of the development phase, when the conference project has been detailed completely. For the decision-making (the final go/no-go), this budget will provide a rather accurate insight into the eventual costs and income.
Furthermore, this working budget will provide a detailed cost budget for monitoring the fundraising plan during the execution phase. A budgetary control system must be set up for this, including a clear procedure describing who is authorised to enter into obligations and to make payments and how this should be administrated. Among other things, this means that:
– an execution administration must be set up for the conference project.
– financial agreements must be made and any contracts should be arranged.
– a system must be thought of to collect, process, and safely store any participants' contributions, earnings from ticket sales, and other earnings.
– the liability and copyrights must be monitored.

The drawing up of a working budget is described in detail in Section 8.1.3 of Chapter 8 and monitoring the budget is described in Section 8.3 of that same chapter.

6.3.4 *Drawing up the production programme*

As mentioned before, all of the product information described and drawn up in the development phase is put together in the production programme. The production programme, therefore, is a collection of separate pieces of information which helps the execution team to carry out the project. In addition, the production programme is the final decision document on the basis of which the client can take the final go/no-go decision for the conference project.

For the steps that should lead to the production programme for the conference project, you are advised to refer to the step-by-step plan for an event project found in Section 5.3.4 (Step 16). You will find an extensive model for a production programme in Appendix C3.

6.4 Step-by-step plan for the execution and completion phases

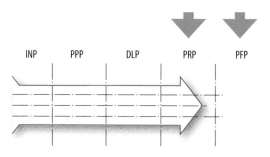

| INP | PPP | DLP | PRP | PFP |

The Application

'Four days ago, we discussed the execution programme (sometimes it's called the production programme) extensively with two supervisors and after making a few adjustments, this final decision document was also approved. We have completed all of our preparations by now. Registration forms for taking part in the conference have poured in from Jakarta and Amsterdam. We have sent all of the participants the instructions on how to access the teleconference. We have put the films and the content contributed by the experts on *Breeze*. The web form for the evaluation has also been placed on the internet. Everything is going as planned, but what we are worried about the most is the susceptibility of the process to disturbances. That is why we are so focused on the test which is to take place next week. We have already held a small trial session with two students in Jakarta and the senior lecturer there. It appeared that it would take fifteen minutes before we were logged in and had a connection. We have solved this problem by now. When we finally did make contact, everything went smoothly, except that the sound was not always perfect. Sometimes you heard the sound of your own voice echoing. We are still trying to solve that problem.'

Once you have provided the production programme as the final decision document, the preparation of the conference project has been completed. In most cases the following steps still need to be taken:

- Step 18: Performance phase
- Step 19: After-care phase

In these phases the scripts and the after-care programme are carried out. Below follows a description of these phases of the conference project. See the general descriptions of these final phases as well in Section 4.3.

6.4.1   Performance phase *Step 18*

This phase can be further divided into three sub-phases in which very practical activities take place which, for the most part, are situated at the conference venue, namely:

Setting up (production phase) *Step 18a*

Set up the conference according to the production programme (script for set- **Exercise** ting up).

In this step everything is made ready for receiving the conference participants, naturally according to the script for setting up the conference.

This involves several activities, among them:
- preparing the room(s) at the conference and the stage and decorations according to the floor plan and lay-out
- checking the service facilities (including both the technical and catering)
- seeing to the accommodation of the participants
- carrying out supporting activities/sub-projects (See also Step 10e)
- arranging special facilities (bank, post office, internet connection, travel

agent, tourist information, signposting, stalls, secretarial department, information desk, participants' registration, issuing documentation folder, photographer, press room, etc).

At the end of the setting up phase the conference is ready to begin or to be opened. The staff has now been provided with a detailed programme and a script for the conference and for the dismantlement. Moreover, there is an *operational programme* (for example in the form of a users' manual) and an *after-care programme* including all of the activities which should be done in the dismantlement phase. These programmes have often been made earlier during the development phase.

Step 18b   The conference itself (operational phase)

Exercise   Allow the conference to take place as intended.

During this phase the conference will take place according to the detailed operational programme and the script for the event. The main difference between a film or video production and a live project such as a conference is that the latter category does not involve a great deal of rehearsing and retakes are not possible. If something does go wrong and it cannot be remedied immediately, then this will always be a determining factor, regardless of how much work was done beforehand. The result is what the visitors experience and what they take home with them. It is therefore of utmost importance that the script for the conference itself is carried out very precisely. The following activities will have to be included such as:

- checking the rooms (perhaps even the dressing room)
- making a sound check and possibly checking the lighting
- placing a pitcher of water on a table and name plates for the speakers
- placing the 'reserved' signs on the chairs
- informing the caterer about the exact final number of visitors/participants
- manning the coat room
- seeing to it that the hostesses attend to the guests
- supervising the speakers/chairperson(s)/artists and special guests
- supervising the arrival of participants, taking attendance
- handing out press files, possibly receiving the press
- sounding the first gong, manning the direction posts, opening the doors to the hall, turning on the lights
- sounding of the second gong, speakers take their place, hostesses request that the guests take their seats

- opening the programme, closing the doors to the hall, possibly turning off any music/turning spotlights on, activating microphones
- taking care of late-comers, seating them in the back of the hall.

What is central during the conference, besides the intrinsic proceedings, is the reception, the supervision and providing service to the participants and the speakers. When a conference or company event is technically complex, the project manager gives cues to perform certain actions that are in the script. In practice, it appears that often unforeseen things happen. Therefore, it is of utmost importance that the conference project manager is always on the scene and can be reached on a mobile phone during the conference, or that he or she is in contact through some other means of communication with the technical crew, the hostesses, the presenters, the speakers, etc. At the end of the conference the evaluation form should be filled in by the participants.

The wrap-up   *Step 18c*

Dismantle the event according to the script for the wrap-up.   Exercise

---

During the hours and days immediately following the conference, the conference venue will be dismantled, cleared away, and tidied up. This is done according to the script for the wrap-up, in which other activities take place such as:
- taking down the decorations and cleaning up the conference room
- cleaning up the facility services, possibly making returns to the rental agent
- finalise accommodation of participants/cleaning up
- arranging transport for the guests/supervising
- dismantling supporting activities/sub-projects/cleaning up
- dismantling special facilities.

Press and public services   *Step 18d*

Organise the press and public services.   Exercise

During the opening or at the start of the conference, it is likely that a press release has been planned in the communication plan (including the distribution of the press folder upon production of the press pass and having reporters sign an attendance list). Make sure this reception goes flawlessly.
Whenever live projects are involved, the service provided to the conference participants should be the main focus during the conference. It is all about keeping the conference goers satisfied and seeing to it that their questions are

answered. Organise the *public service* as described in the communication action plan.

Step 18e Participant survey

Exercise	Carry out the evaluative research study amongst the participants (usually in the form of a survey).

If it was previously decided to carry out an evaluative survey amongst the participants and in Step 15b a research proposal was written, then that research survey will be carried out immediately following the conference. The speakers can also be given an evaluation form to fill in (See Step 14 in the step-by-step plan for such a survey in Section 11.2.1).

Step 18f Business preconditions

Exercise	Monitor the business preconditions during the performance phase of the conference.

At the start of the performance phase a briefing should be organised for all those involved in setting up and running the conference, but also for suppliers (technicians, caterers, hostesses, etc.)

During the performance phase, especially during the *construction,* large financial obligations are entered into and you will be faced with unexpected expenditures. It is therefore of vital importance that the performance budget be well-monitored. Keep a financial project administration as well (for assignments and invoices, among other things. Often there is no time for this because everything is so busy, but you will have to pay the price later if you do not do this. In addition, be sure to monitor the quality of the conference during this performance phase. Furthermore, the project information that is available during this phase will have to be coordinated (involve the information carriers which are mentioned in Appendix A13). Finally, coordinate the execution of all tasks in this phase, on the basis of the scripts.

Step 19

6.4.2   Completion phase

At the end of the completion phase, the conference will have been completed, the survey report will have been presented and the project will have been evaluated (evaluation report).

Aftercare	*Step 19a*

Carry out the aftercare programme.	Exercise

The speakers, volunteers, all of the others involved receive a thank-you note. There may be a follow-up. All this will take place according to the *aftercare programme* which was previously set up.

Research report	*Step 19b*

Report the results of the participant survey, when applicable.	Exercise

Section 11.2.1 contains a step-by-step plan for such a survey. If it is held immediately after the conference, then Steps 15 (processing and analysing survey) and 16 (reporting public survey results) are carried out during the completion phase.

Financial settlement	*Step 19c*

Compose the financial settlement.	Exercise

Upon completion of the conference, the final payments are made and the financial settlement must be drawn up for the client. It is recommended that the format be used again found in Figure 8.3. When it involves a conference that has been carried out by an external organiser, the final invoice of sent by that agency is settled with the client. Sometimes, for instance, a financial or intrinsic account is required by a subsidising agency.

Project records	*Step 19d*

Start project records.	Exercise

It is recommended that all of the relevant project information be recorded in an orderly fashion for the next edition of the conference. This is often neglected because the project manager was too busy already organising the next project during this phase. At the start of the next edition, those involved are often confronted with a huge pile of former documents that have been poorly organised. Try to avoid this from happening.

Step 19e   Project evaluation

Exercise   Evaluate the conference including the syllabus, website, etc. (project *result*) and the project *process* from idea to implementation and draw up an evaluation report.

For the final evaluation of the conference, the following questions can be posed: Has the target group been reached and was it satisfied? Did the conference work out the way it was supposed to? In other words, did the conference achieve the desired effect? Were the methods used during the preparation and execution adequate? Did the control tasks, such as time planning, budgeting, and organising, ensure that the budget was met (or the targets were met), that deadlines were met, that the tasks and responsibilities were carried out by everyone involved, etc? Was the cooperation among those involved to everyone's satisfaction? Has the project manager done a satisfactory job?

It is important that an evaluation report be concluded by providing a summary with points to focus on for the next time. Sometimes, even a blueprint can be made for the next edition of the conference. The team can also evaluate how it functioned during the project.

PART III

The project leaders' toolbox

The Application

Goodwill in the Neighbourhood

'Some time ago, rapidly expanding telecommunication companies saw their number of employees double within a few months. At the briefing for a party for their employees they first indicated six hundred people would attend the event, but a week before the event that number already turned out to have grown to 1,300,' says events organiser J.J. Sometimes that can be a nuisance, because you need permission from the local council for extra parking space. In some cases this has led to a squabble with parking wardens, but even more important is the attitude of the local population. J.J.: 'When you organise a mega-event, you should primarily consider the tolerance of the local population. We provided accommodation for the German 'Mannschaft' during Euro 2000; a mega-event with top sportspeople, a sway of celebrities, a media pavilion with 360 jounalists, 6 TV stations, etc. You can imagine that suddenly it was very busy in Vaalsbroek. Things got even worse when the local authority closed the Mergelland-route, the most heavily travelled scenic route in the Netherlands, to traffic. The result was that the whole area was packed with cars. Inhabitants could not even get out of their own streets. I found out the consequences of this, at my own cost: on Sunday morning the neighbourhood kicked me out of bed to resolve the issue! As the organiser of an event, people hold you responsible for the inconvenience, even if you have little influence over the matter.'

Even More Goodwill in the Neighbourhood

'Of course, conference centre MECC in Maastricht has experience in this as well,' says an events organiser R.H. 'We try to anticipate complaints.' If there is going to be a busy fair we inform the inhabitants beforehand and offer them free entry. That creates goodwill.' In spite of this, things can go wrong, sometimes beyond the control of the organisation. R.H.: 'That was also the case at a fair for the hotel and catering industry. We thought we had done a good job arranging the parking facilities. On top of our own parking spaces we had organised a park & ride service. But as it turned out, visitors of the fair wanted to park their car as close as possible to the MECC and left their vehicles on the drives of houses in the neighbourhood of the MECC. The result of this was that people who lived in the neighbourhood found a strange car on their driveway and could no longer park their own car. Those people angrily informed the newspaper, which blamed us for everything.'

A Traffic-Jam in a Jam-Free City

Sometimes the reverse is true: a mistake, that is corrected, can have fantastic results. R.H.: 'That happened during the car show at the MECC. A conference was linked to this fair, where as an advantage of Maastricht the lack of traffic jams in the city would be highlighted. The worst thing imaginable then happened: the director of the Dutch AA was the first speaker at the conference, yet he was stuck in a traffic jam. As it turned out it was exactly the day that many caravans travel to France through Maastricht. We had the top man of the Dutch AA read the speech through his mobile phone and fed it through the intercom of the conference hall. After a while, when he arrived at the MECC, he was given new instructions and played along: he drove into the cargo lift, entered the hall in his car en continued his speech from behind the microphone. The people in the hall thought it had all been planned like this and gave a standing ovation.'

(From: *High Profile Events*, edited by the author)

7

The Project Organisation

Part II works as a sort of checklist, developed for an event and a conference project. In Part III, some aspects of the project approach are defined. This first chapter discusses the organisational aspects of an event project. First, attention will be given to a possible entanglement of the organisational *structure* of a project with the structure of the permanent organisation. Moreover, a description will be provided of how the organisation of an independent project can be structured. Finally, the harmonisation of the organisational *culture* of a project organisation with the culture of the permanent organisation will be discussed.

7.1   The Project Organisation and the Permanent Organisation

Many projects are realised within permanent organisations, for instance a sports event within a company or an exhibition within a museum. Often problems occur within organisations at the start of a project. This is also the case for institutions and companies in the cultural and leisure industries. These problems are caused by the tension between the vertical, permanent organisation aimed at continuity and the predominantly horizontal and temporary project organisation aimed at a result.

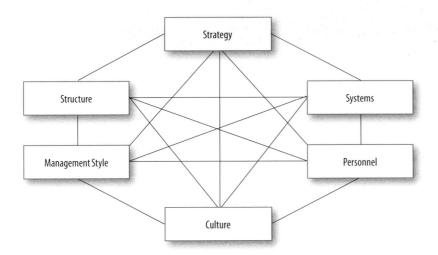

Figure 7.1   *The Six Interrelated Organisational Aspects of the ECH-Model*

In order to understand the organisation better, scores of models have been developed. In Figure 7.1 what is known as the ECH-model, derived from Mc-Kinsey's 7-S framework, has been represented. ECH stands for Equilibrium, Coherence and Heterogeneity. The model proceeds from the assumption that we can look at the permanent or mother organisation in six ways. Because of the interrelation of these aspects, a change in one of the elements will nearly always exert an influence on the other aspects. Before we will highlight the differences between the permanent and the project organisation on the basis of this model, we first need to explain the six elements of the ECH-model, briefly.

1   *Structure*: the distribution of the formal and informal tasks, responsibilities and powers within the organisation and the mechanisms of coordination. Often the organisational structure is visualised by means of an organisational chart.
2   *Culture*: the system of implicit and explicit patterns of thinking, feeling and acting, patterns which are supported by the people who the organisation consists of.
3   *Management (style)*: the characteristic patterns of behaviour of the management at all levels within the organisation, which arise from the understanding of one's job and the view on humankind and society.
4   *Personnel*: the type of people within the organisation and their abilities and skills, also referred to with the term 'human capital.'
5   *Systems*: the information and communication systems and processes within

the organisation that accommodate the functioning of the organisation: controlling and adjusting.

6 *Strategy*: the way in which (and through which) set objectives are reached

By means of the six aspects named above in Figure 7.2 the area of tension between the permanent and the project organisation is visualised.

Permanent Organisation		Project Organisation
Vertical	Structure	Horizontal
Hierarchical		Coordination
Oscillating		Flowing
Activities-Oriented	Management/Personnel	Result-Oriented
Enterprising		Accomplishing
Annual Planning	Systems	Project Planning
Departmental Budget		Sub-Project Budget
Continuous Improvement		Sufficient is Good Enough
Avoid Precedents	Culture	Ad Hoc Reaction
Routine		Situational
Club Spirit		Team Spirit
Continuity	Strategy	**Temporariness**
	Tension	

Figure 7.2   The Area of Tension between the Permanent and the Project Organisation

In the following sections the aspects of structure and culture are discussed more extensively. The handling of the tensions that accompany these two aspects, and the aspect of the management style, can have a great influence on the success of the project approach within an organisation.

7.2   The Organisational Structure

To bring the total set of activities of an organisation under control, the activities that more or less cohere internally are clustered together into groups (departments, teams, working groups, management, or administration). The structure of an organisation indicates how these organisational units relate to each other. Project organisations can be one of a kind, for instance when a festival is organised by several people or groups and a project team is set up for this once-only objective. As mentioned before, projects can also be embedded in a permanent organisation, for instance an exhibition project within a museum or a sports event within a sports organisation.

7.2.1 The Embedding of the Project Organisation within the Permanent Organisation

The traditional structure of the permanent organisation is hierarchical. When represented in an organisational chart it looks like the well-known 'Christmas tree' or 'pyramid.' When a project is realised within a hierarchically structured, permanent organisation an organisational complication occurs. Namely, the structure of a project organisation cuts straight through this hierarchy. If there is no clarity with reference to tasks, responsibilities and powers, tensions can be a result. A project assistant, for instance, has to answer both to his section manager and to the project leader(s) of the project or projects he is involved with. As long as he is working on the project, he therefore has two bosses. To get a clear view on how this can be sorted out in practice, we will describe which three managerial influences have an effect on each employee in the organisation first.

Functional Influence (F)	Hierarchical Influence (H)	Operational Influence (O)
– How	– Personal well-being	– What
– With which approach	– Personal development	– When
– With which means	– Payment, holiday and the like	– How
– With which methods	– Coordination of assessment	– What price
– Development of expertise		– How well
– Who		– On the basis of...
		– Together with...

Figure 7.3   The Three Managerial Influences on an Employee

The functional influence (F) refers to the development and application of the technical expertise of the employee, hence to the 'way in which.' The hierarchical influence (H) focuses on the employee as a subordinate. The operational influence (O) is concerned with the concrete task that the employee is expected to fulfil, hence with what he does. Below a number of aspects are mentioned which these influences are directed at.

When a project approach is not adopted, the employee experiences these three influences in his relation with the manager (See Figure 7.3). If permanent organisations realise projects on a regular basis, the *project matrix organisation* can structure the relations between the permanent organisation and the temporary projects undertaken within it. In this concept the vertical, hierarchical organisation (pyramid) remains intact, but the project dimension is appended to it. In the organisation chart this dimension is drawn horizontally, as a result of which a matrix emerges. This matrix implies, therefore, a *dual power structure*. Both the section manager in the permanent organisation and the project leader answer directly to the permanent organisation and both have their own responsibilities. The project matrix organisation with its dual power structure and its division into three types of managerial influence is represented in Figure 7.4. With the project matrix structure, the tasks, responsibilities and powers of the employees that work on projects within permanent organisations become clear.

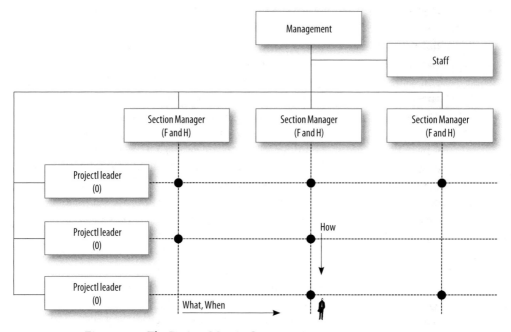

Figure 7.4   The Project Matrix Organisation

The fact that the project leader is situated in the 'lower' regions of the matrix, says little about his position vis-à-vis a section manager for instance. The project leader has an independent responsibility for the realisation of the project result and supervises his own project team, consisting of employees from different sections of the permanent organisation (possibly supplemented with external manpower). He receives a mandate from the board of directors of the mother organisation in the form of an assignment and reports to the board periodically about the progress.

When, for instance, an employee from the publicity department of a museum is adopted into a team for a certain project, this employee will then have two bosses. The three managerial influences then have to be divided. As a rule, this means that the project leader provides the *operational* control and the manager of the publicity department offers *functional* and *hierarchical* control. As mentioned before, the project matrix organisation proceeds from a dual power structure. This structure does not always have to be balanced, however, as is more or less the case in the situation above. There are, indeed, two other possible versions of this structure. In the one case, the powers of the project leader are reduced in relation to the situation above (he then becomes project *coordinator*), whereas in the other case, they are increased (he then becomes the project *manager*). In Section 7.3 these possible interpretations of the role of project leader are developed further.

In large organisations, in which almost all the primary processes are handled like a project or a production (take, for instance, production companies for television programmes), the project dimension is often strengthened within the project matrix organisation. In this case programme leaders are put in charge of a number of project leaders. In the diagram presented in Figure 7.4 they would be placed to the left of the project leaders. Programme leaders in this case cover a programme area, i.e. they direct projects or productions that are alike. Project leaders from the same programme area report to their programme leader and not to the management of the company directly. We call this *programme management* (See also Section 12.2.1).

In conclusion, it is important to draw attention to a development within organisations, which boils down to a gradual replacement of the traditional, hierarchical structure of permanent organisations, with much looser and much more contemporary structures. In the future, the activities within organisations will increasingly be administered by what is referred to as *self-directing teams*. With this, a very different organisational environment emerges for projects. The self-directing teams within permanent organisations in this case will then focus on activities with a permanent character, while project teams will focus on the realisation of temporary objectives. In such a new situation the project matrix structure will have nothing to offer. When this happens, then new ways to accommodate both types of 'equivalent' teams within the organisation will have to be found.

7.2.2   The Organisational Structure of the Project Itself

Now that it has been explained how the embedding of the project organisation within the permanent organisation can be structured, the structuring of the project organisation itself will be examined further. This applies to both projects within permanent organisations and independent projects. With respect to the organisation of activities within a project, what is important is that the staffing, tasks and responsibilities are structured. For some projects it is sufficient to summarise what the tasks, responsibilities and powers are in what is called a *schedule for the allocation of tasks* (See model in Appendix A3). This summary needs to be discussed with everyone concerned, of course. For more complex projects a structure according to the *steering committee – working group model* is recommended (See Figure 7.5). This recommendation applies to projects with policy aspects and/or to projects in which different working groups and departments are involved. Also, organisation-transcending projects can be structured according to the principles of the steering committee - working group model.

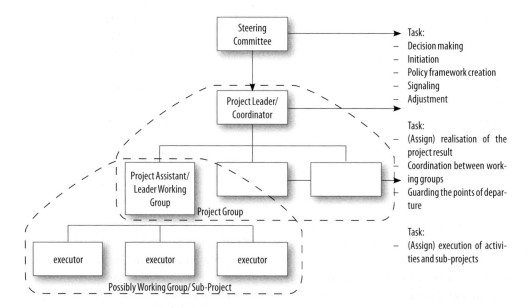

Figure 7.5   The Steering Committee Working Group Model

Working groups or departments focus on content-related, partial results of the project. This can be, for instance, an official opening of an exhibition, a publication or a workshop that is part of a public-event project. In the case of a video production, this concerns, for instance, an art-direction or production department. The business aspects of the project, such as planning, budget control and publicity, are executed by the project leader or his assistant(s). These aspects can also be observed by team members who consider these to be their own specific tasks, or who do this in addition to their content-related task within the project.

A possible disadvantage of this model could be that it can lead to confusing administrative situations for the project assistant, because of its different levels. Hence, it is of the utmost importance that all levels are aware of the limitations of their powers. In this way a situation can be avoided in which the chairmen of the working groups, the project leader, the chairman of the steering committee, the section manager and even the consultants interfere with the project assistant's performance of his tasks. Moreover, with respect to the composition of the steering committee it is important to keep it as small as possible, to ensure its ability to make decisions. It is also recommended only to select people for the committee that actually have a contribution to make. For organisation-transcending projects, for instance, representatives of the participating organisations can take a seat on the committee.

When there is a case of *dual leadership* within a project, for instance when a director and a production manager work together towards the realisation of a stage production, the division of tasks, responsibilities and powers between both leaders needs to be clearly established.

7.2.3   *The Organisational Structure for Multiple Projects*

When a number of related projects are developed and executed, more or less parallel to each other, then they can be accommodated organisationally within what is known as a *programme structure*. This structure is a version of the steering committee-working group model. An example of a programme structure is represented in Figure 7.6.

In Chapter 12 the setting up of an organisational environment for several, related projects, or what is known as the multi-project organisation, is discussed extensively.

Finally, in Figure 7.7 an example of the structure of consultation is presented.

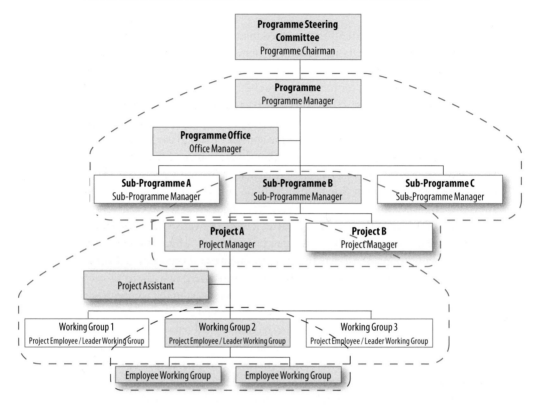

Figure 7.6   *The Programme Structure*

Type of Consultation	Objective	Chairman	Participants	Frequency/Timing
Programme Steering Committee Meeting	– Connection Strategic Objectives – Decision-Making about Start/Stop Projects – Decision-Making Deployment Means	Programme Chairman	Members Steering Committee and Programme Manager	Bi-Monthly on Monday
Sub-Programme Managers' Meeting	– Harmonisation Sub-Programmes – Exchange of Information – Development Team Spirit	Programme Manager	Sub-Programme Managers Office Manager, and Possibly Project Sponsors	Bi-Weekly
Meeting Management Team	– Investigate Feasibility of Recommendations/Choices – Foster Support	Managing Director	Members of the Management Team	Weekly, every Tuesday
Programme Office Meeting	– Progress – Support Sub-Programmes	Office Manager	Employees Programme Office	Every Tuesday From 9:00 to 11:00 Hours

Figure 7.7   *An Example of the Structure of Meetings*

When the basic shape of the organisational structure of the project itself has been determined, for instance the steering committee-working group model, often it is still necessary to establish the tasks, responsibilities and powers for the individual employees. A method that is often used is the formulation of a job description for every employee (See model in Appendix A4). When assigning tasks it is important to strive for an integral set of job responsibilities. Preferably, people will be awarded integral responsibility for the (partial) results, at a public event for instance for a workshop, for the official opening, etc. When a task is too specialised, there is a great danger of people withdrawing onto their own island, and missing the overall view on the project and the synergy between the components.

Finally, it should be mentioned that for effective functioning of a project organisation, more is needed than only the structuring of the organisation and formal agreements. Other aspects also play a part, such as team building, dealing with conflicts and stress, and meeting and negotiation skills.

7.3 The Three Main Characters

The three main characters in every project are the *client*, the *agent* and the *project manager*. Below the characteristics of, and the differences between, these positions will be described briefly.

7.3.1 The Client

We have to take into consideration that we might be dealing with both clients from outside and clients from within the organisation. When commissioned projects are at issue (See also Section 12.2), it will always be an external client. With internal (programme) projects (See Section 12.2) top management plays the role of client vis-à-vis the project manager.

An external client only rarely takes a professional view with respect to project management. Many projects fail because they have the wrong client, a joint client, or even no client. The role the client has to play, involves more than just being the initiator or the financial backer. One can expect from a client that he is involved with the project during the whole process. This means that he guides the risk process by keeping himself informed and by making those decisions that are necessary for the brisk progress of the project. A 'good' client should commit himself to the project emotionally and should have the courage to take calculated risks.

Whenever possible a single client is preferable. This promotes speed and unity of control. The more people believe they have 'the final word,' the greater the chance that conflicting assignments will be handed out or that nothing is done while waiting for a decision. The one who is the most obvious candidate for the position of client, is the person who wants a problem to be solved or an opportunity to be exploited. In large organisations the task of client is placed on the shoulders of a *delegated client*. Within the terms of reference, he will act for the project, as the day-to-day client. We often see this situation at large production companies, in which *delegated producers* carry the day-to-day responsibility for a project. As a matter of fact, this function can also relate to an internal project. As mentioned before, the 'delegated' task of a client can be fulfilled by a steering committee in organisation-transcending projects. Whenever several organisations carry joint responsibility and together share the risk for the process and the end-result of the project, it is recommended that everything is agreed upon in a collaboration agreement. This also applies to co-productions.

7.3.2   Agent

There is an agent when there is a commission for a project, i.e. when a project is realised for an external client. Often the top management of the commissioned organisation plays the role of agent. In large organisations project coordinators and account managers can also have this role. The final responsibility for the project, on behalf of the organisation carrying out the work, rests with the agent. With regard to commissioned projects, it is the agent who controls the project leader.

7.3.3   Project Leader

The project leader is responsible for the realisation of the desired and agreed-upon project result. The given tasks, responsibilities and powers of the project leader depend largely on the client and/or agent. Below the powers of the project leader are again conveyed with reference to three possible versions of project leadership discussed earlier.

The real *Project Leader* has an independent responsibility for the realisation of the project result. The preconditions, however, are determined by the management of the permanent organisation, confirmed in periodic reports to that management.
He heads the project organisation, which can consist of people from different departments, who are partly deployed for a certain period of time. Some-

times people from outside the mother organisation are included in the project organisation. The project leader receives operational authority over the project collaborators, as far as their work involves the project. This situation is represented in the project matrix structure in Figure 7.4.

The *project coordinator* is only responsible for the coordination of the employees from the different departments, who contribute to the project. In this case the operational authority remains with the head of the department of the permanent organisation. An important drawback of a position with such limited substance is the following: because of a lack of power a project coordinator in many cases is unable to function optimally. The fact of the matter is that he is dependent on the heads of the departments within the mother organisation for almost everything, because they have control over the capabilities (people, space, and means). This version of the matrix structure is called the 'coordination structure.' This can be visualised by taking the project matrix structure, but in this case the lines between manger and employee are uninterrupted while the horizontal lines remain dotted. F, H and O in this case have all been placed near the department manager.

The *project manager* is the most far-reaching version. This project manager decides on all aspects that affect the project and is, therefore, integrally responsible. Collaborators are temporarily released from their own department within the permanent organisation for their contribution to the project. Thus the project manager, temporarily, has the *functional* and *hierarchical* authority of the project staff. In this case there is a 'pure project structure.' This holds true as well for independent projects, where the manager of the project possesses all authority, because he is the initiator for instance, there is a 'pure project structure' in the project management.

When the relation between the permanent and the project organisation is structured, therefore, the position of the leader of the project must be clearly indicated. This can be done on the basis of the previous descriptions.

Figure 7.8 depicts from which perspective the three core functions *client*, *agent* and *project leader* operate.

Client	Agent	Project Leader
(internal or external)	(with an external project)	
Control of:	**Control of:**	**Control of:**
– Objective with respect to contents (effects of the use of the result)	– Objective (enjoyable work, turnover, profits)	– Result – Plan of approach
– Result	– Result	– Control aspects
– Preconditions (QOFTIM)	– Preconditions (QOFTIM)	(QOFTIM)
– Consequences	– Consequences	
– Risks (of the project for his own organisation)	– Risks (of the project for his own organisation)	
Oriented on:	**Oriented on:**	**Oriented on:**
Objective and result	Assignment/contract	Work
Management tasks:	**Management tasks:**	**Management tasks:**
– Creates preconditions in his own organisation	– Creates preconditions in his own organisation	– Achieves result – Controls the pre-
– Attends to support		conditions
Has to deal with:	**Has to deal with:**	**Has to deal with:**
– Interested parties	– Capability source administra-	– Project workers
– Agent	tors	– Suppliers
– Policy manipulators	– Project leaders	– Third parties
– Problem owners	– Multi-project managers	– Consumers/users
– Steering committee/final management		
– Financiers		
– (Final) users		
– Administrators		
– Capability source administrators		

Figure 7.8   Differences in Perspective between the Three Core Functions

The Event Manager

The project-leadership role at an event project is fulfilled by an event manager. Central to the professional event manager is the integral development and realisation process of an *event*-project, from the earliest notion to the concrete event, including the aftercare and evaluation. Figure 7.9 shows that the event (project) manager guides the process in many directions.

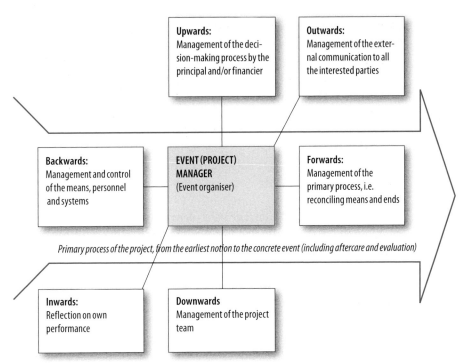

Figure 7.9   *The Event Manager guides (Manages) in Many Directions*

7.4   The Organisational Culture

In this section, the extent to which the culture of the permanent organisation can encourage, or hinder, working by means of projects is discussed.

7.4.1   *How Project-Friendly Is the Permanent Organisation?*

First of all, we should ask this question: What is understood by the term organisational culture? Organisational culture can be understood to mean: a system of implicit and explicit patterns of thinking, feeling and acting. These patterns are supported by the people who make up the organisation. Other terms that are used to refer to this are atmosphere, climate, standards and values. The organisational culture is often reflected very well in that one sentence, or in that one image, with which we make clear to outsiders what kind of organisation we work in. This is reflected for instance, when we talk of the 'island kingdom,' or 'the hornet's nest' or 'the tea party,' in reference to our organisation. While culture is often difficult to measure, because of its implicit character, it is still an important management tool for the daily operation of an organisation. Examples of management through culture are remarks like: 'You have to do it this way, otherwise it will go down badly'; 'This is simply the way we do things'; or: 'There is no reason for it, it's just our policy.'

Culture is made manifest through the kind of people that are employed by the organisation (career objectives, views of society, educational level, dress code), the building and the interior design (modest or grand, old desks in a new building) and the procedures, instructions, forms, manuals, etc. The latter exemplifies, for instance, room for personal initiative, or, the opposite, tight central control of the processes.

That is why cultural differences can be observed between organisations. A museum usually has a culture that is different from a theme park, but an art museum also often has a culture that is different from an historical museum. Differences can also be found within an organisation. A more conservative and bureaucratic culture will be found in the department of a museum which is responsible for the maintenance of the collection, and where the emphasis is on the care of the objects and the correct and complete processing of information, than in the presentation department, which is in much closer contact with the ever-changing needs of visitors. In order to be able to recount more about the affinity of the permanent organisation with the project approach, different organisational cultures have been characterised below.

7.4.2 *Four Types of Organisational Culture*

Within an organisation different cultures can be present at the same time. Cultural differences can easily lead to frictions between the departments. Working with projects also suits some cultures better than others. It is important, therefore, that a manager who wants to introduce working in projects, knows which (sub)cultures are present in his area of responsibility. It is also important for project managers to know this. This way a manager can make an assessment of the friction he will encounter within the mother organisation and adjust his introduction strategy. Moreover, when two organisations are planning to co-operate, it is of great importance that the organisational cultures are geared towards one another. This is true, for instance, when a project is administered by two organisations in a co-production.

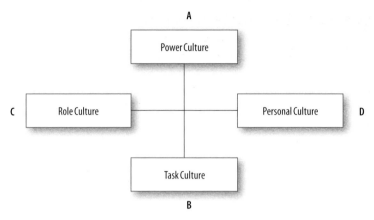

Figure 7.10 *The Four Types of Culture within Organisations According to the
Typology of Harrison*

Figure 7.10 shows the four types of culture that we can encounter within an
organisation. For each we will provide a description. Ideal types are taken as
the point of departure, which we will not, or only rarely, come across in pure
form in the real world. Usually we find hybrid forms, which, nonetheless, can
be dominated by one of the four types of culture.

Cultural differences between organisations or departments are expressed,
among other things, in the following aspects:

- The way people associate   *(Association)*
- Appreciation for certain situations/people   *(Appreciation)*
- The mode of decision making   *(Decision making)*
- When formulating organisational objectives
  attention is paid to: *(With objective attention)*
- The setting of priorities   *(Priority)*
- The adaptability within certain situations   *(Reacts)*
- Dealing with opportunities and threats   *(Danger)*

In the description of the four types of culture below, the characteristics are provided that match with the aspects listed above.

Types of culture

Power Culture

Association	:	is determined by personal power or 'resource power'
Appreciation	:	for personality
Decision making	:	on the basis of power
With objective attention	:	for personal realisation of objective (rules of the central figure are important)
Priority	:	for the maintenance of power
Responds	:	readily to changes in the environment, provided the powerful join in
Danger	:	of growth of the organisation, the personality of the 'heir-apparent'

We often encounter the power culture in expanding organisations in their pioneering phase, but also in family businesses.

Role Culture

Association	:	is determined by following rules, lines of communication and hierarchy, also forms of address are observed
Appreciation	:	for subordination and role performance
Decision making	:	on the basis of procedural steps and formal position
With objective attention	:	to keeping order, clarity and peace
Priority	:	for function/role/position
Responds	:	with difficulty to changed situations
Threat	:	of paper tiger, bureaucracy

The role culture is characteristic of traditional government institutions, but also of, for instance, insurance companies. Also within the larger museums a role culture is often dominant, especially within the control departments.

Personal Culture

Association	:	only when necessary, hence few fixed structures; determined by, for instance, a shared capability source (building, computer); little cohesion
Appreciation	:	for skill and expertise
Decision making	:	through consensus, or not at all, no subordination
With objective attention	:	to talent
Priority	:	for skill/professionalism
Reacts	:	unpredictably, for they are all individuals
Threat	:	of disintegration, for instance as a result of 'Methoden-streit'

Frame 7.1

Frame 7.1 Continuation

We often encounter the personal culture in partnerships of, for instance, architects, lawyers or general practitioners.

Task Culture

Association	:	is determined by the task ahead, the relation between time/person/work
Appreciation	:	for skill as doer
Decision making	:	on the basis of 'what is necessary at this moment for this task'
With objective attention	:	to combination of skills, getting results, rules are unimportant
Priority	:	for results
Reacts	:	readily to changes
Threat	:	of running to extremes

The task culture is characteristic of for instance contractors, but also of production companies. Also within public orientated departments of, for instance, the larger cultural companies, a task culture often dominates.

To be able to gain some insight into the organisational culture of the institution **Exercise** you work for, a small test has been included in Appendix A5. First answer the questions and, then, determine by using Figure 7.10 which cultural type is dominant and with the aid of Figure 7.11, determine what can be deduced from that.

7.4.3   A Few Tips to Increase Acceptance

The level of project-friendliness of the four cultural types is represented in Figure 7.11. With reference to this, a few more tips can be given to project managers, that can increase the acceptance of working by means of projects within a permanent organisation and which can increase the chance of the project being successful.

– In a *power culture* make sure that you get into contact with the empowered, for instance the client(s).
– In a *role culture* make sure that the project approach is recorded in a manual with procedures.
– In a *task culture* make sure that the task and the project coincide.
– In a *personal culture* make sure that you make respected 'friends' with those who are connected to the project.

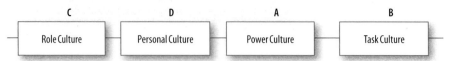

Figure 7.11   The Level of Project-Friendliness of an Organisational Culture

The Project Budget and Budgeting

In this chapter we will explain how project budgets are constructed, and then we will elaborate on budget control. Money plays an important part in event projects. During the different stages of the project, estimates and budgets will have to be produced. In such a budget of expenses, a prognosis of the revenue must also be included. If necessary, a separate financing scheme can be used to show which earnings should cover the project expenses. When a project budget reveals a negative result, additional funding will have to be found. This aspect will be dealt with in Chapter 9.

8.1   Each Project Phase Its Own Budget

At the end of each phase, the current costs of the plans and the expected revenue will have to be mapped. In the initiative phase, naturally, this is still very sketchy, but at the end of the development phase, when all the details have been described or drawn up, a detailed working budget can be constructed for the benefit of the production phase. In the production phase and in the performance phase, usually, no new budgets are constructed. In these operational phases much attention will have to be given to budget control, because that is when most expenses are made. For complex projects three budgets need to be drawn up during the process, and each should show increasing levels of detail, namely:

1 *The estimate of the project expenses*, at the end of the initiative phase (part of the initiative report).
2 *The components budget*, at the end of the preparation phase (part of the project plan).
3 *The working budget*, at the end of the development phase (part of the production schedule).

For less complicated projects the detailed working budget is usually omitted and replaced by the components budget, which then forms the foundation for the budget control during the production phase and afterwards. In Figure 8.1 a framework for assessing the project expenses is presented.

In the framework of Figure 8.1 the point of departure is that for every main type of cost, indicated by thousands, the amount is totalised upwards, whereas for the overall estimate the addition runs downward. The framework can provide something to hold on to when an estimate is made of the project expenses during the initiative phase of an event project. The framework can also be used for the budgets in later phases.

It is recommended that when framing project budgets for the different stages of the process to proceed from the same standard format of expenses.. The standard format that has been used here is four digits and hierarchical. The standard entries are explained further in Section 8.2. Because a standard format is applied, the budgets in the different stages of the project are mutually compatible. In later budgets, the compatible amounts from earlier budgets can be placed in columns next to each other. This makes it possible to get an overview of the cost development during the course of the project and to see the final differences between the last payment and the earlier budgets. Below three brief descriptions follow showing the three budgets of a project and an indication of their level of detail.

8.1.1   *The Estimate of the Project Expenses*

The estimate of the project expenses is a first overall estimate, based on the terms and conditions that have been formulated during the initiative phase. It is called an estimate (or assessment) for a good reason because the word 'budget' suggests greater exactness. This estimate is part of the initiative report. In the estimate of the project expenses, the expenses and earnings are included which are related to the preparation and execution of the project. For a complete survey, it is recommended that all expenses be included, hence also the *indirect* expenses made by, for instance, the mother organisation. If this is impos-

ESTIMATE PROJECT EXPENSES
Name of the Stage Project
Name of Person Responsible for the Project
Date Premiere

Project No.   :
Date   :
For the Benefit Of :   preparation phase

Type of Cost	Description	Expenses		Total
		Material and Third parties	Labour Expenses	
1000	Location Expenses			
1100	–			
1200	–			
2000	Primary Activities (or Direct Production Expenses 'Hardware')			
2100	–			
2200	–			
2300	–			
3000	Secondary Activities (or Direct Production Expenses 'Software')			
3100	–			
3200	–			
3300	–			
4000	Design, Consultation and Support			
5000	Additional Expenses			
6000	Support Facilities (or Supporting Sub-Projects)			
6100	–			
6200	–			
7000	Promotion, Publicity and PR			
7100	–			
7200	–			
8000	Organisation Expenses and Incidental Expenditures			
8100	–			
8200	–			
	Estimate Project Expenses (VAT Not Included)			
	Taxes (VAT)			
	Estimate Project Expenses (VAT Included)			
9000	Revenue (Financing Scheme)			
9100	– Admission Fees			
9200	– Project Subsidies			
9300	– Funds and Sponsoring			
9400	–			

Positive/Negative Project Result

Figure 8.1   A Framework for the Estimate of Project Expenses

sible, then the entries that will come to the account of, for instance, the mother organisation or the client, will have to be highlighted by placing a remark in the estimate. This also includes supplies in kind, which are not charged. This way an overview of the *total* expenses can be maintained.

In the estimate of project expenses, the expenses per main type of expenses are estimated at the minimum. Potentially, at this stage, the most important components of the project can be included in the estimate individually, in a subdivision of the main types of cost. Sometimes it is advisable to take three scenarios into account: the optimistic, realistic and pessimistic. Then, the amounts for the three scenarios can be presented next to each other in columns. If so desired, a number of project versions can be presented in the same way. The estimate made for the amounts, at this stage, is based on experience. Moreover, price estimates and quotes can be requested. It is advised to estimate the earnings as realistically as possible, and it is better too low than too high. For expenses it is the other way around; better to estimate them too high, than too low. However, never estimate them higher than you can substantiate. With each project budget, hence also with the estimate of project expenses, an explanation should be provided which clarifies what the most important entries have been based on. To be able to assess the risk, the explanation should also give an indication of the 'solidity' of the different amounts.

Once the estimate of the project expenses has been approved by the client, the final amount becomes the *term of reference,* and is then called the *budget.* The project has to be realised with this amount. In some cases, the client has already set a budget at the beginning of the initiative phase. In this case, the estimate of the project expenses must fall within the budget. On the basis of an estimate, an assessment is made whether the project is feasible (and, if necessary, sufficiently profitable), or not. The approved budget should be guarded during the further course of the process (See Section 8.3).

8.1.2   *The Components Budget*

After the plan or design has been developed during the preparation phase, a new budget should be built based on the same plan. At the end of this phase the plan needs to be evaluated and then it should be possible to set priorities. If the cost of each component or elementis transparent, then this will be advantageous during the decision process. In the components budget all the elements or components of the plan have been expressed in expenses. This budget, therefore, is more detailed than the estimate derived from the initiative phase, because it is mostly based on quotes from suppliers. Within the entries for the main types of cost, the expenses for all the relevant project components and other expenses within the components budget are referred to individually. The total amount of the components budget, should obviously fall within the approved budget. For a good comparison with the budget, it is recommended that an extra column be included in the components budget with the estimates of the previous phase on which the budget is based. In a components budget an explanation should also be provided which clarifies what the most important entries are based on (for instance on quotes from suppliers). In this explanation the most important differences with regard to the previous budget have to be accounted for. In some cases, the subdivision into the various components is not relevant. In this is the case, then a different budget will need to be made at the end of the preparation phase, based on the required hours and cost of materials. In Appendix A15 an example of such a budget for an Audio-Visual (AV) project has been included. This budget has also been based on the framework with the previously mentioned standard entries. However, it was necessary to make a change (for instance, cost type 6000, Editing) where certain points were concerned.

8.1.3   *Working Budget*

Central to the working budget, and also referred to as the implementation budget, is the detailed *calculation of the cost price* for each element of the project. Calculation here implies that for each arrangement the man-hours, the expenses of the material and the expenses of services by third parties are calculated. The total of calculated expenses in the working budget should also fall within the approved budget. In the working budget all the positions of the four-digit cost type numbers are to be used. For many projects it is not necessary to produce a budget at this detailed a level. Often, an extensive components budget can fulfill the function of the working budget. When a working budget is used, an explanation needs to be given which accounts for the most important differences with respect to the previous budget.

8.2   The Standard Entries of an Event Budget

It has already been mentioned above that it is advisable to use standard entries within the framework for the main types of expenses, so different budgets from different projects can be easily compared.

Do not use the division into standard entries as a kind of straitjacket. For each project, change the names of the types of expenses and the sequence of the entries, if needed. If a certain entry is not applicable, this can be mentioned in the project budget or the entry can be dropped. The standard division of cost types, used here, is in *four digits* and *hierarchical*. The main cost types are indicated by whole thousands. These are standard. They can be subdivided as desired for each project. For these we use hundreds, for instance 2100, 2200, or, in an even finer subdivision, tens, for instance 2210, 2220. On the lowest level we use the numbers 2211, 2212, etcetera. For exhibition projects the hundreds within the 2000 and 3000 range (these are known as the *core expenses*) have also been fixed for the sake of uniformity (See Appendix B2). A brief explanation of the standard entries for the project expenses, as they have been applied in the framework, follows below.

1000 Location Expenses

Included in location expenses are the expenses that have to be made for obtaining the space, the grounds, or the venue ready for the event. Here, one might consider, for instance, the expenses of renting the accommodation, thevenue, the parking space, the expenses, if necessary, of the provisions for the utilities (pipes for gas, water and sewage, and lines for electricity) and the expenses, if necessary, for elementary improvements of the accommodation, to prepare it for being used. This does not include the expenses for the decoration and the furnishing of the accommodation or the venue.

2000 Primary Activities

The types of expenses in the 2000 and 3000 range, together make up what is known as the core expenses. Here the most essential expenses of the project have been categorised. Within this range, first a distinction is made, where possible, between the components or elements of the event. Because of this, the expenses of these elements have become visible in the different budgets. If, for instance, a distinction is first made on the basis of technology (scenery, sound, light, etc.), then this would apply to different components and it would fail to make the budget transparent for each part of the project result.

The above is true, especially, for events that consist of different parts or subprojects. With public events and festivals, for instance, under the heading of primary expenses, the expenses of the *primary* activities or components are included separately. Take, for instance, 2100 Parade, 2200 Workshops, 2300 Cabaret Show, 2400 Exhibition, 2500 Final Party, etc. With productions, for instance an exhibition project or a film or stage production, the *direct production expenses 'hardware'* (the 'carriers' of information or performance) are included here. With an exhibition these are presentation units, for instance 2100 Presentation Unit 1 (consisting of a panel), 2200 Presentation Unit 2 (display case), 2300 Presentation Unit 3 (pedestal with scale model), etc. With an individual stage project the hundreds can be used directly for the expenses of the stage, the gallery, and sound and light equipment, respectively (excluding the expenses of the performances and speakers).

3000 Secondary Activities

With events, such as public events and festivals, it sometimes makes sense to distinguish secondary activities or components, for instance the opening ceremony and the closing ceremony. Main cost type 3000 offers that possibility. Bear in mind, activities with respect to 'content' are at issue here, hence activities aimed at the objective of the project. Catering activities, security and such do not belong here. As it happens, these are support facilities, code 6000. With productions, this cost type is about *direct production expenses 'software'* (the 'information' or 'performances' themselves). With an exhibition project it relates to, for instance, the pictures, texts, objects and models, and with a stage project the expenses of the performances, the artists, the speakers, the teachers, etc. for each component. With a stage production, within the *core expenses* a choice can also be made to make another distinction, namely between the production expenses up to opening night (main cost type 2000) and what is referred to as the daily expenses during the performance stage (3000).

4000 Design, Consultation and Support

The cost type design, consultation and support will cover the fees and the traveling expenses of, for instance, external advisors, designers, stylists and photographers. Also the expenses of the additional staff, such as the expenses of support personnel and the expenses of volunteers, fall within this category. The fees of the artists and speakers are not included in this. These are part of the core expenses, code 3000. The fixed labour expenses for members of the project team are part of the organisation expenses, code 8000.

5000 Additional Expenses

Additional expenses cover all the separate, incidental expenses, such as expenses for transport, insurance, royalties (also for the use of music, pictures and the like), fees, connection charges, encroachment rights and other (government) charges. If a loan has to be taken out for the project, the interest also falls within this category.

6000 Support Facilities

Covered by the cost category, support facilities, are, for instance, the expenses for cleaning, ticket sales, catering, wardrobe, toilet facilities, parking facilities, first aid, signage, decoration of the accommodation and the grounds, signposts, the organisation of access to different parts of the event, means of communication during the production or the event, surveillance and security.

7000 Promotion, Publicity and PR

The cost type of promotion, publicity and PR covers promotion expenses, for instance the expenses of advertising, publicity, press files, flags, and banners. But also the expenses of printing, such as programmes, brochures, posters, folders, stickers, invitations, parking fees, entrance tickets, lottery tickets, including the expenses for mailing and handling of that printed matter, are grouped in this cost category. Moreover, the expenses of public relations and sponsoring fall within the same category, for instance the expenses of the brochure for sponsors, for hosting the sponsors and for promotional gifts. The opening expenses are also included here, for instance the opening of an exhibition, or the expenses of a premiere, including press receptions.

8000 Organisation Expenses and Incidental Expenditures

Included in the organisation expenses are all the expenses that the project organisation makes. Beside the possible labour expenses and compensations for the members of the project team, these also include, among other things, telephone expenses, expenses for stationery, postage, meeting expenses, cost for meeting rooms, travel expenses for the project team, copy and fax expenses, computer expenses and expenses for office supplies. Sometimes the organisation expenses listed above are carried by the mother organisation. In that case, it is advisable to include them in the budget as *general indirect expenses* (also referred to as overhead). With this is meant the expenses that are not made for this project specifically, but those that should be charged to this project, to obtain an accurate view of the total expenses. Sometimes the general indirect expenses should be charged to the specific projects by means of a *surcharge percentage*, in other cases a more accurate formula is sought for these expenses. Part of the general indirect expenses charged to the project are, for instance a share of the housing expenses, the office expenses and the administrative expenses of the mother organisation.

The entry called *incidental expenditures* is meant to catch miscellaneous expenses. This entry is also often expressed in terms of a percentage of the sum of all expenses mentioned above. In the initiative phase of the project, when little is known about the total expenses of realisation, a higher percentage will naturally (fifteen to twenty percent) be included than what will follow in the subsequent phases (eight to twelve per cent, or more, depending on the level of uncertainty). At the end of the development phase, when the uncertainties have been minimised because everything has been described and/or drawn up in detail, a percentage of two to five per cent will often suffice.

9000 Revenue

Revenue includes all the earnings from the project, such as entrance fees/receipts/buying-out premiums, proceeds from sales and programmes, proceeds from catering/parking/toilet facilities (sometimes rent), sponsor contributions in cash or in kind, contributions from funds, donations, proceeds from lotteries, project subsidies from government agencies or guarantees to cover possible shortfalls.

Turnover tax (VAT)

When an organisation developing the project, is liable to pay VAT, the VAT does not constitute a cost component in the budget of the project. This is the case for nearly all the company events and most of the public events. In most countries the turnover tax paid, can be deducted from the taxes that need to be handed over. With respect to the remaining fiscal aspects of an event the reader is referred to Section 8.5.

In addition, the standard division of project expenses used here does not yet fit with what is known as the decimal accounting framework adopted in many permanent organisations. If working in projects is going to become more common within a permanent organisation, such a connection will still need to be established, for instance by making use of a six-digit, instead of a four-digit code.

The above is only a general list of the types of expenses within the main components of the budget. We would be straying too far from the subject, if all budget entries were to be discussed in more detail.

In some cases the aforementioned standard division of expenses for the budget cannot be applied, because subsidisers prescribe their own budget framework. For instance, the Fund for the Performing Arts in the Netherlands has its own framework. See Figure 8.2. The types of expenses used in a stage project fit quite well with the types of expenses that are usually employed in the financial administration of a permanent organisation.

Below the main types of expenses used in this framework will be elaborated upon.

At 100, *Personnel Expenses,* all the expenses are entered, which have to be incurred for the payment of the employees who work on the project. These could include gross salaries, holiday allowances, pension contributions and employer's expenses for employees who will be on the payroll for a determined period. They can also include fees for staff who will deliver a previously agreed upon service for the project, such as a composer, a scene designer, a lighting designer, a clothes designer, a writer, a publicity agent and sometimes even the director. People who are permanently connected with the production, who, as they say, are in a service relationship with the employer, cannot be paid in fees, but they need to obtain an employment contract and therefore enter salaried employment. Depending on the course of the performances (compact playing period, or scattered) contracts for a certain period of time or one-day contracts can be concluded. Please be aware that every country has its own rules and regulations when it comes to salaries and for instance freelancing. Check with your local tax office for more information.

With respect to *200, Housing Expenses,* and *300, Office Expenses,* the following applies. Business expenses are expenses that are incurred to keep the company going. These include, among other things, housing expenses, office and interior decorating expenses, administration expenses, insurance premiums, general expenses for publicity, postage and telephone expenses and accountancy expenses. Often a group will also incur expenses when no production is being carried out. The subsidy received, however, may only be used to cover expenses that will be incurred for the sake of a production. In ths case, it is necessary to attribute business expenses to the production, as precisely as possible.

At *410, Production Expenses,* expenses are included that have been incurred in order to fulfil all of the financial obligations up to opening night, naturally excluding personnel expenses. Roughly the expenses that are at issue here include, among other things, the production of the scenery (material and labour expenses), the expenses for the props and clothes, the expenses for the sound and music recordings, the rental of theatre technology, the rental of the rehearsal room, the rental of the hall for the full dress rehearsal, the try-outs, and the premiere, transport expenses of employees and material, publicity expenses related specifically to the production and royalties.

Under the heading *420, Performance Expenses, or Day Expenses,* all expenses are included that make it possible for the performance to proceed, excluding the personnel expenses. At issue here are, among other things, the expenses for the maintenance of the scenery, costumes, props, expenses for hair-dressing and make-up, transport expenses for the actors, technicians and material, accommodation, and if necessary the rental of the hall, expenses for publicity of the performance and expenses for performing rights.
Under heading *500, Expenses Publicity and Promotion,* promotion expenses are included, for instance expenses for setting up the website, advertising, public-

ity and press files. But also included here are expenses for printed matter such as programmes, brochures, posters, leaflets, invitations and entrance tickets, including the expenses of postage and distribution of that printed matter. The expenses of public relations and attracting sponsors, the expenses of hosting sponsors and the expenses of promotional gifts are also inclued. Moreover, the expenses for the premiere are included in this, including press receptions.

ESTIMATE PROJECT EXPENSES

Name of the Stage Project	:	Project No.	:
Name of Person Responsible for the Project	:	Date	:
Date Premiere	:	For the Benefit Of	: preparation phase

Type of Cost	Description	Amount	Total
100	Personnel Expenses		
110	– Business Leadership		
120	– Artistic Staff		
130	– Administrative Personnel		
140	– Staff Carrying Out the Work		
150	– Other Personnel Expenses		
200	Housing Expenses		
300	Office Expenses		
400	Activities Expenses		
410	– Production Expenses/Research Expenses		
420	– Performance Expenses		
500	Expenses Publicity and Promotion		
Total Cost			
600	Earnings (Total)		
610	– Audience Takings		
620	– Sponsor Contributions		
630	– Media Earnings		
640	– Other Income		
700	Subsidies (Total)		
710	– Subsidies County		
720	– Subsidies Council		
730	– Other Subsidies		
Total Profits			
Budget Deficit			

Figure 8.2   Framework for a Budget of Stage Projects

Under cost entry 600, *Earnings,* all proceeds from the performances are included. These can be box-office receipts or buying-out premiums, but also profit sharing, performance subsidies or guarantees. Moreover, sometimes there are also yields from the sale of posters, programmes, booklets or DVDs or CDs. If a deal has been made with a broadcasting company about the registration of the performance for later broadcasting, then this can also bring in income.

With the application form of the Fund for the Performing Arts an extensive manual is included for the purpose of framing a budget.

The Financing Scheme
All expenses, minus the income, yield what is known as the *exploitation deficiency* of the project. This exploitation *deficiency* needs to be covered. How the author of the budget imagines he will do that can be gathered from what is called the *financing scheme.* Sometimes the financing scheme is integrated into the budget, as is the case with the abovebut sometimes it consists of a separate outline, such as in the budget of the AV-project in Appendix A15. In the financing scheme, it is stated which part of the *deficiency* is covered by one's own means, which part by funds and/or sponsors and which part by subsidisers. Often an appeal is made to more than one subsidiser or fund. Thus, for instance the national government can be appealed to for a subsidy of the personnel expenses, the county can be asked to subsidise the editing expenses and the council a contribution towards the operating expenses. Sponsors can be asked, for instance, to supply material or to make a contribution towards the publicity expenses. By definition, the financing scheme has to break even and is not allowed to show any uncovered *deficiency.*

8.3   Budget Control and Reporting

When the basic principles of the initiative report, including the estimate of the project expenses, have been approved by the client or financier, the total budget for the project has thereby been determined. That budget needs to be guarded during the process. This happens in three ways. In the first place, in each phase a new budget is made on the basis of the most recent data on the project and that budget is checked against the fixed budget. Moreover, the budget is subdivided into partial budgets for different completed components and these partial budgets, in larger projects, are assigned by the project leader, in a 'task-setting' way, to *budget controllers.* These are, for instance, members of the project team and/or leaders of the working groups responsible for a component of the event. The budget controllers are responsible for their part of the budget and have to justify it to the project leader. The project administration, finally, needs to make sure that both the obligations (for instance orders and agreements) and the expenditures of these obligations are booked to the account of the entry in question. Many automated administrations offer budget control of projects. However, the budget control can also be done manually through a budget-control form (See Appendix A2). Each time a budget controller enters into a financial obligation at the expense of his (partial) budget, for instance by filling out an order form or signing a quote, he consults the (partial) budget to check whether the obligation is sensible. Current developments with regard to the possibilities of pocket computers and smart phones allow for project or production leaders to control the budget on the spot. Each transaction can be entered immediately, which means that any given moment and any given location up-to-date information on the (partial) budget can be made available. When the project administration is not kept up by the project team itself but, for instance, by the accounting department of the mother organisation, the bookkeeper has to make sure that the budget controllers regularly receive an up-to-date overview of the state of their budget. In Section 12.3.3 *The Arrangement of the Project Infrastructure*, the setting up of a financial project administration within a multi-project organisation is elaborated upon.

For projects that run for a longer period, it is often desirable that during the development and production phases a budget report be presented to the client. In Figure 8.3 an example of such a report has been included.

In the budget report the assessment of the real expenses is compared with the relevant partial budget for each entry. This will lead to an understanding of the expected result for each entry. The assessment of the real expenses is the sum of all expenditures (usually derived from the financial administration), the ongoing obligations (such as orders and contracts) and an estimate of the pending obligations (an estimate of what is still to be expected). By periodically framing a budget report, insight can be gained into the development of expenses and earnings with respect to the estimates that had previously been provided in the budget.

8.4   Orders, Contracts and Permits

During the course of an event project has many obligations. Most obligations are entered into through orders, for instance to advisors, manufacturers, suppliers, rental companies, artists and other service providers. The project leader has a responsibility to deal efficiently with the available money. Therefore, he

BUDGET REPORT

Name of the Project	: Exhibition 'Energy in 2010'
Name Project Leader	: Rob de Boer
Completion/Opening/Premiere	: May, 2003

Project Number	: 514
Page Number	: 5
Date Report	: March 26, 2009
Current Phase	: Development Phase
File	: 'bugetrpTEN03

Cost Type	Description	First Estimate dd: 02-06-08	Alterations	Current Budget dd: 26-03-00 (All Including)	Expenditures (From Fin. Admin.)	Ongoing Obligations	Assessment Pending Obligations	Assessment Real Expenses/Cover (All Including)	Assessment Budget Balance Surplus+/Deficit−
1	2	3	4	5=3+4	6	7	8	9=6+7+8	10=5−9
	EXPENSES:								
1000	Location Expenses	At Expense Client		At Expense Client	0	0	0	0	0
2000	Direct Production Expenses - Hardware	52.500		52.500	0	0	58.500	58.500	−6.000
2100	– Panels	25.500		25.500	0	0	23.500	23.500	2.000
2200	– Display Cases and Pedestals	27.000		27.000	0	0	35.000	35.500	−8.000
3000	Direct Production Expenses - Software	45.500	−2.500	43.000	7.400	2.110	32.000	41.510	1.490
4000	Design, Consultation and Support	42.925		42.925	14.045	12.590	19.000	45.635	−2.710
5000	Additional Expenses	pm	4.000	4.000	1.200	320	2.480	4.000	0
6000	Supporting Sub-Projects	7.000		7.000	705	1.475	8.620	10.800	−3.800
6100	– Lectures	6.000		6.000	380	0	5.620	6.000	0
6200	– Treasure Hunt	1.000		1.000	0	0	1.000	1.000	0
6300	– Hand-Out	0		0	325	1.475	2.000	3.800	−3.800
7000	Promotion, Publicity and PR	At Expense Client		At Expense Client	0	0	0	0	0
8000	Organisation Expenses and Incidental Expenditures	7.075		7.075	725	120	3.677	4.522	2.553
	Total Project Expenses (VAT Not Included)	155.000	1.500	156.500 (All Including)	24.075	16.615	124.277	164.967 (All Including)	−8.467
	Taxes (VAT)		1.500	1.500					
	Total Project Expenses (VAT Included)	155.000	1.500	156.500	24.075	16.615	124.277	164.967	−8.467
	EARNINGS:								
9000	Revenues	123.000	1.500	124.500				132.967	
9100	– Admission Fees	68.000		68.000				75.000	
9200	– Project Subsidies	40.000		40.000				38.000	
9300	– Funds and Sponsoring	15.000	1.500	16.500				16.500	
9400	– Sales	0		0				3.467	
			32.000	32.000				32.000	
	Total Earnings	123.000	33.500	156.500				164.967	
	Uncovered Deficit	32.000	−32.000	0				0	

Figure 8.3   Summary Overview of the Budget Report

will invite offers/quotes from different suppliers, before he sends out an order for a certain delivery. Roughly, with reference to offering and granting an order the following steps can be distinguished.

8.4.1   *Invite Tentative Offers*

In an early stage of the project, for certain components tentative offers are requested. Through such tentative offers the project team can receive an indication of the cost of a certain part of the event, in order to make the project budget. Because during this stage of the project not everything is known, and because there is still no need for great precision, these tentative prices can be requested over the phone or made based on previous offers and quotes.

Invite Competitive Offers

Competitive offers are requested in particular during the later phases, when there is clarity about the necessary requirements for a certain delivery. To obtain a competitive price, several offers are invited. Often three offers will be sufficient guarantee for a competitive price. When inviting offers, it is of utmost importance that the specifications of the delivery for which a price is requested, both with respect to quality and quantity, are unambiguously described in the briefing for a quote. This reduces the risk of misinterpretations. When suppliers pass on prices by phone, it is always necessary to have them confirmed in writing.

Comparing Offers

If you want to make a good comparison, you have to make sure that all the suppliers base their offer, or set their price, on the basis of the same request. This does not guarantee that you will be sent identical offers. Each company has its own way of framing offers. However, comparing offers requires some skill. It has to be clear, for instance, whether the price includes or excludes VAT, and whether (quantity) rebates are offered. The quantities and the specifications should also be compared closely, in order to be able to make an economically sound choice. Here the price is not the only issue, but also the price-quality relationship. If a lack of clarity remains, it is wise to call the supplier in order to avoid later disappointments. Bear in mind that working with the same supplier more often enhances the working relationship and can lead to fixed discounts.

Issue Orders

It is always advisable to issue orders in writing by means of a written order or an order form. It is recommended that the quantities, technical specifications, terms of delivery and prices be stated explicitly in the written order. Should the occasion arise, the offer on which the order has been based, should be referred to or the possible drawings and descriptions should be enclosed.

In a number of cases the obligations will not be entered into through an order, but through contracts or agreements. Here, one can think of an employment contract, a lease, an artist's contract, a sponsoring contract or a contract with a catering company. With contracts or agreements it is important that the parties are named clearly in the agreement and that the rights and duties of both parties are clearly stated. It is advisable to have contracts read through by a legal advisor, before they are signed. Take your time to read the small print and do not forget that contracts need to be signed by both parties to be legally valid. Appendix A6 includes a model for an employment contract, Appendix A7 a model for an artist's contract, Appendix A8 a model for a volunteer's contract, Appendix A9 a checklist for a sponsor's contract and Appendix A14 a model agreement for an assignment.

Legally, there are roughly two possibilities with respect to entering into an assignment, namely through:

1   An agreement or contract
2   An assignment (letter)

Legally, it makes no difference. An agreement is the most conclusive. In that case the *model agreement for an assignment* included in Appendix A14 can be used. When an assignment (letter) is used, then the other party needs to sign it and send it back by regular post. For, only then will there be a mutual agreement.

An advantage of an agreement is that usually everything is arranged point by point. If a conflict should occur, then it is clear what the parties agreed to exactly. Most assignments do not have this so meticulously formulated in writing. This means that in possible conflicts a decision must be made concerning what would be considered *reasonable* and *fair*.

8.4.2   *The Employment Contract*

With reference to the agreements mentioned above, we will briefly discuss the question: When does an employment agreement exist? Below we took the Dutch situation as an example, but as mentioned before every country has its own rules and regulations. Please ask for information at your local tax office and Chamber of Commerce.

As far as the tax is concerned, it does not matter *how* you arrange it. However, an important sting in these types of relations is that the government quite quickly makes the assumption that there is an employment contract, even if you yourself do not call it that. Using the model agreement for an assignment mentioned earlier, will make clear in most cases whether there is an *assignment* relationship or an *employment* relationship.

This problem does not apply when an assignment is given to a private business.

Permits

For the organisation of certain events a good number of permits will need to be requested from for instance the council, the fire brigade and the police. This involves, for instance, permits for making use of public roads, for using sound equipment or recreational installations in the open air, or for obtaining a liquor licence or a licence from the fire department in which fire safety requirements are listed. For most licences municipal fees have to be paid. To find out which licences are needed, what their terms are and what their expenses are, you can call the information service of the relevant council or municipality.

8.5   Liability, Insurance and Inland Revenue

Within the framework of the organisation of an event a number of liability issues can arise. One can safeguard oneself against these.

8.5.1   *Covering Oneself Against Liability Claims*

The financial consequences of liability claims can be avoided, limited and/or transferred completely, or in part, by means of:

1 Insurance against these risks
2 Complete or partial avoidance by means of the chosen type of business enterprise (structure), or the filing of the general terms of delivery or terms for the performance of services at the registry of the district court
3 Transferral within the framework of the law of ultimate responsibility
4 Preliminary consultation with, and evaluation by, the qualified tax department and industrial insurance board with reference to the implementation of fiscal law (wage and turnover tax).

For events that last only briefly or small projects it is preferable to insure against potential financial consequences as a result of liability. For larger projects of a longer duration the organisation often takes place from within an especially crafted type of business enterprise (structure), usually in the form of a legal person, such as the limited liability company, partnership, association, corporation, cooperative society, or mutual insurance company.

The limited liability company and the corporation are the most common. Because the creation of a legal entity takes some time (about six months) in connection with the framing of the initial agreement, the status, the capital contributed and request for the certificate of incorporation, it is recommended that you work with an already established legal person or that you determine the legal person before the event, so that the actual participation in social (economic) intercourse takes place from within that legal person.

With respect to the risks that possibly need to be insured or evaluated, note the following:

– The liability risk in law, in case of default, tort, neglecting one's obligations and so on.
– Risk in the framework of the law of ultimate responsibility, such as the wrong judgement of whether or not there is an employer-employee relationship, or an employment relationship that is socially comparable with it, which can have consequences regarding the requirement to pay insurance in the framework of social security law, as well as for the payment of income tax and the like

Moreover, the law of ultimate responsibility also extends to turnover tax (VAT).

An accurate assessment and preliminary consultation with the inspector in the initiative or preparation phase is, therefore, of vital importance to avoid or rule out possible risks.

Furthermore, a number of other risks have to be taken into account, such as the weather situation (insurance against rain, however, is relatively expensive), the risk of loss of profits in case of fire or otherwise, as a result of which the event cannot take place but the fixed expenditures carry on through (continuing event insurance).

With reference to a confrontation with damage claims it is sensible to take out a third-party liability insurance and a legal expenses insurance.

Because it would lead us too far afield to discuss all the details in this context, we refer you to the specialised literature on this topic.

It is advisable, moreover, to seek expert advice in such an area, from professionals such as a notary public, lawyer, accountant or fiscal expert.

8.5.2 Fiscal Aspects

Besides the liability risks on account of third-party liability and/or in case of loss of profits, the organisation of an event can be held responsible for withholding and transferring income tax, turnover tax and if applicable social security premiums (both employee's insurance and national insurance).
It is important — if the services of third parties are used — to ascertain whether there is clear and convincing evidence of entrepreneurship, or whether, in view of the factual situation, there is an employer-employee relationship, or an equivalent employment relationship.

For artists there is a special arrangement, which varies from country to country. In the Netherlands we have a wage distribution statement. Moreover, there is an obligation to carry identification papers here. To have these formal documents are inextricably tied to, or are part of the model for an artist's contract provided in Appendix A7.

With reference to the turnover tax (VAT) we can state, in principle, that it is important to find out whether or not there is a rule concerning regular participation in social (economic) interactions in the country where the event takes place.
Besides making the division into a general rate and a lowered rate, in the field of turnover tax many other (special) rules can be applicable with respect to, for instance, sports, leisure, fundraising, donations, gifts and sponsoring, congresses, conferences and training activities, subsidies and cultural institutions.

9

Project Financing

A distinction can be made between *company events, commercial events and non-commercial events depending* on how they are financed. Company events are usually financed from the company's budget. Commercial events must prove their worth on the free market. They are primarily intended for making profit. Non-commercial events are often financed, to a large extent, through subsidies and sponsoring. In this category one can often witness what is referred to as *stacked financing,* in which the expenses are covered by different financial sources. In practice, a distinction between these three categories is often difficult to make. With non-commercial events, for instance, it is very common for them to be financed, in part, by the sale of tickets and merchandising. The main objective is then not commercial, but the sub-objective most certainly is.

In this chapter you will find an elaboration on the financing of these categories of events.

9.1   The Financing of Company Events

Company events are motivational, festive, or a combination of both. Numerous examples abound such as: staff gatherings, product launches, company anniversaries, stockholders' meetings, conferences, incentives, excursions, company sports days or the opening of a building/company. Company events are ad hoc or in accordance with policy and are financed in most cases from the financial resources of the company, for instance from the promotional, communication or the personnel budget. In general, no subsidies or external funding can be secured for these types of events.

9.2   The Financing of Commercial Events

Commercial events include all those events that are primarily aimed at generating profit. Here, we might think of, for instance productions by independent producers or by companies, for example: congresses, pop concerts, fairs, etc. These types of events, which are primarily aimed at making money, can be seen as a product in which an investment needs to be made. Therefore, we must regard these events as *investment projects*. By investing, a part of the capital of a company is turned into liquid assets for a certain period. For an event such as an investment project an investment plan needs to be made, which must be checked for feasibility and profitability. Projects that have to be 'put on the market,' subsequently demand a solid market approach, using market research (SWOT-analysis), a marketing plan (development of the 5 P's), and a prognosis of the turnover (See also Chapter 11). For financing this category of events, a strategic alliance with one or more other companies can sometimes be used, for which the event might also provide an interesting opportunity. Sometimes, a contribution is made towards the financing of the event, but one can of course also consider developing the project at joint expense *and* risk. If this is the case, then we can speak of a co-production.

When evaluating an investment project, we should focus on our expectations of what the level of expenditures and returns will be. For this we can proceed from the project budget. On the basis of this the *cash flows* can be calculated during the course of the project. By cash flow we mean the difference between the earnings that originate, for instance, from the sale of the product (such as admission fees) and the expenditures with regard to the purchase concerning the means of production (project expenses) during a certain period. With investment projects, the purpose is to make profit on the investments during the duration of the project with the periodic earnings. This profit needs to be large enough to meet all the obligations towards the financiers, given that the interest and redemption are not included in the expenditures. The development of the balance of earnings and expenditures should roughly follow the outline provided in Figure 9.1.

The moment that the preparations for the project start is point t_{-1}. The warming-up period of the project (t_{-1} - t_0) is formed by the initiative phase, the preparation phase, the development phase and the production phase combined. During the warming-up period most expenses are made, especially in the production phase. At point t_0, which is the transition from the warming-up period of the project to the performance phase, a deficiency emerges in regard to the size of the total amount of investment I_0. This point is marked by the launching of the product, for instance the premiere of the musical or the opening of the exhibition. From this moment on, the whole investment needs to be earned back. In addition to this, new expenses are also added, for instance the daily expenses of a stage production or the maintenance expenses of an exhibition. However, from that moment onwards earnings will come in increasingly. If everything is alright, then at some point in the *duration* of the project the total earnings will surpass the total expenditures (including the investment): this is point t_1. The period from point t_0 to point t_1 we call the *cost recovery period*. The cost recovery will start slowly, reach its peak and, when for instance the attendance figures drop, it will also decrease again. Because the expenditures continue during the course of the project, there might a time when the expenditures once again are higher during a certain period than the earnings. In that case the graphicline depicting this on the chart will start to drop again. It should be clear that, when only economic motives count, the product will have to be taken off of the market at point t_2 for, that is when the maximum returns remain.

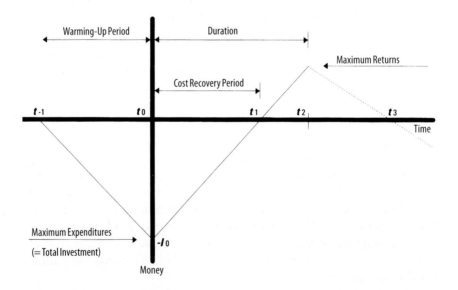

Figure 9.1   *The Schematic Development of the Cash Flow in an Investment Project*

For evaluating the feasibility and profitability of an investment project within your own organisation, a chart such as the one that is shown in Figure 9.1 can give decision-makers a clear understanding of the issue. When a project depends on external financing, the potential financier (for instance a bank or a financial partner who is prepared to guarantee possible losses) will also want to gain a clear understanding of the cash-flow development. Maybe you will also be able to convince them by using such a chart. For high-risk projects it is recommended to draw up a different diagram for each of the three options- optimistic, realistic and pessimistic- or to represent them with three different lines in the same diagram. Finally, such a diagram can be used to calculate the interest expenses. For, from the chart you can deduce how long you can take possession of a certain amount of capital. The *capital possession* is represented in the chart by the triangle under the time axis, from t_{-1} to t_1 to $-I_0$. On the basis of capital possession, the interest must be calculated.

If we want to frame such a chart, we first have to divide the time axis, for instance in months. Subsequently, for each month we can list in a separate survey which part of the expenditures and earnings from the project budget have been spent and received respectively. The sum of the receipts and the expenses is the cash flow for each month. Then, the balance for the first month after the start of the project can be plotted in the lower region of the chart. At that moment, only expenditures will take place. After that we will plot the calculated balances of the subsequent months cumulatively (hence, always added to the sum total of the previous month) in a descending line. From point t_0 onwards the line will go up, because the income per month will be higher than the expenditures.

9.3   The Subsidising of Non-Commercial Events

Within the category of non-commercial productions, all the productions or events that do not belong to the categories of commercial and company events are included. For these (supplemental) subsidies can be requested. Before we take a closer look at the (processing of the) applications, first an explanation on the type of subsidies will be provided, and it will be indicated when they can be applied for and from whom.

9.3.1   Introduction

When non-commercial productions are involved, the profit motive is rarely of primary importance. This does not mean that one should not be allowed to strive towards making a profit (on certain parts). However, only very few cultural productions can be produced and exploited to break even. That is why in many cases money will have to be found in order to realise the plans.

At issue here are, for instance, a streettheatre festival, a village festival, an exhibition, an art production, a tourist event, or a sports event.

Often a non-commercial event is organised by a permanent organisation, such as a museum, theatre group, recreational park or a cultural centre. In this case, such an event is usually financed, either completely or for an important part, from the structural resources of this organisation. Sometimes, however, supplemental funds will be necessary.

For independent initiatives external financing will nearly always have to be sought. In almost all cases there will have to be what is called stacked financing (financing which is put together from smaller amounts derived from different subsidisers/funds/sponsors). This could consist of:

- *Entrance fees* (with stage productions also 'buy-out sums'): box-office receipts, participant's contributions.
- *Contributions from (private) funds*: for this the event has to fit with the objective of the fund.
- *Donations in cash or in kind* (gifts from private individuals or companies).
- *Sponsoring in cash or in kind* (exchange agreement between two parties).
- *Project subsidies by a government institution*: subsidies are granted under certain conditions and most meet specific criteria.
- *Fundraising activities and merchandising*: for instance attracting contributors, sale of CDs, programmes, T-shirts or souvenirs, stimulation of bar turnover, collection of old paper and empty bottles, sale of discount coupons (in cooperation with shopkeepers), lottery, wheel of fortune or bingo, sponsored run or auction.
- *co-production*: a co-production can be considered for several reasons. One reason might be that a co-producer can take care of part of the production expenses and, in some cases, the distribution expenses.

Who to Turn to?

In the Netherlands and Europe you have hundreds of private funds for all sorts of cultural, economic or leisure projects. It is best to seek funding that focuses on the type of project you are working on. What is most important is the *legitimisation* of the project. Only submit an application if your project fits with the subsidiser's objective or the fund itself. If the request is not attuned to this, it will be turned down straight away. It is important, moreover, to request an amount that a subsidiser or funding source is able and willing to give. If it is not known how much a funding source or subsidiser awards, you can call them. Sometimes, they also have an application form or an information folder. The large funding sources and subsidisers publish annual reports, in which you can see who applied for a subsidy for which purpose and who received how much. These annual reports can be found, among other places, on the internet.

When Do You Submit the Request?
Take into account that you often have to start six months, or sometimes even a year, in advance. For, in some cases subsidies are awarded only once a year; many countries operate that way.

One also needs to take into consideration that the money is often available much later than the deadline for submitting the request. Sometimes the production can only really start, then.

Big subsidisers, especially where government funding is concerned, place ads in the national and regional newspapers announcing when the subsidy can be applied for. Applications that come in after the closing date are not processed.

It is advisable, therefore, to obtain the exact information in regard toaspects such as the time span for the procedure and the conditions. All funds are not equally accessible, however. There are funds that are run solely by an administration consisting of volunteers. But subsidisers such as the council, the county or the national government, and funds affiliated with them, usually have a website, brochures and a person who can answer your questions over the phone.

9.3.2   How Is the Application Structured?

The step-by-step plan for applying for a subsidy resembles the following plan:

Step 1: The making of a project proposal in the form of an initiative report, which consists of, among other things:
 – The transformation of the creative idea into a concrete basic concept (with legitimisation)
 – The time planning of the project (how long will it take?)
 – The first draught for the project organisation (who will take part?)
 – The budget with the financing scheme (what are the expenses and how will they be covered?)

Step 2: Orientation on the possible subsidies and funds (including the request of information)

Step 3: The writing of the application, using the data from the initiative report

Step 4: Preparing enclosures

Step 5: Sending the application and staying in contact with the subsidiser

Step 6: Give account afterwards

Step 1   *When Are You Ready to Submit the Application?*

As mentioned before, the moment for submitting the application depends on the deadline stipulated by the subsidisers and funding sources. Of course, this moment is also determined by the stage of development of the project itself!

The difficulty in writing the application is that you do not yet know everything, whereas the subsidiser is requesting all kinds of information. You think that you can only start making arrangements once you are certain that you will receive your subsidy, but the subsidiser, on the contrary, wants to have that information earlier. How do you solve this problem?

You cannot really solve it. What you *can* do, is provide as much clarity as you can to yourself and the subsidiser about what the project will look like, if you get the subsidy you are hoping to receive. A good way to provide clarity is to develop your idea in the shape of a project, i.e. systematically and in phases. In this elaboration the points mentioned above under Step 1 are described systematically. After completing Step 1 there is an initiative report. See the separate steps for the development of the initiative report in Chapter 5. In this initiative report all the basic assumptions of the project, both in regard to the content and the business aspects, are established (See Appendix C1). Such an initiative report, therefore, includes all the information needed to write an application.

Step 2   *What Can You Ask For?*

The point of departure is the budget, which shows how much money you will need. Do not boost your budget entries to the extreme. It is fine to provide a margin, but do not enter implausible amounts. Thus, naturally, you can enter labour expenses when you work with professional people in a project, whereas you should enter an allowance for expenses if you work with volunteers.

Do not ask for too little, either! If you forget essential entries, for instance postage with a large mailing, or advertising expenses when you claim you want to bring the project to the notice of people nationally, then this will look amateuristic and they may wonder whether they can trust you and how professional you are.

The next question to ask is from whom can you should you seek money.

Many subsidisers only give money, if others also provide a subsidy. Almost all of them want you to get some of your income from the public. Hence, divide the amount needed among the public, the subsidisers and the sponsors. How much can you ask from the subsidiser?

Make sure that you know how much money the subsidiser awards on the average to every applicant. That way you can avoid a situation in which you apply for 6,000 euros from a fund that gives a maximum of 1,200 euros. The bigger the difference between the amount asked for and the amount available, the smaller the chance that you will receive the sum available. Hence, if you ask for 3,500 euros and they only award 2,200 euros, then they might award you with a maximum of 1,100 or 2,200 euros. But if the difference is greater, then they might start to think 'that 2,200 euros of ours will do them no good at all, with such a huge budget deficiency!'

If you have little experience in applying for money for projects, look for someone who has more experience and ask him/her whether they would mind looking at your application critically. If need be, ask the subsidiser whether you can send them a first draft, because you are not sure you are doing it correctly. Often they are prepared to give you feedback.

What Does the Application Look Like?   *Step 3*

An application consists of a part concerned with the content or the artistic aspect and a part concerned with the business aspect. In the application it needs to become clear *what* is produced and *why, how* it will be produced, by *whom,* for *whom, when, where, how long* it takes and *how much* the expenses will be. In practice, it often becomes clear during the 'sounding out' of the contacts (Step 2), what needs to be paid attention to explicitly. Governments and funding sources often draw up subsidy forms with questions and a draft/format for the budget.

– How Do You Make Clear What Is at Stake?

Before you start with the application, translate the idea of your project into a concrete basic concept. From this it will become clear how you want to shape the project and why you want to do it that way. In Chapter 5 of this book a separate step-by-step plan has been provided for the development of an idea into a basic concept.

When you are developing the basic concept, at a certain point you should start thinking about who (for instance, when a festival or exhibition is involved) you want to get involved with, and who will help with determining the content of the project. Get into contact with possible artists or groups to check their interest. This also constitutes a difficulty, by the way: the person contacted will ask for concrete information: how much money will I receive, is transport taken care of, who else will be involved?

To all these questions you cannot always give an answer at this early stage. Make clear that you are only researching the possibilities. The same applies when searching for a suitable location. Ask the site manager whether the location will be available and ask for an indication of the price for the budget.

The basic concept provides a clear image of what the result of the project will look like, and what you want to do with it and for whom. Hence, it will be used as the core of your application. When using the basic concept, you should be able to answer all the questions relating to content.

– *How Concrete Do You Have to Be?*

Describe the project which you are applying for a subsidy clearly, and follow the possible questions in the application form. Yet, keep it brief. Make clear immediately *what* you want to produce or organise *where*, for *whom*, with what *purpose*, *when* and with *whom*. Also indicate how many visitors or participants you expect. Of course, you also have to describe the idea, the previous history, and the sources of inspiration which lie at the basis of the project. However, do not turn it into a lengthy life story; mention facts! Outsiders are often able to write everything down clearly and concisely; if necessary, make use of their help.

It is wise to say how much money you would like to receive. This is true as well at the end of this section concerning content. It is very important to *always* ask for a concrete amount!

– *Start From an Optimistic, Realistic and Pessimistic Scenario!*

Construct three scenarios for the project to which you can relate the three budgets. The term scenario evokes a prognosis of 'how the process might unfold and/or what the result might look like.' Construct a scenario in which you have all the money you need to do everything you want to do, a scenario where you can make ends meet and, finally, a scenario that is based on minimal expenses.

– *What Does the Layout Of the Application Look Like?*

A good layout is very important. Not too artsy, easy to make copies of and furnished with page numbers, and, for a large application, it should also include a table of contents. Always carefully number the appendix and attach a list of numbers to them as well. In short, make sure that everything looks well cared for and that they can retrieve everything easily. If a member of the committee first has to search through the papers for five minutes to see how much money and which period it is in fact about, then the chance that you will receive the money will diminish considerably.

Step 4 **Supplements With Your Application**

Make a clear distinction in your application between major and minor issues. The advisory committee that must process the applications, always receives a whole pile of applications at home just before the meeting. The evening before the meeting, and sometimes even in the train on the way, the applications are read through. Hence, it is of the utmost importance that the reader knows in five minutes what the project is about and how much money is being requested. This does not mean that you cannot add information. With the visual arts it is important that you send along pictures of the work of the artists, even if they are well-known names! When you refer to a certain director or to actors, make sure that extensive curriculums are included. Do not assume that people who are known to you, are also known to the committee. It is quite possible that a leading actor in a soap opera, who has been on television every day for five years, is unknown to a member of the committee. The same is true for a well-known artist who regularly exhibits his work.

Do not drop the names of well-known people who might possibly participate in the event, especially if those people themselves do not know that they have been named. Often the *scene* is quite small and if it turns out upon inquiry that you have been bluffing, it will greatly diminish your chances of receiving a subsidy.

– *What Does the Accompanying Budget Look Like?*

Because a subsidy usually has to be applied for long before the start of the production of the event or cultural project, the estimate/budget also needs to be framed long before. This often creates the usual problems, because at that moment many things are not yet known. Make sure, therefore, that the budget handed in is not too tight. What is even better is to base your budget, as mentioned before, on three separate scenarios.

In Chapter 8 a description was given of how you can construct a budget for a cultural production or an event. Opposite the budget of the expenses is the financing scheme. Often, this boils down to a list with names of institutions that you hope to receive money from. Do not forget to include a contribution of your own, even if it is only provisional. In this case you should enter into the budget, for instance: 'hall and organisation expenses: as a reminder (charge to the account of the applicant).' This way you show that your organisation supplies time and space.

The *desirable budget* is the financial translation of the optimistic scenario; which is part of the application for the subsidy. The realistic scenario results in a *working budget*, which can be used to barter with when the subsidiser turns out to be willing to grant some money, but not as much as desired. The *minimal budget* belongs to the pessimistic scenario. On the basis of this last budget the minimum amount can be determined with which the production can still be realised. For strategic reasons it is advisable to keep this last budget as *confidential* as possible.

– *Be Prepared to Terminate a Project When It Is Not Feasible!*

A minimal budget can be very useful, if only very little money is made available. Sometimes employees or participants are unable or unwilling to accept that proceeding with the project will lead to great financial difficulties. Then people will have to be convinced of the fact that it is too risky to go through with the project.

Realise that the person who is commercially responsible, for instance the project leader, will continue to be occupied with satisfying the creditors, the tax department and the industrial insurance board and with clearing up the mess for a long time to come in case of a financial disaster. At that time, the creatives are often involved in new projects again and will feel little need to support the person commercially responsible with the financial completion of earlier projects.

– What Is and What Is Not Accepted?

Assess the expenses as accurately as possible. Mention them all. Do not assume that the chance of receiving a subsidy is smaller, if the budget is kept tight or if wages are cut back. Consult the existing collective labour agreements for the determining the the extent of salaries and remunerations.

Remember that the directors and the business leaders work on the production for a longer period than the time the rehearsals and performances take. Even if it is certain that personnel expenses are not subsidised, do mention them in the budget and as objectively as possible.

– Provisional Budget Entries Enlarge the Risk

Be careful with 'open,' provisional entries on your budget. Provisional entries mean something like: 'I have thought of this expense, but do not (yet) know how much I will have to enter for it in the budget.' This type of 'open' entry forms an uncertainty for decision-making institutions (such as the client, the subsidiser and the sponsor). In general, they will be very reluctant to accept a budget with provisional entries. They will be inclined to scrap these entries, or to quantify them anyway. For, when these expenses turn out to be rather high, the whole project might run the risk of failure and the subsidy will not have received a good destination.

– Do Not Add Up To Your Own Advantage

Be careful with booking income from the number of visitors (visitors times entrance fee), as a rule you do not expect to sell more than 80% of all tickets in your budget, if you want to be on the safe side even bring that down to 60-50%. The sales of T-shirts, programmes, DVDs or CDs, in practice, can turn out to be disappointing, so do not fully add that income to your budget.

9.3.3 How Will the Application Be Processed? *Step 5*

When the application has been submitted, it will be dealt with, in the following way.

Who Will Deal With the Application?
When the applications have been received by the institutions, they are first processed administratively and submitted to an advisor or an advisory committee for a recommendation. This can take up to a month, sometimes. The people that serve on these committees are knowledgeable about the industry to which the projects belong and for which subsidies are requested. The appointment of the members of the committee is carried out by the management of the fund, the delegate or councillor for culture, tourism or sports affairs or by a cultural board. This is usually done on the advice of experts in the relevant field.
While the members of the committee are appointed as representatives of organisations or institutions, they almost always function in a private capacity. They are usually appointed for a certain period.

How Is the Amount Determined?
The committees provide priorities based on an evaluation they have made concerning the contents and the business aspects of the subsidy applications. They are expected, after all, to give advice within the margins of the available budgets of the institution concerned. And, almost always, (much) more money is asked for than is available.
After it has been determined which applications will receive priority so that a subsidy can most likely be given, it often turns out that the budget is still inadequate.

How Long Does the Whole Procedure Take?
On average, advisory committees require two months to come to a recommendation. Subsequently, the civil servants take another month to arrive at a sound recommendation for the county or the council. The subsidisers seek interim contact with the applicant, on a regular basis. It is a common misunderstanding that the size of the subsidy requested, weighs heavily with the subsidisers in determining whether or not a project qualifies for a subsidy. The size of the request, nonetheless, has to be roughly in line with the average of the amounts to be paid out, as mentioned before.
The decision-making and the subsequent official communication to the applicants, whether they wish to receive any money, and if so how much, will take yet another month. This means that the 'lucky' ones will be informed about five or six months after having submitted the application for a subsidy. The

procedures in counties or smaller councils usually take a shorter period. Nevertheless, one should count on a minimum of three months. Of course it is possible to obtain a hint of what the outcome will be by cultivating informal contacts. Therefore, it is always useful to know who is involved in the committees.

How Is the Subsidy Disbursed?

After the subsidy has been granted and the subsidised party has fulfilled a number of requirements, such as the submission of a bank-account number, the registration in the foundation register, the provision of what is known as cash advances will often follow. This usually means that 80% of the promised subsidy will be paid. The remaining 20% is paid after the activities have been concluded and after the financial accounts have been submitted and approved. Because most groups would otherwise experience financial (liquidity) problems if they would have to wait for the remaining 20%, it is usually possible to receive a large share of that 20% earlier, during the production process. But then it must be proven that problems have arisen that have resulted due to insufficient cash advances.

The Procedure for Private Funds

The procedure for private funding is generally shorter, because the number of people involved is usually fewer. The board often takes its own decisions based on its own judgment. When larger funding is involved, there are advisory committees that make recommendations to the board and then it is possible that the process will become just as complicated as is the case in government. There are no general guidelines, however. Hence, it is wise to make contact with the funding source you hope to receive money from and to gather information about the procedures it takes for the process and the time that it will take for the application to be reviewed.

Step 6

9.3.4   Giving Account Afterwards

And, then, when you have realised your production, you still have to account for the subsidy. In general, the provider of the subsidy will take a rough look at the credibility of the settlement of the accounts.

However, always save all of the receipts. Even if you do not have to have a receipt for everything (sometimes an estimate will suffice), you frequently are requested to send along receipts for at least the amount that was subsidised.

In general it is forbidden to transfer the expenses from one main section of the budget to another. For instance, if money for labour expenses is left over, then you cannot use that money for more expensive stage scenery. Often, something can be arranged, after consulting the subsidiser. If it turns out that substantial amounts of money have been moved around at the settlement of accounts at the end of the production period, then this could lead to great difficulties.

9.4 Project Sponsoring

Subsidies from government institutions for arts and culture have been declining over the past few years. Therefore, organisers of events are forced to appeal to the business community. Businesses or Brands, on the other hand, have increasingly been viewing events as means of communication. Companies, out of a feeling of social responsibility, want to make a contribution to non-commercial initiatives. That is why this type of financing of events is discussed extensively in this section.

There is a difference between fundraising and sponsoring. Sponsoring is part of fundraising. Besides sponsoring, fundraising consists of activities mentioned earlier, such as setting-up and maintaining donor records, organising the members' activities and acquiring subsidies. Sponsoring is the most commercial and the most difficult part of fundraising. That is to say, commercial, if you have the idea that sponsoring is a commercial association between a company and a non-commercial institution or project. And difficult, because the institution is looking for a sponsor and the company is aiming to receive a certain return when they close a deal. Determining this return often forms the bottleneck in sponsoring deals. With sponsoring, a distinction can be made on the basis of the social industries, sports, art/culture and academics. Furthermore, some distinctions can be made with reference to the nature and the length of the sponsor relationship. Thus, you have event sponsoring versus the sponsoring of institutions, individual sponsoring versus collective sponsoring, incidental sponsoring versus structural sponsoring and short-term sponsoring versus long-term sponsoring.

Sponsoring and the Business Cycle
Sponsoring is very sensitive to the business cycle. During an economic downturn the sponsor market performs poorly and has a low priority for companies. It is an expense that companies can easily scrap when they need to economise. When there is an economic upturn, however, the sponsor transactions do not go up proportionally. For, it takes a while before companies get over the shock and start thinking about extras such as sponsoring.

9.4.1 Sponsoring as a Means of Communication

Sponsoring is not charity, but it is a means of communication, in which the entrepreneur makes an investment to achieve something that he cannot achieve in another way, or only through difficulty or at a higher cost. Sponsoring emerged when the effect of advertising started to wear off and entrepreneurs started to look for free publicity. Free publicity is more effective than advertisement. For an entrepreneur free publicity can be achieved among other ways, by means of sponsoring, in which the issue is, for instance, the conveyance of an image. Within the business community there are often simple motives to engage in sponsoring; for instance, a manager has an affinity with a certain art form or is a fan of a soccer club and decides to become a sponsor for that reason alone. This appears not to be a good basis for sponsoring in the long term. It is better when a company uses sponsoring consciously as a means to reach a target. The company then asks itself the question who, or what, one wants to reach by sponsoring. The return of sponsoring (what one wants to achieve) can be defined as follows: 'the level of reflection of the image of the sponsored project on the image of the sponsor.' Sponsor partners should realise that the return is more difficult to quantify. Nevertheless, one can ask oneself the question: what can we get out of it?

In the last few decades there has been an excess of sponsorship seekers, such as cultural institutions, cultural projects and sports associations. Because of this oversupply, it is of utmost importance that a certain chemistry exists between the sponsor partners. An event organisation has to be able to excite a potential sponsor; for this to happen the contact between the people who close a sponsorship agreement is important. The oversupply of sponsorship seekers, combined with a slow economy, leads to even fiercer competition on the sponsorship market. Do not be too optimistic about the results of sponsoring! The correct tactics are of utmost importance. As a sponsorship-seeking event you should be very familiar with your own situation and the situation of the business community. When making contact with potential sponsors it is not always wise to start high up in the organisation. The manager might think it is a nice idea, but he leaves the execution to the lower echelons, who subsequently drop the plan. It is important that the sponsor realises that he can achieve his own desires. A good sponsorship plan, therefore, is built by both the event organisation and the sponsor. Sponsoring is a special skill which involves the attraction and strategy of approaching sponsors. This does not mean, however, that the employees within an event organisation, who are not involved with sponsoring, should not have to be aware of sponsoring. On the contrary, every employee or member of the project team should display a sense of involvement with the sponsor. The sponsor must feel welcome when he attends the event; he needs to have the feeling that he is part of the project.

Double Expenses

The management of an institution or the project leader who negotiates with a sponsor, should realise that a hundred thousand euros in sponsoring money means two hundred thousand euros in sponsoring expenses for the sponsor. The company does not only include the sponsored amount in the expense, but also the internal organisation expenses (personnel, facilities) connected with the sponsoring. When the sponsorship-seeking institution is able to alleviate the internal expenses felt by the sponsor, by making an effort to support them in the area of administration, then this can create a great deal of sympathy on the side of the sponsor. This, can lead to establishing continuity in the relationship between the event or the project and the sponsor.

9.4.2   The Sponsorship Contract

Writing down the agreements made in a sponsorship contract is of essential importance. In many cases only the amount and the objective are written down, and sometimes nothing at all has been recorded. In this case the agreements hold as a *gentlemen's agreement*. Some sponsors only want to work in this way. However, when no sponsorship contract is made, there is a chance that the sponsor partners will embark on negotiations dragging on about the details. This can lead to a tense atmosphere, whereas a good atmosphere among the sponsor partners is of essential importance. As mentioned before, it has to do with the relationship between people. It is impossible to provide *the* standard contract for sponsoring. It *is* possible, however, to give a checklist for the framing of a sponsorship contract (See Appendix A9). In the list of topics to be dealt with, attention should be paid to at least the following aspects in the sponsor relationship: the quality of the *parties* (international bank, organiser of cultural projects), the *object* of the sponsoring (art fair, street theatre festival) and the mutual *rights and obligations* (the provision of money versus, for instance, the provision of advertising space or product placement). It might be that the sponsor wants more than is stated in the contract. If this is the case, then you could choose to meet the demands of the sponsor, in view of preserving the good relationship. Then, the sponsored party can charge 'out-of-pocket expenses' for the expressed wishes that went beyond the contract; sponsoring is a business transaction, after all.

Some Practical Tips for Sponsoring

We provide some general tips for matters that demand attention when dealing with sponsoring.

1 Always make a cost/benefit overview. Sponsoring also involves expenses for the sponsored party, for instance an exclusive reception or performance solely for the relations of the sponsor, but also the design and printing of the sponsorship brochure. Moreover, attracting sponsors takes a lot of time. Take into consideration that the sponsorship revenue does not always offset the effort.

2 Ask potential sponsors for information about their company, for instance via an annual report, without immediately making clear that the company appears to be a suitable sponsor. When a very large company is involved, you can request a copy of the sponsorship policy.

3 Approach companies personally, and warm up to people. Make as little use of mailings as possible. If it cannot be avoided, then remember that a extensive mailing might have a higher chance of scoring, but that the follow-up (seeking phone contact after the company has received the mailing) is more expensive and time-consuming than for a small mailing.

4 Make sure that the sponsor has input in the completion of the sponsoring plan.

5 Keep the risk of sponsoring in mind when determining the part of the budget covered by sponsoring. It is advisable not to let the sponsoring exceed 10 to 25 per cent of the minimum budget necessary to proceed with the project. It is very risky to have the project depend too much on sponsorship. It is safer to realise the basic budget, if at all possible, without sponsorship money. Let sponsors finance special wishes and extras.

6 The contact person for the sponsor should be a good listener, a good talker and has to be an open person. It is important that he asks the right questions and finds out during the conversation if there are possibilities.

7 For the formulation of a sponsor plan, preferably, use a mix of the following elements: a few times a lot (only a small number of big amounts); many times a little (relationship marketing); supplementary drives (friends of ... society); fundraising. Give all these elements a place in your sponsor plan to spread the risks.

8 Be careful with the use of the term 'main sponsor.' For it is questionable whether it will still be an attractive option for a company to become a sponsor, if it is not mentioned as being one of the 'main sponsors.'

9 Always remember that sponsoring is done by people who make mistakes.

When a potential sponsor is approached by telephone, it is important to use someone with powerful telephone skills and a good voice.

A possible line of approach follows below.

– *Day 1*

  Ask the receptionist of the company which might qualify as a potential sponsor for the head of the Marketing Department. Do not say anything more, otherwise there might be a greater chance that the receptionist will put you through with the words: 'Here's another one nagging for money.'

– *Day 2*

  Call the head of the Marketing Department, for instance with the following words: 'I won't hide the fact that I am looking for a sponsor. Can I ask you what kind of project would be your ideal candidate for sponsorship?' The person on the other side will be surprised and, consequently, will not easily forget that telephone conversation. After he has painted you a picture of his ideal project, tell the head of the Marketing Department that you will send him a worked-out plan for his ideal project in a week.

– *Day 8*

  Send in the 'ideal project plan.'

– *Day 12*

  Look for a reason to call, for instance to ask how the project plan has been received. Try to evoke an atmosphere of 'our project.' If all goes well, the head of the Marketing Department will start peddling the project internally.

10

Project Planning

In this chapter we focus on the Time aspect (the T in QOFTIM). To realise a project, all kinds of tasks need to be executed. If the project is relatively small and can be carried out by, for instance, a small number of people and when the tasks to be performed can be tracked easily, then you hardly need to plan the time you will need. If the project is more complex, if you do not have a lot of routine with such a project, if there are many people/disciplines involved, if time is very scarce, then you run a greater risk and it is advisable to pay more attention to how time is managed.

According to Section 4.5 a time schedule ensures that:

- The progress of the project activities can be controlled, because you can track their progress and compare it to a planned schedule
- The project result can be delivered on time or can start functioning, because there have been actual intermediate adjustments
- The necessary provisions (people, money, resources, space) are available the moment that they are needed.

A time schedule makes a prognosis about the time scale needed for accomplishing the tasks. There are different planning techniques that can help you to control the time spent within a project. A 'to-do list' is a simple type of time planning. More professional planning techniques are:

- A *bar chart* (also known as a GANTT-chart) is relatively simple and very usable

-   *A script,* which can be applied when everything becomes very concrete
-   A *network plan,* which should only be used for complicated projects (it is often only used by specialists in the field of planning)

Below these three planning techniques are elaborated upon.

10.1   The Bar Chart

A bar chart is relatively simple to make and it is very usable for controlling time within projects in the cultural and leisure industry.

With this planning technique the *time frame* with reference to the activities is displayed on the horizontal bars and important moments or deadlines are marked with *milestones.* This way the activities and occasions and their sequence and connection are visualised in time slots.

With the *time frame* of an activity the total time taken to complete an activity is meant (hence, the duration from the beginning to the end). This duration is usually estimated. The time frame says nothing about the *capacity* that is deployed for a task. When more capacity (for instance more manpower or resources) is deployed to carry out an activity, the total time taken can be reduced and, therefore, the time frame is shortened.

During the implementation of the project the progress of the activities will have to be compared regularly with the prepared planning. This is called *progress control.* Moreover, during the project a vertical *position line* is periodically fitted into the planning. This shows which part of the different activities have been finished at the moment of the snap shot and which part still needs to be carried out. In Figure 10.1 a vertical position line has been drawn, which belongs to the snapshot taken halfway into the second month. This shows a backlog for activity 2.

Time Sheet

Name of the Project	: Exhibition 'Energy in 2010'	**Project No.**	: 514
Name Client	: LEB London	**Date**	: 07–06–02
Completion/Opening/Premiere	: May 2003	**For Phase**	: Preparation Phase

Activities	By	Month 1	Month 2	Month 3	Month 4	Month 5	Month 6
Preparation Phase							
– Activity 1	James						
– Activity 2	Theo						
– Activity 3	R&D						
– Activity 4	Rachel						
Decision-Making 'Project Plan'	Board						
Development Phase							
Production Phase							
Opening							
Performance Phase							
Completion Phase							

Figure 10.1   Example of a Bar Chart in the First Phase of an Exhibition Project

The Five Areas of a Bar Chart

1 In the column to the left there is a short description of the *activities*, sub-divided into phases/components. Such an overview of activities is formulated by means of a break-down analysis. See Section 10.5 Steps 1 to 4 for this overview.
2 In the next column it is stated *by whom* the activity is carried out.
3 In the top horizontal area the general *project data* are provided.
4 In the horizontal area under that the *time bar* is included. The calendar scale is dependent on the 'planning horizon' of the project (for instance a day, week, or month planning).
5 The main area is meant to plot the *time frame* for the different activities and the *milestones*. In the main area the time frame is represented by small bars and the milestones by small circles, triangles or diamonds, including the relations between the different activities.

The Mutual Relationships Between Tasks and the Critical Path

A possible relationship between activities and milestones is represented by means of a vertical dotted line between the bars and the milestones.

When a certain activity is on what is called the *critical path*, this means that this activity cannot overrun its time without having adverse affects, or without it having consequences for the eventual deadline of the project (for instance, the date for the opening of the exhibition). For Activity 4 in Figure 10.1 an *extension* or *leeway* has been drawn. Activity 4 can possibly take longer and, therefore, it is not on the critical path; the other activities are (See the relationship lines).

How Detailed Do You Have to Plan?

When framing a planning, the maker first has to ask himself what the purpose of the planning is. If you want to have a general survey of the whole duration of the project to control the overall development, you should consider having an *overall planning*. An *overall planning* is quite general and provides an oversight of all phases and only the most important activities within them. Time management at a concrete level, hence at the level of activities, demands a detailed insight into the project or a part thereof (for instance a phase or a sub-project); in that case a *detailed planning* is necessary. A mix of these is also possible.

The Time Schedule As Part of the Initiative Report

In Section 10.5 a *step-by-step plan* is described for the framing of a bar chart. For this we must proceed from a planning that has been produced during the early stages of a relatively complicated project. Such a planning is part of, for instance, an initiative report, that is sent to the client or the financier. In such an initiative report or project proposal all the terms and conditions have been included, hence also the conditions with respect to the time aspect. For the first planning of a project a mix is usually chosen of general and detailed information. The part of the time schedule which refers to the first phase is detailed, while the following phases are more general. This way the oversight remains intact, whereas the more detailed section is a good foundation for the management of time in the first phase. The planning in Figure 10.1 shows an example.

10.2   The Script

A script is also a planning tool and is usually employed when the activities have become concrete and when the implementation of the tasks in practice requires a great deal of precision. Often a script is produced at the end of the development phase to be able to manage the time accurately during the production phase of a project, but also during the performance phase. What is important here are, for instance, the time management during the weeks or days leading up to a television recording or the opening of a festival, but also during the recording or the festival itself.

A time schedule in the shape of a script is often part of the production schedule in which all the production information of a project is recorded (See Figure 10.2). The production schedule is described in Section 5.3.

SCRIPT

Name of the Project	:	60 Years Liberation	**Project No.**	:	02
Name of the Client	:	VBN	**Date**	:	March 1, 2009
Completion/Opening/Premiere	:	May 5, 2009	**For Phase**	:	Production Phase

No.	Day/DD	Time	By	Activity	Component	Place	Material/Remarks
01	Mon 03-05	10.00	VHR	Picking up costumes	Performance	Square	At drama club
02		11.15	SDS	Picking up keys	General		At administration
03		13.30	ALL	Cleaning	Reception	Hall	Material from supervisor
04	Tue 04-05	09.00	SRT	Put out drinks	Reception	Kitchen	Crates in the shed
05							
06							

Figure 10.2   Example of a Script for a Public-Event Project

10.3   Network Planning

A network planning proceeds from a different drawing technique and is often used to make complex processes or projects transparent. The advantage of this planning technique is that the mutual relationships between the different activities become very clear. However, this is at the cost of the general overview of activities and is called the *breakdown*.

The framing of a network planning, in my view, does not belong to the basic skills of a project leader in the cultural or leisure industries. It is useful, however, to know that there is such a thing as network planning and to know what the basic principle of this planning technique is.

There are different methods of network planning, but the method presented here starts out from the notion that activities are represented by a small *block* and the mutual dependencies between activities as *arrows*. The block contains basic information about the activity or task. Tasks that are dependent for their completion on other tasks or that simply succeed each other in the planning, are connected by dotted lines (Figure 10.3)

Description of the Task	
Task No.	Task Duration
Starting Date	End Date

Figure 10.3 The Basic Information of a Task in a Network Planning

Nowadays computers are usually used for making a network planning (See also Section 10.4). Not so long ago, however, a roll of transparent paper, pencil and rubber were used for the manual analysis of the production process according to this method. Contemplating the production process, the planner would draw the blocks and arrows from left to right on the paper. Figure 10.4 shows a segment of a network planning.

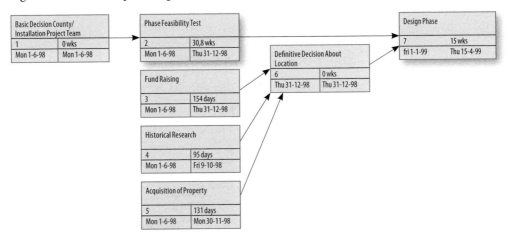

Figure 10.4 A segment of a network planning

10.4   Planning with the Computer

The manual construction of a planning is a time-consuming job. Each time you change something during the framing of the planning or during its implementation, it will have repercussions on the rest of the planning and it will cause changes. Currently there are very useful software programs on the market, ranging from the simple to the ultra sophisticated, that make the framing and the adjustment of the planning much easier.

Nowadays, many software programs containing digital project planning are available.

MS-Project is a relatively advanced package but, nonetheless, reasonably user-friendly.

The big advantage of framing a planning on the computer is that each change is immediately computed and with that the planning adjusts itself automatically. Another advantage is that a planning that was set up in the shape of a bar chart, can be changed into a network planning with the press of a button, see Figure 10.4 (as a result of which the mutual relationships between the different tasks become manifest) or they can be changed into a calendar planning. It also becomes immediately clear which tasks are on the critical path. Moreover, it is possible to show only the main tasks in the list of activities (breakdown), or to change the basic unit of the time scale. Moreover, it is possible to connect capacities (man-hours, budget, resources) with the time schedule, which makes it possible to control them simultaneously. The application of this last possibility, however, demands great skill in working with these types of software packages. Figure 10.5 shows an example of such a computer planning.

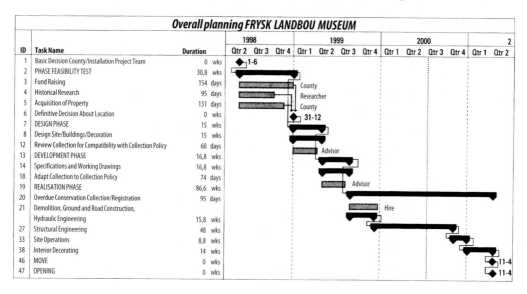

Figure 10.5   Example of a Computer Planning (Bar Chart)

For years there have also been computer programs for the construction of a breakdown for drama productions, such as *Ficfile* or *Movie Magic Scheduling*.

Before a project planning can be constructed, the work process of the project needs to be analysed and, then, structured.

10.5 The Structuring of the Project by Means of a Breakdown

The determination of the approach, the construction of the planning and estimation of the expenses, and the setting up of the project organisation, starts by making an analysis of the overall work process. In other words, what kinds of things have to happen, consecutively, to reach the project result? This is done with the construction of a hierarchical overview of the activities. Such an overview is sometimes called the *Work Breakdown Structure* (wbs), or simply the *breakdown* in short. Whenever possible, the availability of facilities (people, resources, space) should already be taken into account at this point. For the construction of a provisional breakdown you proceed as follows.

Preparatory Step Through the Mind-Map Method

When the basic concept has been developed, it will become clear how the project result will roughly look like. As a first step, to give structure to the project, an analysis needs to be made of the development and production process that will lead to the project result.

For slightly more complex projects it is often difficult to put a logical catalogue of activities (Work Breakdown) on paper. In that case, it is recommended first to perform a creative analysis by using the Mind-Map method, as a preparatory step. Mind-mapping is a creative technique to introduce a first measure of organisation, in a jumble of disorganised information.

For this preparatory step proceed as follows:

Take a big piece of paper and draw a box in the middle, which, in a few keywords, contains the project idea/basic concept, that has become clear in the meantime. Under that write the following question: *What kinds of things will it take to realise this basic concept?* Subsequently, associate freely, on your own, or better, with the whole project team, about the question that you have put in the middle of the sheet of paper. Give all associations a place on the sheet of paper. The Mind-Map grows organically, because more and more associations, key words, questions, etc., are added to it. For this use images, symbols, colours, as much as possible, and, if need be, draw relationship lines between the associations discovered and/or with the box in the middle. Do all of this in a loose style. When the Mind-Map is finished (when the associations stop coming), the chaos in your head is reflected on the paper.

Now, a provisional breakdown can be constructed through the following three steps, on the foundation of this Mind-Map.

Step 1 **Determine the Starting and the End Date of the Project Process**

First the starting and end date of the project has to be determined. Here the period planning should be taken into consideration, hence the period that will be controlled on the basis of this planning. Usually this period begins with the first activity and ends, for instance, when the project result has been completed (for instance at the premiere of a dance production), or when the event has taken place. In many cases the project is considered finished, when everything is over and done with (for instance when the festival has taken place, everything has been cleaned up, settled and evaluated). It depends, therefore, what is considered as the completion of the project.

Also, a planning can only relate to a part of the process, for instance to a finished phase. Below we will assume that the planning refers to the process as a whole.

Step 2 **Make a Distinction Into Phases**

Keeping the project objective and the general course of the project in mind, you see which phases can be distinguished within the project process. Phases are more or less natural stages within the development process of a project, which usually starts with a vague idea and end with a concrete product. Within each phase, a new aspect is central every time. By dividing a project up into phases, you can get a better grip on the course of the process. Sometimes it is sufficient to make the distinction between a *preparation phase* and an *application phase*. In most cases, however, it is sensible to distinguish more phases within the preparation, such as the one provided in Section 4.2 for instance. The naming of the phases and the level of detail in the distinction between them, can of course be adapted to the nature of the project.

Dividing a project up into phases, makes it possible to report to the client by means of a decision document at the end of a phase. Based on this, adjustments can be made during the process, because at the end of each phase the result of that phase can be compared with the terms and conditions that have been determined at the beginning of the project (for instance by the client). This concerns, in the first place, the basic concept as a term of reference with respect to the content, but also, among under things, the budget, the deadline and the organisational preconditions.

Step 3 **The Distinction Between Sub-Projects and Project Components**

After the project process has been divided into phases, subsequently you look for the most important components of the project or search for logical groupings of tasks. Sometimes these components lead to a separate partial result. Within the project *The Opening of the Academic Year,* for instance, a distinction can be made between the official opening with lectures in the afternoon and a party for employees and students in the evening. These components can be seen as two sub-projects, which, can be coordinated separately.

Sometimes even the phases of the different sub-projects are not completely parallel. In that case you can choose to make a separate planning for each of the sub-projects. It is recommended thenthat you produce an overall planning as well.

Within (sub)projects other components can be distinguished. The sub-project *party*, for instance, falls apart into the components hall, performances, catering, invitations, etc.

Construct an Overview of Activities (Breakdown)   *Step 4*

As a next step every part (for each phase and/or sub-project) is further specified into separate activities or tasks. The catering component of the party, can be divided into a number of tasks, such as the search for catering companies, the request for information, the carrying out of negotiations and the handing out of the commission.

The preliminary breakdown provides a hierarchical overview of the tasks that need to be carried out consecutively. Some tasks have to be performed one after the other, while other tasks can be carried out simultaneously. Thus, the granting of the assignment to the catering company can only take place, when the negotiations with that company have been completed. But the making of a plan for the decoration of the party hall can take place at the same time as the making of the guests list.

It will not be possible to get this overview of activities on paper in one go, and that is why it is called a *preliminary* breakdown.

Remark

In Steps 1, 2, 3 and 4 the project process has been unravelled in an extensive overview of the activities, or preliminary breakdown. The breakdown forms the foundation for the Plan of Approach, the Project Planning, Organisational Set-Up and the Estimate of the Project Expenses. Below we will continue, making use of the breakdown to construct the project planning.

10.6   A Step-By-Step Plan for a Bar Chart (GANTT Chart)

In the preceding section the project process has been structured in a few steps with the help of the breakdown. As mentioned before, we can build on this for the framing of the project planning. Therefore, we will continue below with the same step-by-step plan.

Step 5   **Put an Overview of the Activities in the Planning**

The preliminary breakdown, as a result of the preceding steps, forms the foundation for the what will appear in the left column of the bar chart. The point here is a general breakdown with the most important clusters of tasks. The overview of tasks, with the division into phases, in the second column of Figure 10.5 is an example of a general breakdown.

The time schedule which has been constructed at the beginning of the project, is, as mentioned before, a mix of the 'general' and the 'detailed' (See example in Figure 10.1). In that planning only the next phase was developed to the level of concrete activities or tasks. For the following phases, usually only the duration of the phases and the milestones are included (possibly supplemented with the most important components).

In this way overview is maintained, while the planning for the next phase is detailed enough to control effectively the progress during this phase.

Step 6   **Determine Who Will Carry Out the Tasks**

After the data from the preliminary breakdown have been entered in the first column of the planning, the names are mentioned of those who will carry out the task and/or who will carry primary responsibility for the different components for each activity. These data are entered in the planning in the column 'By.'

Step 7   **Determine the Calendar Scale**

For each planning a calendar scale has to be chosen for the time axis. The calendar scale is dependent on the units of time in which the time frames of the tasks will be discussed (See the next step). Sometimes existing planning forms can be used. There are planning forms with different calendar scales. The calendar scale can be expressed in years, trimesters, months, weeks, days, hours, or even minutes.

The overall planning of a space travel project, for instance, is set up in years, while a detailed planning of a television recording of a live show is represented in seconds. When everything becomes very concrete and needs a great deal of precision such as in the latter example, people no longer work with bar charts, but with a script. See Section 10.2.

Step 8   **Make an Estimate of the Time Frame of Each Activity**

The completion of a task takes time. This is called the *task duration* or *time frame*. The time frame for each task is made visible with a bar in the main area of the planning. When you want to supply tasks with a time frame, you can start with the first task, but you can also start with the final deadline. In this case you will have to plan *backwards*. Depending on the project and the phase the planning refers to, the time frame will have to be stated in months, weeks, days, hours or minutes.

When you need to make an estimate concerning the duration of a task, you can make use of:

– Knowledge from personal experience
– Intuition.

The most realistic estimate is provided when the one who has to carry out the task is asked how much time he thinks he will need for the execution of the task in question. This makes him jointly responsible for the planning constructed and for the realisation of the activities within that planning.

To build up a body of knowledge from personal experience for the planning of future projects, it is very useful to record the real duration of activities during the implementation of the project (for instance in an Excel sheet) in the planning itself. When doing that you should ask yourself the following question: Could I have foreseen that, or in other words did you overlook something? In this way you can gain a more realistic sense of the time that different activities require.

Mark Milestones and Deadlines

Step 9

A milestone is an occurrence which indicates that a group of related tasks (for instance a component or a phase) has to be completed. Hence, it marks a deadline. Milestones are moments and do not last any length of time. In the main area of the time schedule milestones are marked by a triangle, circle or diamond.

Introduce Relationships and Determine the Critical Path

Step 10

Determine which relationships exist between the tasks and milestones. Mark these relationships by means of a vertical dotted line between tasks and milestones that are dependent on each other (See Figure 10.1). It might be the case that a task can begin when another task has been completed, for instance, by 25 or 50 %.

Subsequently, determine the critical tasks. These are the tasks that cannot overrun their time without this having immediate consequences for the eventual deadline of the project. In the construction of the planning, but most certainly also during the implementation of the planning, critical tasks deserve special care. Seen as a whole, the critical tasks are what is referred to as the critical path.

Step 11 **Close the Planning**

Whether, with the set up of the time frames, you start with the first task and work forwards, or whether you start with the last milestone and work backwards, in both cases the planning will have to be closed. This means that all the tasks have to be realised eventually within the total available time. If you did not succeed in doing this the first time, then you will have to solve this *planning problem*. Sometimes you can have more overlap between tasks than you had the first time. Also, you can check if it is possible to shorten the time frames, for instance by deploying more capacity (man-power or resources). In extreme cases, you sometimes have to drop components, or you have to see whether the ultimate deadline can be moved to a later date.

It is advisable to make changes in the initial points of departure of the planning in close consultation with those who will have to make things happen during the implementation.

Step 12 **Make the Planning Definitive**

In the preceding steps a *draft planning* has materialised on the basis of a preliminary breakdown. After this planning has been 'closed' in the previous step, it is important for easy reference, that a definitive breakdown be drawn up.

The time frames in the main area of the planning will have to show a logical (step-by-step) section from the top-left to the bottom-right corner.

When the definitive planning is finished, it will be presented to the internal or external client of the project for approval.

If working through projects is taken seriously, then the planning will often be part of a decision document (for instance the initiative report, project plan or production schedule) which is produced at the end of a phase, for phased decision-making. From a project proposal, often in the shape of an *initiative report*, a planning, such as the one represented in Figure 10.1 has to be an integrated part of that report.

Step 13 **Engage in Progress Control During the Implementation**

When the project has really gotten on its way, progress control will have to take place during the execution of the activities that have been previously entered into the planning. This is an often neglected part of the planning process. Only by regularly conducting progress control during the implementation, can you manage the real course of the planned activities.

It is wise to turn progress control into a fixed item on the agenda in meetings of the project team or in production meetings. During each meeting the up-to-date status of the activities is then indicated by a vertical *position line* in the planning. The planning that has been represented in Figure 10.1, has already been used for progress control. This is clear from the vertical position line drawn halfway into the second month. The conclusion that you can draw from this, is that the real progress of Activity 2 is behind schedule. Because this is an activity on the critical path, an adjustment is required. If no action is taken, there is a great chance that the ultimate deadline of the project will be overrun.

11

Project Marketing and Communication

As mentioned before, a project's justification can be found in its environment. In this chapter the fine-tuning of the project within its environment will be discussed. The point of focus here is that the introduction of (commercial) projects into the market and the communication with the projects' target group(s). Moreover, it also concerns the communication with other important target groups such as sponsors, subsidisers, the media, permit granters, local residents, etc.

For an event project the communication can be an aim in itself, when, for example the event is a means of communication (See also Chapter 3). However, what should be stressed is the marketing of, and the communication regarding the event itself. In Section 4.4 the steps of the marketing and communication track of a public event have been introduced. It is recommended that you read this section first, before you start reading this chapter.

11.1   The Marketing and Communication Track Summarised

Because public events usually depend on the number of paying visitors in order to have a break-even situation (if events do not have a commissioning client that makes a budget available), priority will be given to the promotion of the event. That is why the most important deadline for a public event will be the point at which it becomes necessary to start promotional activities. For example, these activities could consist of an e-mail, flyer, poster, website, viral marketing, TV commercial, radio spot and a free-publicity offensive. The promotional activity used must contain important information about the event, which might be for example, the date of the event. The deals between the sponsor and media partners should already been sealed, partly because of the need to include logos on printed promotional material. On average, depending on the number of visitors expected, promotional activities start three to six months before the event. This usually starts by releasing small bits of information (a whisper campaign) with information becoming increasingly more detailed as time goes on.

The steps discussed in Section 4.4 are usually integrated into the project phases in the integral project-management concept. Thus, in the initiative phase attention is given to the first steps of the marketing and communication track, which concern the positioning/profiling of the project (respectively the project mission and project image), a test of the project result by means of the SWOT-analysis, the communication field (target groups and objectives) and the communication strategy (message). These elements are part of the first decision document (initiative report or project proposal). The communication plan, the fundraising plan and possibly the marketing plan are written during the preparation phase, and these plans have been based on the communication strategy. Hence, these plans are part of the integral project plan. The communication *action*-plan (usually written as a script) is normally made in the development phase, and is, therefore, part of the production schedule. A sizeable part of the actual realisation of the communication plan takes place in the production phase. Finally, during, or directly after an event, the evaluative public opinion poll is carried out.

The marketing and communication track sketched above is schematically represented in Figure 11.1:

Step	Activity	Central Question	In Phase
1	Choose positioning		
	a Choose positioning on content (project mission)	What do we want to signify with this project and to whom?	Initiative phase (initiative report)
	b Choose positioning on image (project image)	Which image do we choose for the project?	
	c Choose legitimisation	With which social issue, or with which government policy do we want to connect the project?	
2	Perform SWOT-analysis	Is the project result (product) viable in the market and environment? In other words, map the strategic issues (feasibility question)	Initiative phase (ininitiative report)
3	Formulate communication strategy	Make inventory of the communication target groups with matching target (Communication Field) and formulate message	Initiative phase (initiative report)
	a Communication target group	With which parties do we need to communicate? Distinguish into: – market/project target group – funds/sponsors – other parties	
	b Communication target	Which effects do we want to achieve within those communication target groups?	
	c Communication message	Which message needs to be communicated to each target group, to achieve the matching communication target	
4	Frame marketing plan	How is the product introduced into the market? For this, use among other things the SWOT-analysis and the 5 P-s of the marketing mix	Preparation phase (in project plan)
5	Frame fundraising plan (does not apply to all events)	With which funds, subsidisers, companies can an appeal be made for a financial contribution? On the basis of which arguments? For which return service? (by sponsoring)	Preparation phase (in project plan)
6	Frame a communication plan	Which instruments do we choose from the communication mix? (This can be done in the shape of a Communication matrix, see Figure 11.6)	Preparation phase (in project plan)
7	Formulate a communication action plan	Who will do what concretely, and when, and with what? (The planning of the communication activities can be done in the shape of a communication script, see also Figure 11.7)	Development phase (in production schedule)
8	Implementation of the communication action plan	Implement with the use of the script	Production phase
9	Perform evaluative survey of the public	Have the different targets/effects been realised?	Performance phase (in evaluation report)

Figure 11.1   *The Steps in the Marketing and Communication Track*

11.2   The Development of the Marketing and
        Communication Track

In the following sections the steps that should be followed during the marketing and communication track mentioned above will be discussed extensively.
In Chapters 5 and 6 these steps have been integrated into the general step-by-
step plans which are discussed.

11.2.1   *Choose the Positioning*   *Step 1*

After it has been made sufficiently clear in the basic assignment underlying the
project what the project team has been asked to do, the project result (product) should be positioned as a first step in the marketing and communication
track. For the positioning of a product three fundamental questions are central, namely:

1 *Positioning on content*: How do we want to *position* the project? In other
   words, what will this project signify and to whom? We do this by formulating a project mission, with which the project distinguishes itself from other
   similar projects. For instance: *The event 'Art-4-U' is a meeting place for young
   people, where people are actively involved in art and culture, from within their
   own world of experience.*

2 *Legitimisation*: How does the possible subsidiser, or how do other social
   groups, see the project? The *legitimisation* of the project is of importance
   here. In other words, to what extent does our project connect with the policy
   of the subsidising government agency and/or with social issues? If we would
   like our project to connect with the policy of our subsidiser, which, for instance, is aimed at education or innovation, then we need to take that into
   account in our communication strategy (communication message) as well.

3 *Positioning on image (or profiling)*: What image should we choose for the
   project? In other words, which perception do we want our customer to have
   of the project/product? How do we want to come across? We do this by describing the image of the event, whereby it will further distinguish itself.
   When you are concerned with creating an image, then the atmosphere and
   experience aspects of the event enter into play. Possible images are: *young,
   modern, sporty, fast, dynamic, for the whole family, for everyone, exclusive,
   experimental, educational, quiet, contemporary, cool, innovative* or *cosy.*

11.2.2   *Perform the SWOT-analysis*   *Step 2*

When, through the development of the basic concept, a general image has
emerged of the project result (product), it is important to test this product.

The SWOT-analysis is a tool used to represent in a systematic way the internal strong and weak points of the product, and the opportunities and threats from the environment.

SWOT is an abbreviation for the components Strengths, Weaknesses, Opportunities and Threats.

A SWOT-analysis provides insight into all the factors that are important in a certain situation. This insight can serve as a point of departure for determining which action should be taken.

For conducting a SWOT-analysis you proceed as follows:

Step 2a   *Formulate the subject of the analyses*
Write the project result in the centre of a sheet of paper or on the board in a catchword.

Step 2b   *Brainstorm about the four components*
Strengths: the internal characteristics/behaviours/aspects of achievements that form the strong points of the project result.
Weaknesses: the internal characteristics/behaviours/aspects that form the weak points.
Opportunities: occurrences, developments, tendencies, factors and changes in the environment, that offer positive opportunities for the project result.
Threats: occurrences or changes in the environment that can become obstacles for the successful completion of the project result.

In Figure 11.2 the basic shape of the SWOT-analysis is represented.

	Positive	Negative
Internal:	Strengths – – –	Weaknesses – – –
	Object of Analysis: (here: project result)	
Environment:	Opportunities – – –	Threats – – –

Figure 11.2   *The Basic Shape of the swot-Analysis*

The SWOT-analysis consists, of an internal and an external analysis.

Internal analysis: This analysis is aimed primarily at the strong and weak points of the project result (product) itself. Moreover, in this analysis the internal organisation can also be involved. In other words, it is possible to check whether the (project) organisation is sufficiently equipped to achieve, to maintain and to extend a certain market position with the project result. For this an inventory has to be made of the strong and the weak points with reference to, among other things, the competence of the employees, the marketing policy and the financial position of the (project) organisation.

External analysis: Here one first must look for the opportunities and threats in the medium-range environment, hence, it should investigate which parties in the direct environment of the (project) organisation that it can more or less exert influence on. Here one might think of, among other things, customer/ market, suppliers, similar projects, media, regulatory and subsidising government organisations.

Whether or not a project will succeed depends, heavily on the degree to which a project is accepted by the people that have a direct interest in the project. With commissioned projects these are primarily the client and the future users. With one's own projects, when they are concerned with a product that is going to be introduced onto the market, hence when there is a product that external customers (viewers/visitors/participants/audience) will have to come and visit or attend, it is necessary to know what the visitor or participant wants. The event has to be attuned to the needs and expectations within the target group. One has to put oneself in the position of the consumer, as it were, before a product can be introduced onto the market. Therefore, it is often advisable to perform some general market orientation (demand side) during this stage. Sometimes thorough market research is necessary for this, however, it can often be done in a relatively simple way, for instance by calling a number of potential or permanent clients, telling them which product you want to develop and asking them whether they would be interested in it. Talk with others about your initiative as well, and try to find out whether there is sufficient demand or interest in the project result. For big events it is also important at this stage to map the supply side of the market. You should then pose the following question: What is currently happening in the country or the world in this area and which trends and patterns can be discerned? The opportunities and threats in the macro-environment need to be surveyed as well as in the immediate environment. This environment consists of uncontrollable variables. For this purpose, one can investigate political/legal, economic, socio-cultural, technical and demographic developments.

Step 2c   *Confront the aspects that have been found*

Now, compare the aspects that have been found through the SWOT-analysis with each other. In this way, the most important points of interest (also known as *strategic issues*) are brought into the picture. Then, formulate which actions need to be taken on the basis of these points of interest.

First concentrate on the threats and weaknesses that you have found and think of extra measures you might take to overcome or avoid these. If need be, use 'Why' questions to probe deeper into the causes of certain problems. Negative factors that you can change only slightly, or not at all, deserve your attention, but not your energy.

Then, look at your opportunities and strengths and think of how you can make maximum use of these and how you can extend them in order to reinforce their position or to achieve the project result that you have applied the SWOT-analysis to. The presence of positive factors usually means that there are people or institutions that, in principle, can/want to invest energy in strengthening the product. The question is how can you mobilise that energy.

It is true that in general, energy which is aimed at positive factors usually obtains better results than energy invested in resistance!

Step 3   ### 11.2.3   *Formulate the Communication Strategy*

After it has become clear how the project result should roughly look like (basic concept), and what (project objectives) needs to be achieved and with whom (project target groups), one can then start to ponder about the communication strategy. As a first step, the communication field needs to be mapped.

The central question here is: With whom (communication target groups) do we need to communicate and with what aim (communication objective)? Try as well to involve the results of the SWOT-analysis in this effort. The term communication target groups is meant to refer to the project target groups, but also the other parties, such as potential partners for cooperation, sponsors, subsidisers, licence providers, the media, local residents, etc.

Communication objectives are for instance: Attracting visitors (with project target groups), acquiring subsidies (with subsidy providers), securing sponsored funding (with companies), receiving attention in the media (with the media), etc.

Subsequently, thought needs to be given to what the message should be that is communicated to each communication target group, in order to reach the communication target. For instance, in the case of a potential sponsor: 'This event is a unique opportunity for you to communicate directly with your target group.' Or if a subsidiser is involved: 'This event fits exactly with the objective of your subsidy scheme or your fund.'

The communication strategy falls into three categories of communication target groups, namely:

a   Product target groups (main and sub-target groups of the project)

b   Fund-raising target groups (companies, subsidisers, funds, potential partners for cooperation, etc.)

c   Other parties (the media, licence providers, institutions concerning, for instance, property rights, etc. Thus, ordinary companies who function in the capacity of supplier are not included in the communication strategy. For those a systematic and organised approach is not necessary.)

Communication *Target Group*	Communication *Objective*	Communication *Message*
a Product Target Groups		
–		
–		
b Fundraising Target Groups		
–		
–		
c Other Parties		
–		
–		

Figure 11.3   *Format for a Communication Strategy*

The Communication Strategy is often an integral part (chapter) of the Initiative Report/Project Proposal. It does not necessarily have to be presented in the form of a diagram, such as the one above, but it can also be described in the text.

11.2.4   Framing the Marketing Plan   *Step 4*

Naturally, a marketing plan is only important for projects with end-products (project results) aimed at the market. When it involves a company party, for instance or a product launch this is not the case. (With a product launch the event is used as a *means of communication* to introduce another product, for instance a new car, onto the market.)

The marketing plan is often an integrated part of the project plan, but it can also be presented as an independent plan. In a marketing plan, it is made clear *how* one wants to introduce the product (project result) onto the market. For the framing of the marketing plan the marketing mix (5 Ps) is usually used. These 5 aspects, in combination with each other, should lead to the the project target group's wishes and needs being satisfied. They are about making choices with respect to:

- Product, which (partial) product for each target group (Product/Market Combination, also known as PMC)
- Price, price level, price differentiation
- Place, where is it offered, how is it distributed
- Promotion, how is it brought to the public's attention
- Personnel, posture, image, etc.

In Figure 11.4 a format is provided for a Marketing Matrix.

Product Target Groups	Product	Price	Place	Promotion	Personnel
Main Target Group					
Sub-Target Group					
–					
–					
Secondary Target Group					
–					
–					

Figure 11.4   Format for a Marketing Plan (Using the Marketing Matrix)

Here, also, we should point out that the marketing plan does not necessarily have to be presented in the form of a diagram, but it can also be described in the body of the text.

Step 5

11.2.5   Framing the Fund-raising Plan

In the communication strategy the fund-raising target groups have also been included. As mentioned before, this refers to, among others, subsidisers, funding sources, companies, and potential partners for cooperation.

In the Fund-raising Plan the way in which the fundraising/sponsoring will be approached, needs to be worked out.
In Section 9.3 *The Subsidising of Non-Commercial Events,* the whole subsidy track is described. In Section 9.4 *Project Sponsoring* the approach towards sponsoring is elaborated upon.
In Figure 11.5 a format is provided for the Fundraising Plan.

Fundraising Target Group	Fundraising Target	Fundraising Message (Possible Return Service)	When to Apply	When to Expect a Reaction	Who Applies
a Subsidisers/Funds					
–					
–					
b Sponsors					
–					
–					

Figure 11.5   Format for a Fundraising Plan

11.2.6   Frame a Communication Plan

Step 6

A communication plan can also be an integrated part of the project plan, but it can also be an independent document.

The communication plan is also a further elaboration of the communication strategy from the Project Proposal/Initiative Report.

When the communication plan is an integral part (chapter) of the Project Plan, it usually consists of two parts:

– The Communication Matrix (See clarification below)
– The Communication Planning (the planning of the communication activities, for instance in the form of an independent bar chart)

In a communication matrix for each target group the following aspects are considered:

a *Communication target groups*: The target groups can be copied from the Communication Strategy, which is included in the Project Proposal. The fundraising target groups are included in the Fundraising Plan, see Section 11.2.5

b *Communication objective*: What does a target group need to know and/or how does it have to change/be influenced and/or which effect do you want to achieve with the target groups?

c *Communication message*: The message that needs to be communicated to achieve the communication target for this target group

d *Means of communication*: Which means or communication instruments will be used to reach this target group? The communication mix is used for this. The instruments in the communication mix can be divided into the following categories:

- Advertising (for instance magazine, internet, television, billboards, or an event)
- Public relations (for instance publicity drives, press conferences, press releases, word-of-mouth)
- Promotions (for instance competition, stunts)
- Direct marketing (for instance direct mail, digital newsletter)
- Personal approach (for instance promotion team, presentations, personal sales)

A point of interest here is that one often has to start thinking about activities in the field of publicity and promotion at a very early stage. Thus, for publicity in the form of, for instance, special offers (for readers), or a special editorial attention, they have to be contacted via a weekly and monthly magazine, four to five months before the event itself, since free publicity is hugely important for (public) events. It is important to generate free publicity both before the event, by issuing press releases, and after the event, by inviting the press to attend the event.

Gaining free publicity is an important task which should be delegated to a team member who focuses completely on press contacts, writing press releases, and inviting and assisting journalists. This responsibility includes writing press releases in the tone appropriate for the specific media to which the press release will be sent, including all correct data and preferably possessing news value. A good press release will be one that a journalist will be able to copy effortlessly. It is important that an up-to-date list is available of all of the deadlines applicable for the editorial team and advertising by the different media (daily, weekly and monthly newspapers/magazines, TV and Internet sites). An effective way to involve the media in the event and to gain free publicity is to launch promotions (for example, competitions and interviews and meet & greets with artists).

For writing a press release see Appendix A10.
e *Style and tone*: Which style and tone will be used for the communication?
f *Frequency and timing*: When is a means of communication deployed? This can also be represented in a separate bar chart for the communication activities
g *Sender*: In whose name is the message sent to the target group? (For instance in the name of the client, or the management of the mother organisation, or the project leader, etc.)
h *Feedback opportunities*: In what way can the target group submit feedback? (For instance through e-mail, reply card, telephone, etc.)

i *Return service*: What can we offer in return (for instance, local residents who will be inconvenienced, the press who needs to be 'enticed,' etc.)?

Communication Target Group	Commu-nication Objective	Commu-nication Message	Means of Commu-nication	Style + Tone	Frequency + Timing	Sender	Feedback Oppor-tunities	Possible Return Service
a Production Target Groups								
(Marketing Communication)								
–								
–								
b Other Parties								
–								
–								

Figure 11.6   Format for a Communication Plan (in the Form of a Communication Matrix)

The communication plan does not necessarily have to be represented in a diagram, but can also be presented in written form.

As mentioned before, sometimes there are good reasons for presenting the communication plan independently from the project plan. Such an independent communication and/or marketingplan might consist of the following items:

a General description of the project
b Objective and scope of the project
c Concrete project results
d Agreements about the communication responsibilities (part of the project organisation): who assumes final responsibility for the communication of the project, who carries out the communication plan, who coordinates it, etc.
e General communication objective for the project, formulated on the basis of knowledge, attitude and behavioural level
f Making of an inventory of the target groups with corresponding objective and message (is communication strategy)
g Choosing the means of communication to be deployed, preferred style and tone, frequency, sender and feedback possibilities (in the shape of a communication matrix, see Figure 11.6)
h Planning of the communication activities

The points from *a* up to and including *f* can usually be derived directly from the integral project plan. Point *h*, the planning of the communication activities, can, of course, also be put in a separate GANTT-chart (bar chart). Then, point *g* remains, choosing the means of communication to be deployed, etc. For this, once more, the communication matrix mentioned above can be used.

11.2.7 Framing/Implementing the Action Plans

Step 7/8
The communication action plan is the actual execution of the communication plan. In this communication action plan all the communication activities are included in a kind of script. This action plan is usually formulated in the development phase and can be included in the Production Schedule. However, this action plan can also be presented as a separate document. A format for a communication action plan is provided in Figure 11.7.

No.	Day/ Date	Action	Aimed at Communication Target Group	Media to Be Used	Message	By	Expenses	Remarks

Figure 11.7   Format for a Communication Action Plan (in the Form of a Script)

Step 9
11.2.8 Perform an Evaluative Public Survey

To find out whether the objectives of an event have been realised, an *evaluative public survey* is often performed.

Below a step-by-step plan is described for the construction and execution of such a public survey in the service of a public event. The step-by-step plan should be seen as something to hold on to, and not as a straitjacket. Hence, do not be afraid to depart from it if it is necessary or sensible. In the step-by-step plan there are occasional references made to forms and tables that have been included as appendices.

The step-by-step plan contains the following steps:

Orientation Phase (results in a *research proposal which*, is a sort of plan of approach)
Step a   Describe the reason for the public survey (context)
Step b   Exploration of the problem: formulating central problem
Step c   Formulate research questions

Step d   Choose research method
Step e   Describe population and choose a sample
Step f   Budget hours, facilities and expenses
Step g   Construct time schedule and possibly organisational set-up

Research Phase (results in a *research report*)
Step h   Desk research
Step i   Constructing survey
Step j   Do lay-out of the questionnaire
Step k   Produce the schedule for taking the survey
Step l   Test the survey
Step m   Construct a coding system and a processing table
Step n   Copy the survey and conduct it
Step o   Process and analyse the surveys
Step p   Report the findings of the survey

Below the steps are further elaborated upon.

Orientation Phase

Describe the Reason for the Public Survey   *Step a*
This involves a description of the context in which the survey is being conducted. The occasion for this can be, for instance, that you want to find out who visits the event, because there is a possibility that new target groups can be tapped
into. It is also possible that you do not have a clue about whether or not the
right means of communication have been used. Because a public survey is relatively expensive, it is recommended always to do a cost/benefit analysis first.
For serial events it will be of great importance to determine in the first editions
whether the targets have been reached. When a certain routine develops, the
importance of doing public surveys diminishes, except when, for instance,
dropping attendance figures raise new questions.

The Exploration of the Problem: Formulating the Central Problem   *Step b*
With public events there are often great uncertainties with regard to the following three aspects:
– The *make-up of the public* of the event (for instance: age, level of education,
   origin)
– The appreciation of the public for the event (for instance: parts of the event,
   location, accessibility, provision of information, price/quality, repeat visits)

- The effectiveness of the means of communication deployed (for instance: Through which communication medium was contact established? Has the discount coupon been used?)

The central problem of a public survey in most cases relates to one of these three factors.

The central problem of a survey falls apart into:
- The *objective* of the customer
- The *central question* for the researcher(s) (which is really the formulation of the assignment)

With respect to the *objective,* the important thing is what the customer wants to achieve. For instance: 'The customer wants to gain more insight into the effect of the communication activities.'

The *central question* is a translation of the objective into the form of a question or assignment. The accompanying question could be, for instance: 'What is the effect of the communication activities used?'

The researcher gets a feel for the reason, the objective and the central question of the research by holding a briefing with the customer (for instance the project leader of an event). The researcher can also present the customer with a list, such as the one shown below. Then, the customer can indicate which topic he wants to gain more information about by means of the public survey.

Project	
Gender	
Origin	
Age	
Motivation Visit	
Interests	
Communication Medium	
Evaluation	
Size Party	
Level of Education	
Transport	
Occupational Group	
Price/Quality	
Date	
Weather Conditions	
Prognosis Number of Visitors	

Figure 11.8   Example of Aspects to Be Researched in Public Survey

Formulate Research Questions

Step c

When the central problem has been formulated, the research questions can be derived from this. By means of the research questions the research is made more concrete. By formulating the research questions, a clear image emerges concerning the questions that need to be included in the questionnaire, in order to be able to answer the central question of the research. Examples of research questions that fit with the question formulated above are: 'Through which medium of communication has the visitor become aware of the event?' And: 'Did the visitor make use of the discount coupon in the newspaper?'

Choose Research Method

Step d

There are two types of research, namely desk research and field research. In desk research you check whether existing sources (literature, reports of earlier research, internet, etc.) can already provide answers to one or more of the research questions. With regard to public surveys this is indeed often the case. For all the questions that have not been answered the researcher must conduct his own research, and this is called field research. Forms of field research are for instance interview/questionnaire, observation and experiments. The following steps refer to these methods.

Describe the Population and Choose a Sample

Step e

As mentioned above, for a public survey a questionnaire is often the most obvious research method. Before you can start with the research, first the set of research units which the research is focused on, also known as the *population*, needs to be indicated. The population are all the visitors to the project, or the part that is going to be researched. When the population consists of many people, then not all of them need to be polled, but only a sample will suffice. On the basis of the number of expected visitors the size of the sample can be determined. In the literature the following ratios are taken as a basis.

For a hundred visitors the sample is eighty, for a thousand it is 278, for five thousand it is 357, for ten thousand it is 370, for fifty thousand it is 381 and for a hundred thousand the sample is 384.

Everyone in the population must have an equal chance of being included in the sample. Depending on the number of visitors, for instance, every hundredth, tenth, or fifth visitor should fill in the questionnaire.

It is advisable to place the pollsters at the exit. A special corner can, also, be created, where visitors can fill in the questionnaire. In case visitors need help, the pollsters can give them support. The cheapest way to do this is to hand every visitor out of five, ten, or a hundred, a questionnaire and ask them to fill it out and drop it in a letter box at the exit on the way out. There are several ways to encourage a visitor to participate in a survey. Thus, a visitor can be offered a drink, but also a discount coupon for the catalogue of the exhibition, for instance. Another possibility is to give a nice little gift, or to raffle a work of art or a holiday arrangement among those visitors who participate in the survey. In all cases, it has to be determined beforehand what kind of present the participant will receive and how this can be realised.

Step f   **Budget the Hours, Facilities and Expenses**
On the basis of the (prognosticated) data from the different steps an estimate can be made, at the start of the research, of how much manpower, facilities and money will be needed. On the basis of this inventory a budget in time and money can be constructed. To save expenses, sometimes students and volunteers can be used to conduct the survey. However, the processing (by means of for instance SPSS) and the reporting are often tasks that can only be performed by specialists.

Step g   **Construct a Time Schedule and Possibly an Organisational Set-Up**
At the start of the research study a time schedule can be made, on the basis of the steps. This can be visualised, for instance, in the form of a GANTT-Chart (bar chart). There should also be a clear indication of when the customer can expect the completion of the possible intermediate and end results shown in this chart. For the planning technique, see Chapter 10, *Project Planning*.

The organisational set-up mentions who is involved in conducting the research study and which role everyone is to perform. Thus, it indicates who carries the end-responsibility for the research in the research team, who will carry out the research, who will perform the role of customer, and so forth.
As said before, the *Research Proposal* is formulated on the basis of the results obtained during these first 7 steps and then submitted to the customer for approval.

Research Phase

Step h   **Desk Research**
After the research proposal has been approved, the research study can actually get started. As was described in Step d, in desk research one checks whether existing sources (literature, reports of earlier research, internet, etc.) can already provide answers to one or more of the research questions. This is often the case with public surveys. After the desk research, your own research (field research) follows.

Constructing the Survey

To find answers to the research questions that remain after the desk research has been done, usually questionnaires are used in the public survey. Central to the construction of the questionnaires is the phrasing of the questions. These survey questions emanate from the research questions formulated earlier. Also the order in which the questions are posed is important. It is advisable to start with a topic that is not sensitive, for instance, start with 'communication' and not with accessibility if the latter is not optimal. It is best to end with personal questions such as postal code and education.

In the questionnaire a text block always needs to be included with a compulsory respondent number, date and, if the survey is done in different places, also the location. Optionally also the day of the week, the weather conditions, the pollster's number and the time of the questioning can be included. See Appendix A17 for an example of a survey form.

Do the Lay-Out of the Questionnaire

The questionnaire should be in line with the style of the project or the institution that has organised the project. The logo also has to be placed on it and the letter type and letter size need to be determined (for instance Times New Roman, 11 points). Below follow some suggestions for the lay-out:

1 The logo of the project, specification of the survey and, possibly, the logo of the organising institution
2 Text block which the pollster is required to fill in, with a respondent number, date and maybe the location and optionally: day of the week, weather conditions, pollster's number and the time of the questioning.
3 Text block with instructions for the respondent
4 Questions about communication media
5 Questions about accessibility and the evaluation of the event
6 Personal questions
7 Optionally, dotted lines for possible remarks
8 Word of thanks for the cooperation
9 If something is raffled off, a text block in which the respondent can fill in his name and telephone number, if he/she wants to stand a chance of winning the 'prize.'

See Appendix A 17 for an example of a questionnaire form.

Produce the Schedule for the Taking of the Survey

Suppose the event lasts for 20 days and on 5 of those days the survey will have to be conducted. The number of days that surveys will take place needs to be assigned then. It is recommended, for instance, to spread out the days and always to choose a different week for the survey. Depending on the survey method a schedule is produced. In this schedule the days that surveys will be conducted are mentioned and the person(s) who will conduct the survey on a given day, and at a specific location.

Step l **Test the Survey**

When the survey has been put together and laid out, it will have to be tested. Hand the survey out to five people with different backgrounds. By having the questionnaire filled in by people who were not involved with its construction, it can be tested whether or not the form is clear. If the test subjects have problems filling it in, the survey can be adjusted or clarified where necessary. In this way once can avoid incomplete questionnaires from being returned during the survey, or that a great deal of explanation is necessary during the survey. Moreover, the time it takes to fill out the questionnaire can be measured, so that this can be mentioned on the form.

Step m **Construct a Coding System and a Processing Table**

Before the survey is conducted it is advisable to prepare in advance for later processing. Surveys are usually processed by using the computer programme spss. To accommodate the data input into spss, a coding system and a processing table need to be set up. For this the computer programme Excel can be used.

In the *coding system* for each question mention is made of: the number of the question, a description of the question, an abbreviation of the question, also called the code, and what sort of data can be entered for the question.

In the *processing table* all the respondent numbers are listed vertically. For instance, if 180 surveys are conducted, then the numbering on the vertical axis in Excel is 1 to 180. On the horizontal axis the numbers of the questions are listed. For multiple questions with one possible answer, you therefore have, as is mentioned in the coding system, only the question number 1. For multiple questions that have several possible answers, you have question numbers 2.1, 2.2, 2.3, etc. If a question offers as a possible answer 'other, namely', then this answer simply receives an 'input number'. However, behind this input column, there is an extra column in which the written answer can be filled in.

Step n **Multiply the Survey and Conduct It**

When the survey has been tested it should be copied on one side only and stapled together. Then the survey can be conducted. The people who will be administering the survey will need to be instructed about the selection rule (who do you address) and about the non-response records (what is the profile of the non-respondent and those who do not return the survey).

Points of Interest for this Instruction

Before the survey is started all the questionnaires need to be numbered, to make sure that no double numbers emerge and every respondent number is unique. For each day that a survey is conducted, a number of questionnaires has to be prepared. The first text block (date and optional information) has to be filled in by the researcher or the pollsters.

Checklist: What Does the Pollster Take Along

– Pre-numbered questionnaires
– Forms to record the non-response
– Pencils with eraser (plus sharpener) and pens
– A table that is big enough to seat about 8 people near the person that hands out the questionnaires (depending on the method of questioning)
– Small gifts for the people that filled in the questionnaires

Selection Rule

It should be clear to the pollster that he is not supposed to select suitable candidates himself. In principle, for instance, every tenth, fifth, or third visitor that comes along is surveyed. When the pollster is still dealing with a visitor, then he will just let the next person to be surveyed go by. He will then take the next first visitor, when he is available again, after which he will try to stick to the selection rule as much as possible. When the number of visitors to an event falls behind the prognosis, then the selection rule will have to be adjusted.

Non-Response Records

For each day and each pollster non-response records have to be kept. In these records you register which questionnaire (number) has been ignored and which has not been returned at all. With that the profile of the non-respondent is entered, for instance the sex, age category and a remark about the company the non-respondent belongs to (a couple, alone, with child, without child).

When the survey is handed out at the cash register, it is not possible to keep complete non-response records. Only refused forms can be kept track of in that case. All the non-response forms are compiled into the *total response records*, which is kept next to the processing table.

Process and Analyse the Surveys   *Step o*

As a first step in the processing of the survey, the data should be entered into the processing table. Subsequently, the processing table and the non-response records are handed to the person who enters them into spss. The person who will analyse the data with the help of spss will have to study the survey, the coding system and the processing table, so that he can ask questions when something is not clear.

Step p **Report the Findings of the Survey**

The results of the public survey become available after an analysis of the data has been made by means of SPSS. The research report needs to provide answers to all the research questions that have been posed in the research proposal and, thus, to the central question of the research. A written report will suffice, but often the results of a survey are presented orally.

The Setting up of a Multi-Project Organisation

For an increasing number of organisations in the cultural and leisure industries, project activities have become one of the core activities of the organisation. Projects can arise from one's own company mission, but they can also be produced under commission of an external client or together with a co-producer. Business risks are increasingly taken when implementing projects. To be able to control these risks, the management must take steps at the organisational level. This means, first of all, that the ability to work through projects has to be developed as a core competence within these organisations. Employees have to be trained to work in this (new) way. In so doing a mutual *project language* can be developed within the organisation. The provision of tailor-made central guidelines or a project protocol for a company can also play an important role.

Whether the method of working through projects is successful or not depends greatly on the commitment and active support of the top management. Among other things, this management should focus on the coordination, direction, planning and monitoring of a large number of projects simultaneously, which sometimes, but not always are similar in content. The degree and way in which management must pay attention to these functions, is dependent on the design of the project portfolio.

12.1   What is Multi-Project Management?

Multi-project management is a type of management which is engaged with all those aspects of the project approach that rise above the level of the individual project. Sometimes attention needs to be paid to the connection between the content of projects. A mutual source of capacity is almost always there, namely the 'own' organisation executing the projects. This means that also the distribution of capacity (such as people and resources) and the determination of priorities need special attention in multi-project management. This management, on the one hand, supports the individual projects and, on the other hand, it serves the higher interest of the overall organisation. It has to ensure that the risks involved in taking on and executing project obligations are manageable for the top management of the organisation. The risks involve the margins of the six control aspects of projects, namely: quality, organisation, facilities, time, information and money (QOFTIM). The multi-project management does this by, among other things, designing the right infrastructure for a project approach to projects. Moreover, it coordinates all project activities within the organisation, monitors the manageability and the efficiency by developing systems and procedures, and sets priorities. Often, one or more line managers are responsible for multi-project management, whether or not they are supported by a project coordinator or a project office.

12.2   The Project Portfolio

The most important parties involved in a project are the client and the agent. Both can be organisations that have several projects in their portfolio. Both parties have to manage their assignment portfolio. In many cases this has to be done alongside the regular activities in the continuous organisation (not approached as projects).
Within the project portfolio of a multi-project organisation, different groups of projects can be distinguished. Each category demands its own approach from management.

A distinction on the basis of project ownership:
1   *Programme projects*
2   *Assigned projects*

A distinction based on the direct connection between content and planning:

3 *Serial projects*
4 *Mega-projects*
5 *Edition projects*

There remains one residual category, namely:

6 *Incidental projects*

Below descriptions of the diverse categories of projects follow, in which the most important points of interest for the overall management have been indicated.

12.2.1 *Programme Projects*

Projects that arise from the company's own activities *programme* are based on the mission of the organisation. Hence, these projects will, to a greater or lesser degree, show similarity with respect to content. You can consider an exhibition programme of a museum, an educational programme of a centre for art education, the stage productions of a theatre company, but also the maintenance projects within a maintenance programme of a technical services department as Programme Projects. The result of these projects is dependent on the supply of your own organisation or department. Programme management, through the link with the mission of the organisation, is closely connected with strategic management. Programme projects, as a rule, are initiated and developed within your own organisation and are characterised by a certain uniformity in the end result. Projects succeed each other within a programme organisation, as a result of which a certain degree of continuity emerges, a phenomenon that would be strange in an individual project. For the organisational structuring of projects within a programme, the model of *programme structure* can be used. See Figure 7.6.

A programme is sometimes described as: 'a group of coherent projects which are managed in a combined and coordinated manner, and which is not necessarily finite in its existence and through which a continuous flow of projects can be channelled.'

An important point of interest in this category for multi-project management is the guidance during the process of initiating the projects and comparing their content with the mission of the organisation. Capacity planning and financial planning are useful tools within a programme organisation. Depending on the ratio between project activities and regular activities, an organisation with many programme projects will be structured as a permanent project organisation (for instance, a theatre company) or as a project matrix organisation (for instance, a music school in which regular lessons are alternated with projects). The emphasis in these projects lies on hierarchical relationships within the organisation, because the programmes are predominantly realised by that organisation.

12.2.2 Assigned Projects

Contrary to programme projects, assigned projects are projects which have been executed on the assignment of another organisation. Hence, there is always a relationship between an external party commissioning and one's own organisation acting as client. What is characteristic of this category is that between these sorts of projects there are no relevant relationships with respect to content. Each time objectives change and the end result might be different. Assigned projects are connected, however, in the sense that they often have a claim on the same capacity source, namely your own organisation (take, for example, people, equipment, space, and machines). Examples of organisations which almost exclusively execute assigned projects are: contractors, production companies, research institutes, consultancy and architect's firms, automation and advertising companies. These are, almost without exception, referred to as permanent project organisations. Increasingly, also organisations in the cultural and leisure industries are executing assigned projects for external clients. Thus, for instance, an art centre might take on an assignment provided by a school to develop an educational project, or a museum might organise an exhibition for a local council. Another important point of interest for this project category is to monitor the risk and profit margins of each project. Important tools for this are the (financial) project administration and a system for monitoring contracts. Commissioned projects are mainly carried out by agent organisations.

The distinction between programme projects and assigned projects is about project ownership. Who is the actual client: your own company, or an external company or person? Within the project portfolio another distinction can also be made. There are groups of projects in which several individual projects share a direct relationship in their content or planning, which is true of serial projects, mega-projects and edition projects.

12.2.3 Serial Projects

The characteristics of serial projects are that they are all done so that sometimes a great number of projects are being produced at the assembly line. This could be like a drama or game series of a television producer, a periodic publication of a publisher, but also an upgrading of the interior design of all the pump stations that have been built in a certain series by an oil company.

It should be clear that the phasing and planning for serial projects looks quite different from individual projects. Take the example of the planning of a television series. Often the initiation phase (concept development) and the preparation phase (plan formation) are still aimed at the overall series level, but the development, production and performance phase is primarily aimed at the individual project, namely the one episode. Finally, the evaluation and aftercare phase is primarily aimed at the series level again.

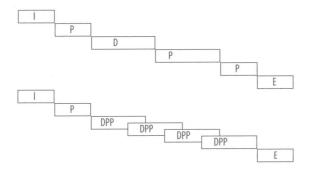

Figure 12.1   Phasing of an Individual Project and a Serial Project

Because of the series-effect, a certain routine emerges which is not common in the case of individual projects. The efficiency, which is created because of this, is a point of special interest for the overarching management of these types of projects. Moreover, monitoring the concept of the series, with the development of each sub-project and the commitment of people and resources for a longer period, demands the necessary attention of the multi-project management.

12.2.4 Mega-Project

A mega-project is a big and complex project, which can be divided into a group of individual projects, that are characterised by a large degree of interrelatedness. It has *one* project mission, *one* end result (as an economic unit) and many (sub)projects with an equal number of (sub)results. The control of this type of project is primarily aimed at the coherence of the end result. Mega-projects exist in all different fields. Here, one might think of, for instance, the development of a major new transport link, but also a world exhibition like Expo 2011, European or World Championships or Olympic Games. In addition, the concept of holding the Liberation Day festivals on the 5th of May in the Netherlands, consisting of thirteen regional festivals with a thematic coherence, can be seen as a mega-project. One of the characteristics of this type of project is that the implementation is often contracted. This means a lot of attention is given to contracts and little to the planning of (your own) people and resources. For the commissioning organisation the emphasis is on the control of time and money in particular. Such a group of connected projects is always aimed at achieving previously determined end results, and finishes when the result has been achieved. The Liberation Day festivals and the European and World Championships, also have the characteristics of an edition project, discussed below, and therefore have less of a finite character.

The phasing of a mega-project is not characterised by such a clear demarcation as the individual projects. In practice, projects can even exist in all possible phases at the same time.

Within the project organisation, the mega-project often follows the basic pattern of the steering committee - working group model. Because the work is contracted to so many suppliers, with this sort of project the emphasis is placed on the contract relationships. This means that much attention needs to be paid to the definition and maintenance of these relationships. A mega-project organisation, therefore, is often a client organisation.

12.2.5 Edition Projects

Edition projects also have a form of continuity. Their chief characteristic is that they are repeated periodically and that they are always aimed at the achievement of a similar kind of result. Sometimes edition projects form part of a programme, for instance an annual sports event within the programme of a community centre, or what is known as an arts menu on offer at an arts centre. An example of a separate and much larger edition project is the project Sail Amsterdam or the Prague Quadrianale. Edition projects, therefore, have a routine quality and that often plays a role in the degree in which such a project is approached as a project.

Finally, in the project portfolio a residual category still needs to be discussed, namely incidental projects.

12.2.6 *Incidental Projects*

Incidental projects are more or less individual projects, often connected to an incident, and therefore by definition once-only. Here one can think of projects within one's own company that are aimed at: a new development, a move, an opening, an automation project, a quinquennium celebration or a policy development. Each incidental project has its own mission and its own result, even though that result is much less concrete within the framework of policy development. Moreover, the project organisation and project planning are free-standing. Often there is use of the same capacity sources as the continuing activities and other projects within the organisation. Because of this, these projects are sometimes experienced as extras that disturb the normal activities.

Having made the distinction regarding the categories of projects mentioned above, the different types of connection between the individual projects appeared to be central. From the description of the different project categories we can sum up the following kinds of dependencies or connections between projects:
- Shared capacity sources (in a particular programme, assigned and incidental projects)
- Mutual dependency with respect to the end result (in particular serial and mega-projects)
- Thematic connection (in particular serial and edition projects, but also programme projects)
- Mutual dependency within the planning framework (in particular serial and mega-projects)
- Connection between (external) preconditions (in particular programme, serial, edition, and mega-projects)

From this coherence between the projects the most important points of interest for the multi-project management arise. These were mentioned previously in the description of the categories.

The project portfolio of many organisations in the cultural and leisure industries contains a mix of the above-mentioned project categories. Moreover, projects can share characteristics of more categories simultaneously. Thus, an annual summer festival, as a programme project of a theme park, also has the characteristics of an edition project. Evidently, each category demands its own approach from the overarching management. An additional point of interest for the multi-project management within many organisations is the distribution of the capacity available between, on one hand, the projects and, on the other hand, the continuing activities and the individual projects. When within this type of organisation the need emerges to tackle activities through projects, there will have to be a redistribution of the capacity available between the regular activities and the projects. Such a change in working method is often experienced as a change of culture in such an organisation, which is sweeping and sometimes calls for a great deal of resistance. In such cases this process is a central point of interest for the overarching management. Sometimes, professional support is necessary at this level.

In literature there is a great deal of confusion about the notion of multi-project management. Some authors define our concept of a mega-project as a multi-project, while others talk of multi-project management in the case of the management of projects for external clients. In both cases, there is a rather narrow definition of the concept of a multi-project. We have decided to refer to a multi-project organisation when the project activities have become one of the core activities of the organisation (whether or not alongside regular activities).

The notion of programme management can also be interpreted in different ways by different authors. Sometimes, only the serial projects mentioned above are included, or the combination of the programme projects and serial projects are mentioned. We believe that the distinction made above is the most useful.

12.3 Four Core Tasks of the Multi-Project Manager

Each multi-project organisation is different; this means that the multi-project management needs to be tailor-made for each organisation. The manager who is responsible for the management of the project within his own organisation must carry out the following four core tasks:

1. *The training of assistants*, to change the project approach into a core competence of the organisation and to give the initial impetus to a mutual project language

2. *The management of the project portfolio*, to attune the projects to each other and to the regular activities and to guarantee an overall control

3. *The organisation of a project infrastructure* to enable the management of the project portfolio mentioned above with the help of systems and procedures

4. *The provision of central guidelines* to create a common project approach within the organisation and to stimulate the development of a mutual project language.

The core tasks 1, 3, and 4 include establishing the preconditions within one's own organisation, so that the organisation can develop and/or execute more projects simultaneously. Developing these preconditions falls under the direct responsibility of the top management of the multi-project organisation. The second core task is aimed at the control above project level. For this, tools are used that are part of the project infrastructure. Below the four core tasks are elaborated upon.

12.3.1 *The Training of Assistants*

When project activities become so extensive that they become part of the core activities of the organisation, the project approach needs to be developed into a core competence. This means, among other things, that the staff members who are involved in the development and execution of projects should receive project management training. It is of great importance that not only the (potential) project leaders and project assistants are sent on a course in project management, but that also the staff members of the supporting departments, such as Administration and the Technical Department, and the line managers and board of directors, so that they can become acquainted with the how to handle activities when carrying out projects. In this way, an understanding can be developed throughout the organisation of the principles, the possibilities and the limitations of working by means of projects and common ground can be created.

12.3.2 *The Management of the Project Portfolio*

Daily control is important when managing the project portfolio. This is achieved by planning, monitoring and adjusting the project portfolio. The kind of attention that the overarching management should give to projects in the portfolio is greatly dependent on the nature of the connection found within certain categories. This connection, in turn, determines what needs to be co-ordinated. When it concerns a thematic connection in regard to the end result, the standardisation of output, might be of importance. When little is contracted out and the coherence is supplied by the use of the same capacity source, the resource planning deserves a great deal of attention. For the benefit of central control, decision-making and checks, standardisation of the working method (project approach, project language, and procedures) is important. The *project protocol*, discussed later, is an important instrument for achieving a standardisation of the working method. When entrepreneurial risks are taken, the control of time and money is important. Furthermore, in most multi-project organisations the pursuit of an ongoing balance between the capacity that is needed and available (people and resources) is central. For programmes, for instance, the stress will be on testing the concept in regard to the mission of the organisation. With serial projects attention is particularly paid to the effects of the overarching concept of the series. With mega-projects the focus is on controlling the mutual end result. And, with assigned projects, attention is paid to monitoring the risks and profit margins and contracting third parties.

With respect to the execution of this daily control, a choice can be made between: central or decentral, formal or informal, complete or partly and implicit or explicit. There is no ideal alternative. All this is dependent, among other things, on the nature, size and complexity of the projects, on the number of staff involved with the projects and their professionalism with respect to the management of projects, but also on the culture within your own organisation. Each multi-project organisation will have to choose its own version or combination with respect to the daily management of the project portfolio.

A great pitfall that is attached to introducing multi-project management is bureaucratization. This can be prevented by pursuing a maximum on the delegation of powers and responsibilities in the planning and monitoring process. Project leaders need to have as much freedom as possible to arrange the necessary capacity (people and resources) for their project themselves. Naturally, this can take place in consultation with the section and industry heads, who usually administer this capacity. The overarching management only interferes if disturbances occur in the capacity balance or if the targets might not be met. To make this possible, a project infrastructure needs to be established within the organisation.

12.3.3 *The Arrangement of the Project Infrastructure*

Within a professional multi-project organisation it is clear *at any given moment*:
– In which way, by whom and on what basis, projects are accepted
– In which way project obligations between parties are recorded
– What the status and state of affairs is for each project
– What the names are of the core positions client/agent/project leader
– What the freely available space is for each capacity source (people, space, resources) and the prognosis of what is needed
– Which management information is needed, at which management level for each capacity source

For this the project infrastructure contains tools and procedures, in order to make the daily management of the project portfolio possible. The project infrastructure can be simple, but sometimes it is also very extensive. The tools that are used for the daily control of the project portfolio, are for instance determined by the composition and size of the portfolio and of the management view of the top management. The tools that are related to the overall level, and possibly the cluster level, are described below.

Project Administration
Within the project administration a distinction can be made between projects that have an external client and projects that have an internal client. In this administration important information is recorded of all of the projects during their different stages. In those projects that have an external client, you should think of data about that client, about the project itself and, of course, about the previously constructed and/or approved decision documents and management plans of each project. Ideally, the project administration provides an up-to-date overview of all of the agreements and obligations that the organisation has made with external parties, within the framework of the project (for instance, about the assignment, about co-production and about the rental of temporary capacity). Of course, in this administration all of the agreements that the organisation has made with the internal client (the person carrying responsibility for the project or project leader) are also recorded. A good project administration represents the exact state of affairs of the project at any given moment and, thus, it is an important tool for top management during the decision-making process.
The project administration, at a minimum, consists of a database with the core information for each project, linked to a file management system.

The File Management System
Each project generates documents in the form of paper, USB sticks, compact discs or files on a computer. Here we can think of tenders, orders, invoices, agreements with external clients and suppliers, permits, project plans and reports. The multi-project organisation has to be able to retrieve these documents at any given moment. Instructions will have to be recorded about who can keep these documents, for how long and in which form. A choice will have to be made for a centralised (by, or in the name of, the multi-project manager) or a decentralised file management system at the level of each project, by the project leaders.

The Financial Project Administration

For smaller organisations it will suffice to designate a cost section for each project in the financial administration of the company. When the actual production or implementation phase is included in the activities of the organisation for many projects, and therefore, many entries have to be made, integrating a project administration into the company administration is highly recommended. A software package for company administration *Exact*, widely used in Europe, offers the software application *E-Project*. The financial administration for projects is aimed at the control and settlement of the financial aspect of projects. Moreover, this administration is aimed at the financial control of the total project portfolio and at the supply of financial information to individual project leaders (as budget controllers). This administration registers all the expenses made for each project and the state of affairs with respect to the financial obligations towards possible external clients. In many cases, however, the financial administration of the project is unable to register obligations made with, for instance suppliers, alongside payments.

The connection between the company administration and the project administration deserves necessary attention as well. An important problem encountered here is namely that the financial administration of the project starts from the moment the obligation has been made, because of the budget control, while for the company administration, on the other hand, the moment of payment is important. Another problem is how to define the expense types. A company administration generally has a standard division of expenses with cost entries such as personnel expenses, housing expenses and office expenses. For a project leader, it is often very inconvenient to have to work with these cost entries. With a project, other types of expenses are significant. See also the standard cost types for event projects in the Finance Chapter. Project leaders monitor their budget on the level of these types of expenses. Also, project leaders have to provide a budget overview periodically, in which, besides the expenses, the ongoing and foreseen future obligations have been included (See Section 8.2). When the financial administration of the project and the company administration cannot be sufficiently attuned, this means that in practice the project leaders will use separate financial control instruments.

The financial administration of the project has a close relationship with the capacity administration. The capacity (people and resources) times the rate, namely, supplies an insight into the expenses.

The Capacity Administration

The capacity administration entails the registration of the planned, the available and the actually used capacity of each employee in hours, but also other capacity sources, such as recording equipment, studio space and machines. Capacity is also referred to as facilities or resources within projects. The most important capacity source is the total number of hours worked by employees within the organisation.

The components of the capacity administration are:

- *Capacity planning* (at the individual, group and organisation level): without a capacity planning or a time schedule no one in the organisation can demonstrate whether or not he can, or cannot, handle another project. Moreover, the capacity or resource planning can fulfil an important role in the setting of priorities.
- *Capacity account*: at issue here are tools such as the time account for assistants and equipment. In this way the real capacity spent can be checked with the planned application. When the recording of time is introduced for the staff, the management must realise that this can be experienced by the staff as limiting their personal freedom. You can only count on reliable time accounts when it is clear for everyone how it will serve the management and that it is not meant as a means of controlling the staff.

For the orderly registration of hours commercial software packages are also available.

- *Capacity expenses* (capacity x rate = expenses): by linking the capacity administration to the financial administration the expenses of the staff, space, or machines can also be revealed for each project in the financial administration.

For the planning and maintenance of capacity in more complex project situations, advanced planning software such as ms-*Project* of Microsoft can be used, or the more simple package *Turboproject* from imsi (which is compatible with ms-*Project*).

The Overall Planning and Guidance

The overall guidance of the development and execution of projects is given shape, by the phasing of the projects and by the submission for approval to the higher management or (external) client of the phase results in the form of decision documents. In the case of internal projects the overarching master plan or annual plan of the organisation serves as a frame of reference for the measurement of achievements within the projects. Thus, an important management tool exists at the central level, which makes it possible to decentralise the responsibilities to the people responsible for the individual project.

In a big multi-project organisation, the division of responsibilities and powers can be designed in a way that is common for a division structure. This is done through project and cluster plans, as an elaboration upon the overarching master plan or annual plan at the organisational level.

The time scheme within a multi-project organisation can be in the form of a bar chart at the cluster or organisational level, in which the phasing and the time periods for all projects are included. Such a time scheme can be created in a relatively simple way by using one of the many software packages in this field. For this the packages named above, MS-*Project* made by Microsoft or the simpler and cheaper, but also very useful package *Turboproject* from IMSI, can be used. Within the space of a few hours the inexperienced user can produce simple time schemes with these packages.

12.3.4 The Provision of Central Guidelines

Central guidelines include all the central guidelines, agreements and instructions for everyone who is involved with working in projects within the organisation. By means of these central guidelines we can achieve uniformity with respect to working in projects within the organisation. These central guidelines are formulated by the overarching management and apply to everyone who is involved with projects in the organisation. These guidelines are included in what is known as the *project protocol*. A step-by-step plan for the construction of such a protocol is provided in Section 12.4.

Central guidelines can be divided into three categories, namely:

- *Guidelines concerning content*: these are related to the requirements which are set for the content of the product process. Here, you might think of, for instance, guidelines for the writing of educational programmes or for the structuring of the content of conferences, or for the development of content for exhibitions
- *Guidelines with respect to working methods*: this is not about the uniformisation of content, but about the uniformisation of the process. Uniform working methods, on the one hand, ensure controllability of the processes and, on the other hand, controllability of the activities. This is concerns guidelines that are based on the project approach, which were discussed in the previous chapters. But **must** be focused on the practice within your own organisation. Thus, guidelines can be provided about the role of the project leader, about the creation of, and cooperation within, a project team, or about the feedback of intermediate results to the higher management. These guidelines may differ for different project profiles and can be included in a protocol. In Section 12.4 we will return to this topic.
- *Administrative guidelines*: these ensure uniformity with reference to the

administrative aspect and the documentation of projects. Here, guidelines need to be considered that relate to the project administration discussed earlier, the financial administration of the project and the file management system. Guidelines can be provided, for instance, for constructing the initiative report or project proposal, for the contents and preconditions of contracts, for the organisation of cost estimates, budgets, budget reports and plans and for structuring of project documents. In this way, a certain routine can begin to emerge, the comparability can be improved.

12.4   The Making of a Project Protocol

The project protocol makes clear how the organisation plans to handle projects and their management. In this way, working by making use of projects becomes embedded in the organisation. When the project portfolio consists of a great diversity of projects, it is recommended that a limited number of *project profiles* are formulated. By using project profiles the central guidelines can be differentiated. Moreover, in the project protocol, tools and procedures can be described, if need be for each project profile. Here, you can think of, for instance: how do projects get started, how does the feedback and decision-making at the management level take place, but also how do the project administration and records need to be organised and which information is collected and placed where and by whom.

12.4.1   The Step-by-Step Plan for a Project Protocol

The following step-by-step plan serves as a tool for the establishment of a project protocol.

The analysis of the project portfolio and the description of the project profiles   *Step 1*

For this step, for instance, the nature, size, risk level and (organisational) complexity of the projects in the project portfolio are examined. Often the diversity is so great that it would be wise to describe a limited number of project profiles on the basis of this analysis. With the description of these project profiles the point of departure is that for each profile a concomitant approach can be described as unambiguously as possible. These project profiles must cover the variation of projects in the portfolio. As an example, here is a short description of three project profiles:
- *Small projects* are projects that have access to a maximum budget in the tens

of thousands of euros, which generally can be developed and realised by one person, as the one responsible for the project, possibly with limited support by colleagues. In these cases a project team does not need to be formed.

– *Intermediate projects* are projects which have access to a budget of several hundreds of thousands of euros, possibly for an external client, in which several employees of your own organisation are intensively involved. For this, a project leader is appointed and an internal project team is formally established

– *An extensive and complex project* is a project which has access to a budget of several hundreds of thousands of euros or more, and which has possibly been developed together with a co-producer for an external client. For this, it is often necessary to create a real project organisation, for example according to the steering committee - working group model. In this everyone's tasks, responsibilities and powers are further described.

It is important that each project profile is described as clearly as possible indicating the delimitations.

Step 2   **The description of the management of the project portfolio**
Here a description is provided of how the multi-project management above the projects is organised, who are responsible for it and who might also play a role. Furthermore, a description is given of the tools that will be used at the overarching level and what they are for (decision-making, setting priorities, monitoring, charging hours). These tools involve, for instance, the project administration mentioned earlier, the financial administration of the project, the capacity administration and the file management system.
In addition, it needs to be determined what information will be available for the overarching management, what purpose it will serve and to which extent this information will be available to the project leaders of the individual projects. To gain access to this information, the overarching management will also need to receive data about the projects. Moreover, it will have to be determined which project information is salient here and with which tools and in what way the information needs to be provided. Here, a method that might be employed, for instance, is one in which the project leaders supply budget reports periodically to the overarching management.

Step 3   **The description of central guidelines as the heart of the project protocol**
It is also the task of the multi-project management to ensure that tools will be available at the project level, and that for a uniform application of these tools possible guidelines can be provided. The fact of the matter is that the basis for

having control over the portfolio as a whole is depends on each individual project.

In the previous section three categories of central guidelines (with respect to content, method and administration) were described. The central guidelines concerning the method form the core of the project protocol. When there is great diversity in the project portfolio, these guidelines should be concentrated on the project *profiles* that have been described in Step 1.

When the organisation has many similar projects, the guidelines concerning content can also be included in the project protocol. However, when this is not the case, the project protocol will primarily contain guidelines, agreements and instructions about the method, the administration and the documentation. In some cases it is advisable to make a separate protocol for the guidelines concerning content, with regard to the development of specific projects within the organisation, for instance the development of educational programmes or exhibitions.

Possible guidelines with respect to the method at project level are the following:

- Concerning the initiation phase:
  - Guidelines for the description of project specifications in, for instance, a project proposal or a project tender (both often take the form of an initiative report. See Section 5.1 and Appendix C1)
  - Guidelines for the framing of norms for the control aspects (QOFTIM). This has to do with the guidelines for the formulation of cost estimates and budgets (See Chapter 8), time schedules and capacity planning (See Chapter 10), the set-up of a project organisation with task/responsibility/ powers planning and planning of consultation (See Chapter 7). Instructions with respect to realistic margins which the organisation wants to use for estimates and planning also fit in here
  - Points of interest and procedure with respect to the acceptance of both internal and external projects by the own organisation. In other words: on the basis of which criteria the decision is made by whom, whether or not to accept a project?
  - Guidelines on the degree in which and the way in which a project needs to be approached and dealt with as a project. It may be useful to link these guidelines with a few project profiles
  - Guidelines for project start-ups (PSU-s)
  - Guidelines for internal and external communication about the project, during the course of the project. In other words: *who* is allowed to say *what* about the project *to whom*?

 – Concerning the preparation and implementation:
  – Guidelines for the adoption of internal adjustments, originating from your own organisation or from the internal or external client
  – Guidelines about management tools for quality, organisation, facilities, time, information and money (QOFTIM), such as procedures for the monitoring of the project budget and for progress control (See Chapters 4, 7, 8 and 10)
  – Guidelines for reporting, hence the procedure for feedback given to the internal or external client, in the shape of decision documents or budget reports (see Chapters 4, 5 and Appendices C1, C2 and C3)
  – Guidelines for the supply of information in the service of the multi-project management at the overarching level
  – Guidelines for periodic project progress meetings
 – Concerning the evaluation:
  – Guidelines for project evaluations, their reporting, including the distribution. All this is meant to bring to the surface and circulate the most important lessons learned. With the evaluation phase the creative process comes full circle and the most important criterion of what is known as the *learning organisation* is met.
  – Guidelines with respect to procedures for a possible follow-up after the project.

12.4.2 *Beware of Rigidity*

In conclusion, we would like to offer a word of caution concerning the use of guidelines and tools:

1 Give people space, because creativity and a sense of responsibility are stimulated when people feel they have some freedom of movement. This implies that people are allowed to make mistakes.
2 Let everything proceed in a decentralised fashion, unless central regulation yields some demonstrable added value. In other words: do not regulate for the sake of regulation; that smothers the organisation.
3 Keep central guidelines and tools simple.
4 Make sure that people themselves also really benefit from them.
5 Do not abuse the guidelines.

A sensible use of central guidelines and tools is important, because their efficiency depends greatly on the people that are to provide the right information in time. That is why abuse should be avoided. When people, for instance record working times, it is not meant to be used by the management to monitor the number of hours people have worked. Employees who have noticed that this is the case will immediately shift to 'socially desirable' behaviour. This way the reliability of the information provided will disappear. This means that only information that is absolutely necessary should be requested. For instance, in order to bill hours reliably to external clients, it is not necessary at all to know how many hours someone worked that week. He only needs to record how many hours he worked on a certain project that week.

Appendices A
The Tools

Appendix A1:   The Time Schedule Form

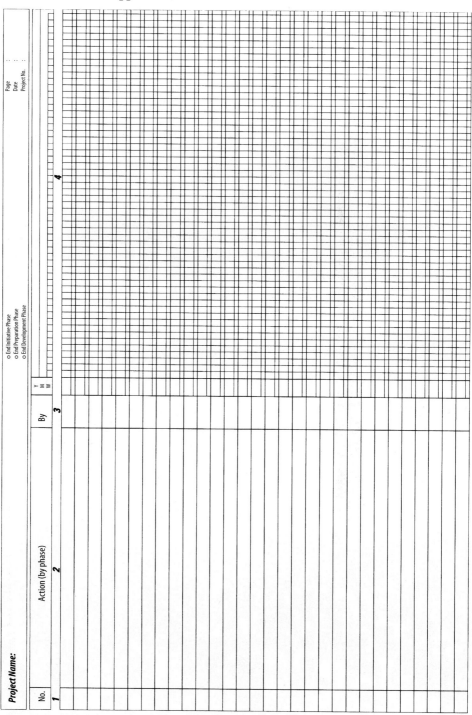

Appendix A2:   Budget Control Form

Project Name:
All amounts incl./excl. VAT

Date   :
Page   :
Project No.   :
Date Working Budget :

Cost Type	Description	Order				Payment				Balance	Remarks
		Date	Receipt No.	Supplier		Date	In Cash	By	Amount	Sub-Budget	
1	2	3	4	5		6	7	8	9	10	11

Appendix A3:   Schedule for the Allocation of Tasks

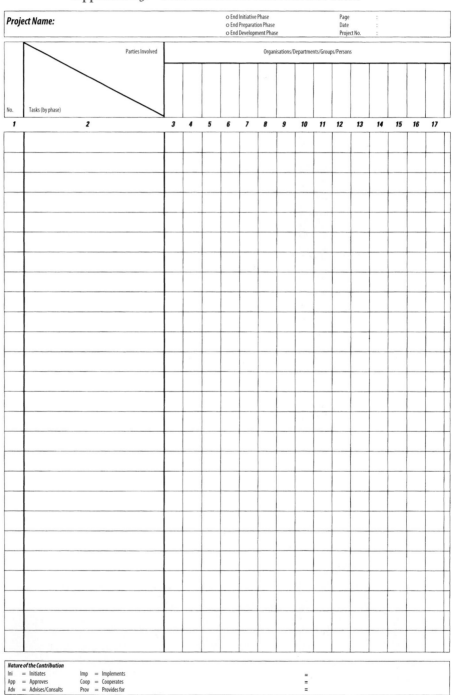

Project Name:		o End Initiative Phase		Page	:
		o End Preparation Phase		Date	:
		o End Development Phase		Project No.	:

Parties Involved — Organisations/Departments/Groups/Persons

| No. | Tasks (by phase) | | | | | | | | | | | | | | | |
| 1 | 2 | 3 | 4 | 5 | 6 | 7 | 8 | 9 | 10 | 11 | 12 | 13 | 14 | 15 | 16 | 17 |

Nature of the Contribution

Ini	= Initiates	Imp	= Implements		=
App	= Approves	Coop	= Cooperates		=
Adv	= Advises/Consults	Prov	= Provides for		=

Appendix A4:   Job Description

Job Title:

Department/Working Group

Implemented by
Name:
Address:
Postal Code + City
Home Phone:
Other Phone:
Fax:

1   Description of the task, including possible sub-tasks:

2   Accompanying responsibilities:

3   Possible powers, for example with respect to the budget:

4   Estimated time required for the task:

5   Supervises:

6   Is supervised by:

7   Special arrangements:

Appendix A5:   Test the Organisational Culture

Objective

In section 7.4.2 the four types of culture that can be found in an organisation are described in more detail (Harrison's typology). In the description ideal types have been taken as the point of departure, however, in their purest form we would be unlikely to come across them in the real world, if at all. Usually we encounter mixes, which, nevertheless, are dominated by one or two of the four cultural types. Not every organisational culture supports working through projects equally well. If you are considering the introduction of working through projects in your organisation, it is useful to know which cultural type is dominant in your organisation. To find this out, you should take the test below. It is also possible to find out, by means of the test, to what extent working in projects fits with your personality.

Instruction

Make a choice:

A I am taking the test to find out what the dominant culture is in the organisation I work for and to find out how project-friendly my organisation is

B I am taking the test to examine which organisational culture I prefer and, thereby, to find out to what degree working in projects suits me.

Exercise Finish the following eight sentences. From the four organisational characteristics offered, always choose the situation which:
- You think is most applicable to your organisation (for A)
- Appeals to you the most personally (for B)

Step 1 1 When someone in your organisation has an argument with his manager, then:
   a he usually admits that talking it over will not offer a solution
   b he can start an appeal procedure to get a binding resolution
   c it is an open question whether it is so important that a great deal of time needs to be spent on it
   d we will talk to them both and help them resolve the issue

2 When someone in your organisation has a difference of opinion with a colleague, then:
   a a discussion will take place in which the strongest party wins
   b they will present the conflict to their manager, who decides

c they work out together what is best for the company and that is then adopted

d they discuss it, and then each proceeds with what they think is best

3 When someone is no longer satisfied with his work, then he will:
   a fight for a promotion
   b put in a request for a change, or a transfer
   c start making a different contribution within the total amount of work to be done
   d start doing a different line of work or look for a different job

4 When someone is no longer able to manage quite as well:
   a he will entrench himself in his work and try to make his position as strong as possible
   b he will usually be kicked upstairs or transferred
   c somebody else will take over his job and he will start doing less demanding work
   d we agree that he is to do less work and we will help him to accept this fact

5 People in your organisation make an effort together because:
   a you only achieve something in the organisation if you work hard at it
   b you are expected to perform well
   c the job needs to be done and you are all responsible for its completion
   d you are interested in the work and it has become part of you

6 When someone within the organisation needs to give up something to achieve a certain objective, then:
   a this will usually be a lower-ranking employee who will resign himself to it
   b it is checked whether he can get compensation
   c it is not pleasant for the person in question, but the fact is that it is beneficial for the job
   d we help the person to accept that, or he leaves

7 When suddenly an executive manager drops out, then:
   a the board of directors will assign someonewho they believe is suitable and competent
   b the assistant manager, if he has the qualifications, is appointed to his position
   c we will look for a man/woman who is able to cope with this job

d we will choose someone who as a person enjoys having people's trust

8 When the introduction of implementing different working conditions is being reviewed within your organisation, then:
   a the management will allow it within reason, as long as they do not believe it is harmful
   b there is consultation (for instance, within a committee that makes a proposal)
   c this will be implemented if people find it acceptable, and when arrangements are made to deal with the problems internally
   d those who are able to use them, will use them, the others will not.

Step 2 Add up all the times that you chose answer *a*. Do the same for answers *b*, *c* and *d*. Next, check in Figure 7.10 (Section 7.4) which organisational culture receives the highest score. Read over the relevant characteristics of the four types of culture in Section 7.4, again, and see if you can acknowledge the score. Subsequently, derive the degree of project-friendliness from Figure 7.11.

Appendix A6:   Model for an Employment Contract

This example contains exchangeable texts, starting with 'or'. These refer to the duration of the agreement (the middle one refers to a project!)

(Taken from the *Ondernemerswijzer* (translated from Dutch) by publisher Kluwer)

We, the undersigned,
Work Ltd in Companytown (hereinafter: employer) and
P. Working, living in Labourville (hereinafter: employee) hereby declare to have entered into the following employment contract:

1. Duration
Employee takes service with employer for an indefinite period of time as of January 1st 19..... as............................

or:
Employee takes service with employer as of...................as...................... ....
......................for the duration of.......................weeks/months/ years; the agreement, therefore, terminates legally on.........

or:
Employee takes service as of...................as.......................................with employer for the performance of services in the framework of project x, specified in............................ The agreement, therefore, terminates legally at the moment these services will have been completed.

or:
Employee takes service as of the January 1st 19.............as.....................
......................with employer for the time that the.................................. in the service of employer, P. Vowel, will be absent because of................. ....
The agreement, therefore, terminates legally at the moment that P. Vowel resumes work.

The first two months will constitute the statutory probationary period, during which both employer and employee can terminate the agreement at any moment without reason given.

If employer, or employee, wants to terminate this agreement after the expiration of the probationary period, then for this the employer will observe a term of notice of at least .... months, and the employee will observe a term of notice of at least .... months.

2. Working Hours
The working hours will be from Monday to Friday from 08:00-17:00 hours with a one hour lunch break. The employer is empowered to assign overtime work.

3. The Nature of the Duties
Employee will in the main perform the following duties
....
For a brief period, the employer is empowered to assign different duties as well, if the business circumstances call for it.

4. Remuneration
The starting salary amounts to _........................gross a month.
Employee will receive a holiday allowance of ....% calculated on the fixed gross monthly incomes (so exclusive of overtime work and other allowances) that have been paid during the relevant holiday-allowance year. The holiday-allowance year runs from May 1st to April 30th [or: The holiday-allowance year is equal to the calendar year.]

or:
The starting salary amounts to _........................gross a month.
Employee will receive a holiday allowance of ....% calculated on twelve times the fixed gross monthly salary in ....[for instance April or May] if during the whole holiday-allowance year there was a continuous period of gainful employment. The holiday-allowance year runs from May 1st to April 30th [or: The holiday-allowance year is equal to the calendar year.]
If there was an interrupted holiday-allowance year, or if during the holiday-allowance year part-time employment was turned into full-time employment, or vice versa, the holiday allowance is calculated proportionately.

5. Holiday
Employee has a right to.........................days of holiday per holiday year, to be taken up in consultation. The holiday-allowance year runs from May 1st to April 30th [or: The holiday-allowance year is equal to the calendar year.]
Employee has to take up at least ....days of holiday in unbroken succession. Employer is empowered to designate at most ....collective days off per holiday year.

6. Collective Labour Agreements
Insofar this agreement does not prescribe otherwise, the regulations apply that have been set down in the Collective Labour Agreement for................................
....

7. Allowance for Expenses
With reference to the costs of work travel the employee receives a compensation which is related to the distance from home to work and which fits within the that rate allowance for travel costs employed by the treasury.

or
With reference to the costs of work travel the employee receives a compensation of _............ a month. On the amount that exceeds the flat rate allowance for travel costs appropriate for the given distance from home to work, the required statutory deductions will be withheld
–   Car costs
–   Phone costs

8. Pension
Employee is a participant in the Company Pension Fund/Business Pension Fund. The contribution will be withheld from his salary on a monthly basis.

9. Special Provisions
Employee is bound to comply strictly with the provisions of the Company Code; a copy of this code has been handed to him.
–   Pledge of secrecy
–   Additional job
–   Restraint of trade
–   Property summons

Drawn up in duplicate and signed in Companytown on December 20th 19....

Work Ltd   P. Working

(Signature)   (Signature)

M. Ployer
Director

Appendix A7:   Artists Contract Model

We, the undersigned,
Work Ltd in Companytown (hereinafter: employer) and
P. Working, living in Labourville (hereinafter: employee) hereby declare to have entered into the following employment contract:

1. Duration
Employee takes service with employer for an indefinite period of time as of January 1st 20..... as..............................

or:
Employee takes service with employer as of....................as...................... ....
.........................for the duration of.........................weeks/months/years; the agreement, therefore, terminates legally on.........

or:
Employee takes service as of...................as..with employer for the performance of services in the framework of project x, specified in............................ The agreement, therefore, terminates legally at the moment these services will have been completed.

or:
Employee takes service as of the January 1st 20..............as......................
........................with employer for the time that the.................................... in the service of employer, P. Vowel, will be absent because of.................. .... The agreement, therefore, terminates legally at the moment that P. Vowel resumes work.

The first two months will constitute the statutory probationary period, during which both employer and employee can terminate the agreement at any moment without reason given.

If employer, or employee, wants to terminate this agreement after the expiration of the probationary period, then for this the employer will observe a term of notice of at least .... months, and the employee will observe a term of notice of at least .... months.

2. Working Hours
The working hours will be from Monday to Friday from 08:00-5:00 p.m. with a one hour lunch break. The employer is empowered to assign overtime work.

3. The Nature of the Duties
Employee will in the main perform the following duties
....
For a brief period, the employer is empowered to assign different duties as well, if the business circumstances call for it.

4. Remuneration
The starting salary amounts to _.......................gross a month.
Employee will receive a holiday allowance of ....% calculated on the fixed gross monthly incomes (so exclusive of overtime work and other allowances) that have been paid during the relevant holiday-allowance year. The holiday-allowance year runs from May 1st to April 30th [or: The holiday-allowance year is equal to the calendar year.]

or:
The starting salary amounts to _.......................gross a month.
Employee will receive a holiday allowance of ....% calculated on twelve times the fixed gross monthly salary in ....[for instance April or May] if during the whole holiday-allowance year there was a continuous period of gainful employment. The holiday-allowance year runs from May 1st to April 30th [or: The holiday-allowance year is equal to the calendar year.]
If there was an interrupted holiday-allowance year, or if during the holiday-allowance year part-time employment was turned into full-time employment, or vice versa, the holiday allowance is calculated proportionately.

5. Holiday
Employee has a right to..........................days of holiday per holiday year, to be taken up in consultation. The holiday-allowance year runs from May 1st to April 30th [or: The holiday-allowance year is equal to the calendar year.]
Employee has to take up at least ....days of holiday inconsecutively.
Employer is empowered to designate at most ....collective days off per holiday year.

6. Collective Labour Agreements
Insofar this agreement does not prescribe otherwise, the regulations apply that have been set down in the Collective Labour Agreement for....................................,

7. Allowance for Expenses

With reference to the expenses of work travel the employee receives a compensation which is related to the distance from home to work and which fits within the rate allowance for travel expenses employed by the treasury.

or

With reference to the expenses of work travel the employee receives a compensation of _............ a month. On the amount that exceeds the flat rate allowance for travel expenses appropriate for the given distance from home to work, the required statutory deductions will be withheld

– Car expenses
– Phone expenses

8. Pension

Employee is a participant in the Company Pension Fund/Business Pension Fund. The contribution will be withheld from his salary on a monthly basis.

9. Special Provisions

Employee is bound to comply strictly with the provisions of the Company Code; a copy of this code has been handed to him.

– Pledge of secrecy
– Additional job
– Restraint of trade
– Property summons

Drawn up in duplicate and signed in Companytown on December 20th 20....

Work Ltd   P. Working

(Signature)   (Signature)

M. Ployer
Director

Appendix A8:   Volunteers Contract Model

Contract Number: Place:
   Date:

The Undersigned:
1 Name   :
   Address   :
   Postal Code + City   :
   Telephone/Fax   :   /
   Represented By   :
               Hereinafter Referred to as Employer

2 Name   :
   Address   :
   Postal Code + City   :
   Telephone/Fax   :   /
   Birth Date/Nationality   :   /
   Social Security No.   :
   Giro/Bank Account No.   :
               Hereinafter Referred to as Volunteer

Agree to a volunteer's work agreement for a definite/indefinite*) time period under the following conditions:

A Starting Date/Time: ....

B Probationary period................weeks/months*/Details: ....

C With Project/Department: ....

D Nature of the Activities: ....

E Name Supervisor: ....

F Holiday: Absence because of holiday will be discussed by the volunteer .... days/weeks in advance with the supervisor.

G Compensation: The volunteer has a right to compensation for the actual expenses incurred. By this is meant the expenses that he/she had to incur to be able to do the job. These include, for instance:

– Travel expenses (travel to work is/is not* included)
– Other possible expenses that the volunteer had to incur

The expenses are declared once a week/month/quarter* via an expense form. The volunteer will/will not *) get a fixed compensation for work travel, in the case he/she will, this will amount to .... per ....

H Protection of privacy: The volunteer will keep secret everything that will come to his/her notice in his/her capacity as a volunteer with reference to the project/the organisation. This also applies after the termination of the volunteer position.

I Insurance: During the presence of the volunteer the employer does/does not *) take out a liability and accident insurance for him/her.

J Term of notice: For both parties a term of notice of .... days/ weeks/months*) applies.

K Prevention as a result of illness: If the volunteer is prevented from doing his/ her work as a result of illness, he/she will inform the employer about this as soon as possible.

L Particular return services : ....

M Other provisions : ....

Thus, signed in duplicate : .... Date:.......................

Signature Employer   *Signature Volunteer*

* strike out whichever is not applicable

Appendix A9: Checklist Sponsor Contract

Parties:
What applies to written agreements in general, applies here as well: parties need to be designated in a coherent way (for instance as sponsor and sponsored party). Also, it will have to be examined what authority the parties have to make contracts in a legally valid way.

Considerations
The inclusion of a more or less extensive clause for 'considerations,' is also advisable in sponsor contracts. A consideration 'frames' the contract and provides the opportunity to introduce the object of sponsoring (for instance, the festival, the exhibition). Furthermore, all sorts of 'biographical' and other information relevant for the interpretation of the contract (for instance, subsidies fallen through, expected invitations for foreign tours) can be mentioned. Moreover, if need be, reference can be made to important documents (for instance, correspondence, promises) and to specific, applicable regulations (for example copyright law, media law, the code of advertising practice, the society for sports sponsoring).

Core Performance
The sponsor makes available:
– Money (cash, financing)
– Services (transport artists, publicity/promotion)
– Facilities (use of grounds)
– Goods (circus tent)
– Act as guarantor for possible losses
– Advice and support

The sponsored party makes available (return service), for instance:
– Communication opportunities in the service of promotion of the company
– Association of the name of the sponsor with the sponsored party with the right for both parties to refer to that association
– Use of the name of the sponsor in all promotional material, for instance in programmes and on clothes and game attributes
– Connection of the name of the sponsor with (a part of) the project, for instance a hall in a museum

Other Agreements Involve:
- The duration of the agreement
- The way in which money, services, facilities and goods are made available
- The way in which the name of the sponsor is carried (consultation or approval by the sponsor required?)

Additional requirements for the sponsored party:
- Co-signing by members
- Representative and/or behaviour not unfriendly to the sponsor
- No politically or religiously controversial behaviour
- The keeping of transparent accounts and accounting for the money spent
- No transference of contractual rights to third parties

Additional rights for the sponsored party:
- Guarantee for the freedom of expression
- Safeguard against product liability
- No interference by the sponsor with the content of the activities of the sponsored party

Additional requirements for the sponsor:
- No transference of contractual rights to third parties

Additional rights for the sponsor:
- Exclusivity (also: main sponsor)
- Special treatment at the event (preview, free tickets and the like)
- Attendance of meetings of the sponsored party

Other:
- Termination arrangement
- Yes/no during project
- With bankruptcy, etc.
- Conditions for dissolution of contract or expressly described defaults
- Prohibition of mutual reference after conclusion
- Making an inventory of the specific applicable regulations with required harmonisation and warranties
- The appropriate law between the parties and arbitration agreement (judge, binding advice, arbitration)

Adaptation of the checklist by Professor Grosheide, Master of Laws

Appendix A10:   Model for a Press Release

Media attention is part of the marketing communication. To receive media attention the (public) event will have to make use of press releases. Below a number of criteria for a good press release are listed.

The press release has to:

1   Contain an important message (form:headline/lead/text)
2   Be written well and clearly (see press release model below)
3   Be sent in the appropriate manner
4   Be sent at the right moment

Important Message

With this the following should be taken into account: news that is of local or regional importance, does not necessarily have to be of national importance. That is why it is sometimes advisable to make two press releases: one for the national media and one for the regional media. The news reported is not a promotional story, but needs to convince the editorial staff. Editors are allergic to advertising, anything that looks like advertising is immediately thrown in the bin.

Well and Clearly Written

Here, think of the following matters: always put 'Press Release' at the top. Come up with a stimulating title (*headline*) for the editor, so that he does not put the press release aside. The core message has to be crystal-clear from the first section (the *lead*, like the first lines in bold type in a newspaper article). This *lead* should not be longer than 50 words. The release itself provides an answer to the following six questions: *who, what, where, why, when* and *how*.

Press releases leave a lot of space between the lines. Use 1.5 spacing between the lines of the text, and use a relatively wide margin (4 centimetres). This space gives the journalist the opportunity to make possible notes on the press release. Naturally, the pages of the press release should be numbered.

Sent in the appropriate manner

It is recommended to make a list of the names of those who write about the topic in newspapers and magazines or who pay attention to it on the radio or television. Do not address indiscriminately to 'the editorial staff...', but at least name the desk where it belongs. It is even better to approach the relevant editor or journalist directly. It only makes sense to send a press release by e-mail, if you have the exact electronic address of the desk or the editor/journalist, otherwise it may take a long time before it reaches the right place. It is also recommended to send along an introductory note with the press release. A few lines is enough, as it is merely a formality, a courtesy.

When the media are also invited for a gathering (for instance a press conference or press presentation), this needs to be mentioned in a separate letter. In that case it is recommended to send along a reply card, so the organisation knows who to expect. This is in regard to such provisions as sandwiches and drinks, but also press files, etc.

Sent at the right moment

The press release needs to be sent at the right moment. In order to write an article or to make a report, the media plan ahead. Weeks before, an agenda is compiled; at that point an examination is made of what will happen in the weeks ahead. The first contact with the press can therefore best be scheduled two months before the event takes place at the very latest. A second press release can be sent, for instance, a month in advance, and the last one or two weeks before the event.

A press release has its own lay-out. Below a list of possible parts of a press release follows.

1 *Name and address* of the organisation that hands out the press release, usually with a logo. Often printed stationery is used for a press release.
2 The *designation* PRESS RELEASE in bold letters
3 *If need be, an instruction about an embargo* (exact date and time). If a press item is not allowed to be published before a certain time then this is indicated here. Do not place an embargo of more than two days. Usually an embargo does not apply.
4 *Date*: written in full and given completely. With a press release the aspect of time is very important, therefore a journalist has to be able to see quickly how current a message is.
5 *Headline*: in the headline the essence of the current news item is represented precisely (who + what) in an objective, concise and powerful way.
6 *Lead*: this is the first section. This contains the most important information. For an example, examine the first part of a newspaper article (what + who and subsequently where, when and sometimes how, why or with what/ whom).
7 *Text*: this is divided in sections, divided by extra space and headings. In the text there is an explanation and clarification of the aspects mentioned in the lead, in descending degree of importance (to you as author). Place the background information and history at the end. You should remember that cut-

ting the last lines is the easiest way to shorten a press release. The intermediate headlines, just like the main headline, should be objective and cover the content of the relevant block of text as accurately as possible.

8 A *closing-off sign* indicates where the text of the press release ends. The text below the closing-off sign, no longer belongs to the information that the media can take over. The nature and number of appendices, and possible notes to the editors are provided after the closing-off sign.

9 *Further information.* After several lines of extra space the one(s) who can provide extra information is/are mentioned: name institution or company, address, department, name contact, position, telephone (business and private), who can provide reports/pictures? The contact should be easy to reach as the morning papers still gather a lot of information in the evenings.

Appendix A11:   Parties Involved in Conferences

For conferences the following (groups) of people can be called in:
Called in for the preparation:
- (Internal) conference committee
- Organisation bureau of a conference centre
- External conference advisor for the organisation of the conference

Specialists called in for the preparation and during/after the conference:
- Trainers: programming and group-dynamic methods with an eye to inter-action and communication processes, deployment of panel chairmen and discussion leaders
- Organisation advisors: strategic aspects and aspects concerning transformation
- Public relations officials/advisors: promotional, advertising and mass communication aspects
- Linguists/journalists: translations, copywriting of information and reporting, training of public performances
- Publishers: production, graphic design of written conference material, language issues, market research, publishing of a conference book
- Marketing experts: marketing of the conference, market research, advertising, media planning for several promotional activities
- Artists: exhibition, imagination or making of conference theme(s) more dynamic
- Automation experts: simulation, teleprinting, word-processing, database, feedback information
- Audio-visual experts: arrangement of prefabricated slide/film/video programmes, recording/operation of equipment during the conference, editing a videolog

Officials called in for a specific task during the conference:
- Conference chairman or chairman for the day
- Speakers
- Rapporteurs
- Panel chairmen
- Discussion leaders
- Voting panel
- Discussion forum
- Artists
- Interpreters

- Hostesses
- Control crew
- Technical staff
- Photographers

Appendix A12:   Group-Dynamic Forms

Examples of suitable means and methods that can lend form to the communication and interaction process (for instance at conferences).

Interaction between participants on stage:
– Question rounds
– Interview panels
– Response panels
– Teams of listeners
– Forum discussions
– Observation teams
– An empty chair on the stage (for participants with a strong urge to respond)
– Voting machine (interaction with the whole audience)

Interaction among participants themselves
– Zoom groups
– Philips 66
– Meta-planning method
– Delphi (before, during and after conference)
– Synectics
– Brainstorming and other creativity techniques
– Inner/outer circle
– Pairs/threesomes
– Incident method
– Pro/contra game
– Lawsuit role play
– Simulation game

Dynamic presentation techniques:
– Demonstrations
– Play, improvisation, radio play, role play
– Warm-ups
– Film, video, wide-screen projections
– Speakers with 'visuals'
– Video portraits

Appendix A13:   Information Carriers Conferences

This appendix provides you with a number of examples of information carriers at a conference, at different stages in the organisation process.

Before the conference consider such information carriers as:
– Advance announcement, invitations and registration forms
– Conference book or paper, syllabus or documentation file
– List of participants
– Conference programme, programme booklet
– General publicity about the conference
– Press release, articles, folders, dispatch lists, media contacts and the like
– Preliminary reports, research results, theme descriptions
– Small printed material such as badges, tickets, stationery, floor plans, posters, conference cards, emblem, hotel vouchers, a word of welcome for the hotel room, signposting and the like
– Media plan in case of different, related (preliminary) conferences and events
– Information with respect to the pilot-testing of the conference design on a test group

During the conference consider such information carriers as:
– Programme presentations
– Necessary small printed material
– Lectures, introductions and reprints of these
– Discussion questions, theses, starter information and questions for discussion, etcetera
– Registration of discussions, lectures and the like
– Possibilities for the adjustment of the programme during the conference itself (to fall back on)
– Itinerary, routine information
– Supplementary programme and tourist information at the information desk
– Evaluations (begin and end)
– Reading table
– Audiovisual information
– Teleconferencing programme
– Word-processing programmes/database in the service of prompt information supply

After the conference consider such information carriers as:
- General conference report, possibly also specific reports
- Reporting back to the participants, target groups and other parties involved (evaluation results, possible follow-up activities and the like)
- Press publications
- Videotape and audiotapes of (parts of) the conference
- Evaluations of (parts of) the conference
- Plan for and communication about follow-up activities

Appendix A14:   Model Agreement for an Assignment

The undersigned..(name and place of business/residence of the client), hereinafter referred to as client, and.......................................(name and place of business/residence of the agent), hereinafter referred to as agent, declare to have agreed to the following:

1   Agent shall perform the following services for client:
    .... (list of the activities)

2   Client shall pay agent for the activities listed under 1 the remuneration of ....euro an hour/as fixed amount.* Moreover, agent has a right to compensation for expenses incurred for......................(specification)

3   The services to be rendered will be performed by the agent independently. Agent is employed by client. Furthermore, agent is free to determine the date and time to perform the activities at his own discretion, on the understanding that they have to be completed no later than ....(date).

4   ....(time period over which declarations/forward invoices are submitted by agent) agent needs to submit his declarations/invoices by means of specified bills to the client, who is obliged to pay these bills within .... (term)

5   The client can terminate this assignment agreement at all times. In that case he owes the agent a remuneration in the proportion of the work accomplished until then and the quality thereof. The agent cannot terminate this agreement, unless:
    – the agreement is for an indeterminate time and does not end by its fulfilment
    – the agent terminates this agreement due to weighty reasons and he is not prepared on reasonable grounds to carry out the assignment according to the instructions afforded to him

In case the agent has a right to terminate the agreement, the client owes the agent a remuneration in the proportion of the work accomplished up until then.

When the agent terminates this agreement without the occurrence of one of the instances just mentioned, he owes the client damages, consisting of the difference between the agreed upon amount of the remuneration due and the price which the client will have to pay to a third party for the completion of the assignment.

6 The agent is not liable with respect to the client for damages to the client incurred by the agent during the carrying out of this assignment. This is unless it is a matter of malice or culpability.

7 To this agreement the stipulations of Dutch law are applicable.

8 All disputes about the implementation of this agreement are subject in the first instance to the verdict of the acting judge in ....(city)

Thus agreed upon and drawn up in duplicate in.......................(city)
on......................(date)

Client   Agent

Appendix A15:   Budget Audio-Visual Project

Basic Data Audio-Visual Project

Type of audio-visual project	:	Documentary
Working title	:	***'Max Havelaar Against the Current'*** *(FICTIONAL PROJECT!!)*
Length/display time	:	52 minutes
Language version	:	Dutch

Parties Involved:

Production company	:	STEENHUIS Productions, Amstelveen
Producer	:	Jan Steenhuis
Director	:	Wouter Stapel
Cameraman	:	Rob de Boer
Sound	:	Jeltje Vos
Editor	:	Ben van Groeningen
Technical services	:	AV-Service
Sound studio	:	AV-Service

Tapes:

Format	:	Betacam-SP
Tape format on-line	:	Digibetacam
Tape format off-line	:	VHS

Time Schedule

Pre-production	:	21 days
Recording time	:	22 days
Recording period	:	October 08 - November 08
Travel Days	:	8 days
Off-line editing	:	25 days
On-line	:	8 periods
Date completion	:	December 15 2008

Expenses Budget Audio-Visual Project

Name of the Project: *'Max Havelaar Against the Current'* *(FICTIONAL PROJECT!)*
Type of Project: Documentary (52 min.) On Betacam SP
Project Number: 804
Name Party Responsible for the Project: *Jan Steenhuis/STEENHUIS Productions*
Date Report: July 30th 2008
Completion/Opening/Premiere: December 15th 2008
Phase: Development phase

Cost Type	Description	Material and Third Parties	Labour Costs	Total
1000	*Location Costs*	–	–	–
2000	*Direct Production Costs* (Technical Equipment and Organisation)	87.200	–	87.200
2100	– Equipment and Material	30.520		
2200	– Per Day and Transport	53.000		
2300	– Other Direct Production Costs	3.760		
3000	*Direct Production Costs (People)*	–	46.000	46.000
3100	– Remuneration Recording Period		39.600	
3200	– Remuneration Travel Days		6.400	
4000	*Development and Preparation*	–	34.950	34.950
4100	– Development Costs (Preparation Budget)		28.200	
4200	– Remuneration Preparation Recordings		6.750	
5000	*Additional Costs*	34.400	–	34.400
5100	– Insurance	6.300		
5200	– Rights Manuscript	15.000		
5300	– Rights (Benelux)	13.100		
6000	*Editing*	29.650	29.300	58.950
6100	– Off-Line Editing	6.500	27.500	34.000
6200	– On-Line Editing	23.150	1.800	24.950
7000	*Promotion, Publicity and PR*	–	–	–
8000	*General Costs, Unforeseen and Profits*	–	–	63.850
8100	– Financing Costs			3.000
8200	– Unforeseen (9%) x € 264,580			23.812
8300	– Overhead (5%) x € 254,580			13.226
8400	– Producers Fee (9%) x € 264,580			23.812
	Estimated Project Costs (VAT Not Included) **Taxes (VAT)**			**325.430** *(All Including)*
	Estimated Project Costs (VAT Included)			
9000	Financing Scheme/Earnings			325.430
9100	-Share Financing STEENHUIS Productions			22.930
9200	- Share Partners			170.000
9300	- Contribution Funds and Sponsors			132.500
	Positive/Negative Project Result			0

Explanation of the Budget of the Audio-Visual Project

1000	**Location Costs**	
	Not applicable	

2000	**Direct Production Costs (Technical**	
	Equipment and Organisation)	**87.280**
2100	Equipment and Material	30.520
	• ENG-set 30 Days (600)	18.000
	• Light 30 Days (150)	4.500
	• Sound Equipment 8 Days (240)	1.920
	• Betacam Tapes 50 (50)	2.500
	• Helicopter	2.000
	• Production Stores	1.600
2200	Per Day and Transport	53.000
	• Tickets	12.000
	• Overweight	4.000
	• Local Transport	7.000
	• Hotel	16.000
	• Per Day	8.000
	• Cooperation Third Parties	3.500
	• Interpreters/Translations	2.500
2300	Other Direct Production Costs	3.760
	• Visas/Carnets/Vaccinations	760
	• Representational Costs	2.000
	• Photo Material/Labour	1.000

3000	**Direct Production Costs**	
	(People/Crew)	**46.000**
3100	Remuneration Recording Period	39.600
	• Director 22 Days (450)	9.900
	• Producer 22 Days (450)	9.900
	• Cameraman 22 Days (700)	15.400
	• Sound Technician 8 Days (55)	4.400
3200	Remuneration Travel Days	6.400
	• Director 50% of (450) 8 D.	1.800
	• Producer 50% of (450) 8 D.	1.800
	• Cameraman 50% of (700) 8 D.	2.800

4000	**Development and Preparation**	**34.950**
4100	Development Costs	
	(Preparation Budget)	28.200
4200	Remuneration Preparation	
	Recordings	6.750
	• Director 5 Days (450)	2.250
	• Producer 10 Days (450)	4.500

5000	**Additional Costs**	**34.400**
5100	Insurance	6.300
	• Negative Insurance	2.500
	• Breakdown Insurance	3.000
	• Liability Insurance	500
	• Equipment Insurance	300
5200	Rights Manuscript	15.500
5300	Rights (Benelux)	13.100
	• Archived Film Material	7.000
	• Transfer Costs	1.600
	• Making Music	2.500
	• Legal Costs	2.000

6000	**Editing**	**58.950**
6100	Off-Line Editing	34.000
	• Betacam to VHS, 25 Hours	3.000
	• Equipment 25 Days (200)	5.000
	• Editor 25 Days (450)	11.250
	• Direction 25 Days (450)	11.250
	• Translation Raw Material	3.500
6200	On-Line Editing	24.950
	• 8 Periods of 4 Hours	14.400
	• Tapes, Betacam Master IT	
	& Dutch Version	250
	• Direction 4 Days (450)	1.800
	• Worked-Out Script	1.500
	• Title Translation/Subtitles (NOB)	6.000
	• Travel Expenses Post-Production	1.000

7000	**Promotion, Publicity and PR**	

8000	**General Costs, Unforeseen**	
	and Profits	**63.850**
8100	– Financing Costs	3.000
8200	– Unforeseen (9%) x € 264,580	23.812
8300	– Overhead (5%) x € 254,580	13.226
8400	– Producers Fee (9%) x € 264,580	23.812

Estimated Project Costs		
(VAT Not Included)		*325.430*
Financing Scheme		

9000	**Earnings**	**325.430**
9100	Subsidies/Contribution Participants	263.750
	• EO-Television	25.000
	• RNTV/Broadcasting Company	70.000
	• NCDO	75.000
	• Foundation 'Doen'	50.000
	• Solidaridad	43.750
9200	Sponsoring	38.750
	• FNV	25.000
	• Commission P.I.N.	10.000
	• Socially Responsible	
	Entrepreneurship	3.750
9300	Venture Capital	22.930
	• STEENHUIS Productions	22.930

Appendix A16:   Risk Analysis for Projects

This risk analysis is best applied *at the end of the initiative phase.*This is the moment when the decision is made whether the project should startor not. Read section 5.2 before applying this risk analysis. The risks that are listed in the analysis below are of a general nature. For specific fields, risks can be added or left out when they do not apply to the project. You can also adjust the 'weight' of the risks. In doing this, the total number of 'points' to be scored will also change. You will have to interpret the result of the analysis yourself, although an 'indication' has been provided at the end.

Risk		Value	Factor	Weight	Risk	Highest Possible Risk
A	**The Approach**					
1	To what degree does the mother organisation have experience with the project approach?	sufficient	0			
		reasonable degree	1			
		insufficient	4	x 4		16
2	To what degree are the members of the project team familiar with the project approach?	very	0			
		reasonably	2			
		hardly	5	x 5		25
3	Has a conscious choice been made for the project approach, with a clear assignment for the project leader/team?	yes	0			
		no	6	x 6		36
B	**The Coherence of the Content**					
1	Is the basic concept of the project sufficiently connected to the objective(s) and target group(s) with respect to content	yes	0			
		reasonable degree	3			
		no	8	x 6		48
2	Are the points of departure with respect to the content of the project sufficiently familiar to all the people involved with the project?	yes	0			
		most of them	1			
		insufficiently	5	x 5		25
3	Is it clear how the project result will look?	yes	0			
		somewhat	3			
		not at all	6	x 6		36
4	Is there sufficient demarcation with respect to other projects?	yes	0			
		reasonably	1			
		insufficient	5	x 4		20
5	Is the field the project is related to sufficiently known to the people involved?	yes	0			
		reasonably	2			
		not accurately	5	x 5		25

Risk		Value	Factor	Weight	Risk	Highest Possible Risk
C	**The coherence of the process**					
1	Is it clear who is the client, and/or who sets the policy and the preconditions?	yes no	0 5	 x 5		 25
2	To what extent is the project unique?	not at all somewhat very unique	0 2 5	 x 5		 25
3	If there are other projects or sub-projects, does the progress depend on the fine tuning between them?	yes somewhat strongly	0 2 5	 x 3		 15
D1	**The Management of Time**					
1	What is the estimated duration of the project?	0-3 months 3-6 months 6+ months	0 1 3	 x 4		 12
2	Does the project have a deadline?	no yes, flexible yes, definitive	0 2 4	 x 4		 16
3	Is there sufficient time to realise the project within the determined period, with the people and means available?	ample sufficient insufficient	0 1 6	 x 5		 30
D2	**The Management of Money**					
1	Is there clarity about the expenses and the benefits the project will create?	yes reasonable no	0 3 6	 x 5		 30
2	To what degree can the financial coverage of the project budget be met?	completely somewhat not at all	0 3 6	 x 6		 36
3	Which percentage of the estimated expenses is assumed to be covered by sponsoring and funds?	0-5% 5-10% 10-20% more than 20%	1 3 6 9	 x 6		 54
4	When an investment project is involved, how is the financial-economic feasibility assessed?	favourable reasonable doubtful	0 2 6	 x 6		 36
D3	**The Management of the Remaining Aspects**					
1	Can the other commercial preconditions be fulfilled, such as facility and quality requirements and the like?	almost certainly probably unsure	0 1 5	 x 4		 20

Risk		Value	Factor	Weight	Risk	Highest Possible Risk
2	Is it expected that the necessary permits, permissions and the like will be obtained?	almost certainly	0			
		probably	1			
		unsure	6	x 6		36
E	**The Attuning of the Project to the Environment**					
1	What will the attitude of the future consumers of the project result be?	positive	0			
		interested	1			
		reserved	5	x 5		25
2	When a market project is involved, how is the demand/need for the product assessed?	positive	0			
		uncertain	6	x 6		36
3	What is the attitude of the rest of the environment towards this project?	positive	0			
		interested	1			
		reserved	4	x 5		20
4	Has enough time been planned for the attunement to the environment and decision-making?	sufficient	0			
		reasonable	1			
		insufficient	3	x 4		12
F	**The Internal Project Organisation**					
1	Which employees are to assist in the project?	mostly internal	0			
		internal + external	1			
		mostly external	3	x 4		12
2	How many disciplines are involved in the project?	one	0			
		two	1			
		three or more	3	x 4		12
3	Is a co-production at issue?	yes	0			
		no	5	x 5		25
4	The number of project staff that is involved with the project for more than 80% at peak times	1-5	0			
		5-15	2			
		more than 15	4	x 5		20
5	The ratio of experts on content vis-a-vis experts in the field of project management?	good	0			
		reasonable	2			
		bad	4	x 5		20
G	**The Cooperation within the Project**					
1	To what extent are the members of the project team excited about the project?	very	0			
		reasonably	2			
		not much	6	x 6		36

Risk		Value	Factor	Weight	Risk	Highest Possible Risk
2	Is there a chance that the composition of the project group will change considerably during the project?	small chance average chance great chance	0 2 5	 x 5		 25
3	How expert are the experts on content in the field of this project?	very reasonably limited	0 1 5	 x 5		 25
H	**Project Leadership**					
1	Is it clear who is in charge of the development and realisation of the project?	yes no	0 8	 x 5		 40
2	How expert is the project leadership with respect to project management and phased decision-making?	very reasonably limited	0 2 6	 x 5		 30
3	To what degree does the project leadership possess social skills and the ability to kindle enthusiasm?	high reasonable extent not much	0 1 6	 x 6		 36
4	How involved are the responsible line managers with the project?	highly reasonably limited	0 2 6	 x 5		 30
						(970)

$$\text{Risk Percentage} = \frac{\text{Total Risk}}{\text{Total Highest Possible Risk}} \times 100\% = \qquad \%$$

Remark: Take action on the most important risk factors.

Indication: When the percentage is higher than 50%, the start up of the project *in this form* is inadvisable!

Warning: the outcome of the analysis should always be personally interpreted!

Appendix A17:   Questionnaire (Example)

 KAAP✳ HELDER art from a natural source.

Survey

Art and Culture North Holland

17

Respondent number:	Date:
Day of the week:	Wednesday/Thursday/Friday/Saturday/Sunday*

Instruction for Filling Out the Survey

- **Filling out this survey will take approximately 5 minutes**
- **Encircle the correct answer, or write the answer on the designated dotted lines**
- **The survey can be filled out in pencil, pen or felt-tip**
- **You can make corrections by crossing out a mistakenly encircled answer and encircling the correct answer.**
- **Only one answer per question is possible, unless otherwise indicated!**

1   **In what way were you informed about the project Kaap Helder?**
(More than one answer is possible)

By a flyer:	1	Sent to my house
	2	Through museum, Tourist Office, hotel, etcetera
By an article in:	3	Weekly or monthly magazine
	4	Regional daily
	5	National daily
	6	Local weekly
	7	Entertainment folder
	8	Rails, Checkpoint, or NRC
By an advertisement in:	9	De Volkskrant, NRC or Parool
	10	Kunstforum
By information:	11	On the internet
	12	On poster or bill board
	13	Radio
	14	TV
	15	Through Den Helder city council or the Royal Dutch Navy
	16	Through friends, relatives or acquaintances
	17	Other namely:..................

2   **Would you please indicate whether you engaged in the activities below and, if you did, which mark (1 to 10) you would give it?**

		Done	Mark
1	Visited the 'Bathyscaaf'	no yes	....
2	Visited theatre performance 'BUNKER'	no yes	....
3	Children present visited the children's workshop	no yes not applicable	....

3 **How would you rate the following components of the event?
(please mark with a figure between 1 and 10)**

Mark

   1   Visual art   ....

   2   Photo exhibition 'Gezichtseinder'   ....

   3   Photo chronicles of 'Nieuwediepers'   ....

   4   The architecture exhibition 'Helderder'   ....

4 **Would you please give a mark (1 to 10) for the following aspects**

Mark

   1   Accessibility of the location   ....

   2   Information leaflet you received at the entry   ....

   3   Captions attached to the art works   ....

   4   Price-quality ratio   ....

   5   Parking space   ....   Not applicable

   6   Customer-friendliness of the staff on site   ....

   7   The atmosphere at the location   ....

5 **What was the most important consideration to visit 'Kaap Helder'?**
   1   The art
   2   The location
   3   The combination of the art and the location
   4   Other, namely..

6 **Would you visit a next edition of 'Kaap Helder', again?**
   1   No
   2   Yes
   3   I do not know (yet)

7 **What is your postal code? ......**

8 **Have you come especially from home for a visit to the 'Kaap Helder'?**
   1   No
   2   Yes (skip question 9)

9 **Where have you come from, if you have not come especially from home for this visit?**
   1   From work in the area
   2   I had an engagement in the area
   3   From a holiday or guest address in the area
   4   I am travelling through
   5   Other, namely................

10 **Did the 'Kaap Helder' signposting help you find the Oude Rijkswerf Willemsoord?**
   1   No, the route was unclear
   2   Yes, the route was clear
   3   I did not follow the signposting

11 **What is the size of the company you came here with?**
    1   I have come alone
    2   There are .... persons (yourself included), of which ...... persons are younger than 13 years.

12 **How old are you? .... years**

13 **How many times a year (on average) do you visit an arts event and/or an art museum?**
    1   Never, 'Kaap Helder' is an exception
    2   ....times a year

14 **What is the highest level of education that you have completed? If you are at school momentarily: what school are you in at the moment?**
    1   Primary school
    2   School of lower vocational training
    3   School of lower general secondary education
    4   School of higher general secondary education
    5   School of intermediate vocational training
    6   School of higher vocational training
    7   University

15 **Please indicate which of the following descriptions apply to you (You can mark more than one item.)**
    1   I sometimes follow television or radio programmes about art
    2   I visit a performance by a professional theatre company at least once a year
    3   I visit a performance of classical music at least once a year
    4   I have read a book last month
    5   I read one or more news magazines a week
    6   I work or study in the cultural sector (not education, unless a teacher of the arts)
    7   I am a student or still go to school

Thank you for your cooperation!

Appendices

B   Phase Models for Events

- Conferences
- Exhibitions
- Stage Productions
- Video-/Film Productions
- Fairs

Appendix B1:   Phase Model for Conferences
(This model has been worked out as a step-by-step plan in Chapter 6)

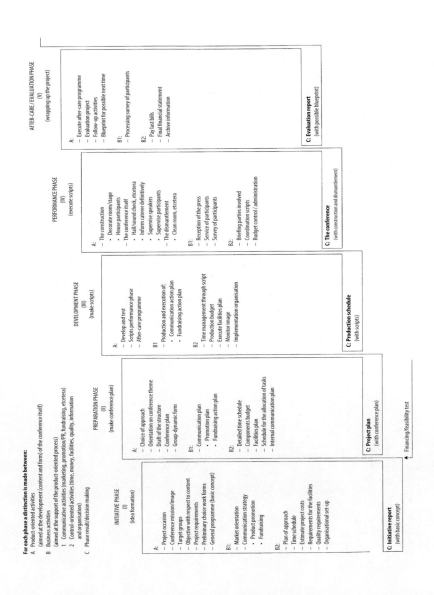

Appendix B2:   Phase Model for Exhibitions

For each phase a distinction is made between:

A Product-oriented activities
(aimed at the development (content and form) of the conference itself)

B Business activities
(aimed at the support of the product-oriented process)
1 Communicative activities (marketing, promotion/PR, fundraising, etcetera)
2 Control-oriented activities (time, money, facilities, quality, information and organisation)

C Phase result/decision making

INITIATIVE PHASE
(I)
(idea formation)

A: Project leader
– Project occasion
– Project mission/image
– Target group(s)
– Objective with respect to content
– Project requirements
– Definition of the partial products
– Description of the idea (basic concept)

B1: Project leader/assistant for publicity
– If need be market orientation
– Communication strategy
  • Product promotion
  • Financing/fundraising

B2: Project leader
– Plan of approach
– Overall time schedule
– Estimate project costs
– Requirements for the facilities and location
– Quality requirements
– General set-up for the project organisation

C: **Initiative report**
(with basic concept and preconditions)

PREPARATION PHASE
(II)
(exhibition concept)

A: Project leader/curator
– Possible research of the content
– First orientation of the objects
– Conservation research
– Story line
– Exhibition concept and draughts
– Reflection on the supporting programmes

B1: Project leader/assistant for publicity
– Communication plan
– Promotion plan
  • Fundraising
  • Negotiations financiers

B2: Project leader
– Detailed time schedule
– Components budget
– Plan for the adjustment of the hall/location
– Possibly take out an option on the hall/location
– Internal communication plan

C: **Project plan**
(with conference plan)

DEVELOPMENT PHASE
(III)
(production data)

A: Designer/curator
– Definitive choice objects
– Write texts
– Definitive style
– Produce plans
– Definitive design
– Technical description
– Develop supporting programmes/publications

B1: Project leader/assistant for publicity
– Possibly formative public survey
– Production and execution of:
  • Communication action plan
  • Supplementary fundraising
– Production plan for the opening
– Invitations for the opening

B2: Project leader/production leader
– Production schedule
– Production budget
– Loan (for use) contracts
– Implementation organisation

C: **Production schedule**
(with detail drawing and technical description)

PRODUCTION PHASE
(IV)
(building exhibition)

A: Production leader/project leader
– Preparation location/hall
– Construction exhibition
  • Any pre-fabrication in the workshop
  • Building up location/hall
  • Arranging exhibition
– Realisation supporting programmes/publications

B1: Assistant for publicity/project leader
– Promotional campaign
– Preparation opening/reception of the press

B2: Project leader/production leader
– Coordinate and organise production
– Progress control
– Budget control/administration
– Security plan
– Briefing attendants

C: **Installed exhibition**

OPENING PHASE
(V)
(receive visitors)

A: Project leader/warden
– Presentation of the exhibition to visitors
– Surveillance and security
– Supervision and maintenance exhibition
– Execute supporting programmes

B1: Project leader/assistant for publicity
– Promotional campaign
– Opening/reception of the press
– Visitors' service
– Public survey
– After-care programme

B2: Project leader
– Progress control
– Budget control/administration
– Support attendants
– Travel schedule for touring exhibition
– Disassembly plan

C: **Opened exhibition**

AFTER-CARE / EVALUATION PHASE
(VI)
(wrapping up the project)

A: Production leader/project leader
– Execute disassembly plan
– Evaluation project
– Possible follow-up activities
– Blueprint for possible next time

B1: Project leader/assistant for publicity
– Processing data public survey
– Thank-you letters
– Any processing of complaints

B2: Project leader
– After-care assistants
– Pay last bills
– Produce final financial statement
– Archive information

C: **Evaluation report**
(with possible blueprint)

Financing/feasibility test

Appendix B3:   Phase Model for Festivals and Public Events

(This model has been worked out as a step-by-step plan in Chapter 5)

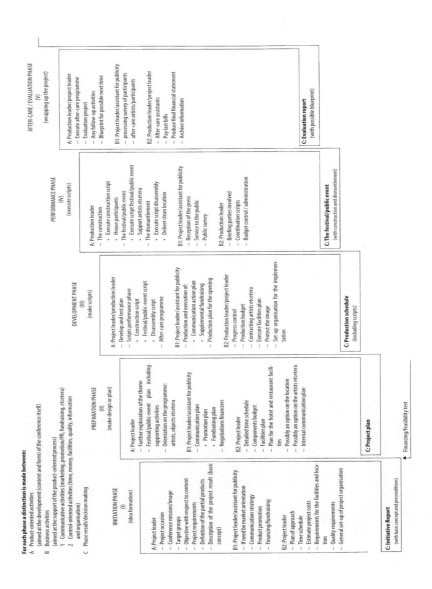

For each phase a distinction is made between:

A Product-oriented activities
  (aimed at the development (content and form) of the conference itself)

B Business activities
  (aimed at the support of the product-oriented process)
  1 Communicative activities (marketing, promotion/PR, fundraising, etcetera)
  2 Control-oriented activities (time, money, facilities, quality, information and organisation)

C Phase result/decision making

INITIATION PHASE
(I)
(idea formation)

A: Project leader
– Project occasion
– Conference mission/image
– Target groups
– Objective with respect to content
– Project requirements
– Definition of the partial products
– Description of the project result (basic concept)

B1: Project leader/assistant for publicity
– If need be market orientation
– Communication strategy
– Product promotion
– Financing/fundraising

B2: Project leader
– Plan of approach
– Time schedule
– Estimate project costs
– Requirements for the facilities and location
– Quality requirements
– General set-up of project organisation

C: Initiative Report
(with basic concept and preconditions)

Financing/feasibility test

PREPARATION PHASE
(II)
(make design or plan)

A: Project leader
– Further exploration of the theme
– Festival/public-event plan including supporting activities
– Orientation on the programme: artists, objects etcetera

B1: Project leader/assistant for publicity
– Communication plan
  • Promotion plan
  • Fundraising plan
– Negotiations financiers

B2: Project leader
– Detailed time schedule
– Components budget
– Facilities plan
– Plan for the hotel and restaurant facilities
– Possibly an option on the location
– Possibly an option on the artists etcetera
– Internal communication plan

C: Project plan

DEVELOPMENT PHASE
(III)
(make scripts)

A: Project leader/production leader
– Develop and test plan
– Scripts performance phase
  • Construction script
  • Festival/public-event script
  • Disassembly script
– After-care programme

B1: Project leader/assistant for publicity
– Production and execution of:
  • Communication action plan
  • Supplemental fundraising
– Production plan for the opening

B2: Production leader/project leader
– Progress control
– Production budget
– Contracting artists etcetera
– Execute facilities plan
– Protect the image
– Set-up organisation for the implementation

C: Production schedule
(including scripts)

PERFORMANCE PHASE
(IV)
(execute scripts)

A: Production leader
– The construction
  • Execute construction script
  • House participants
– The festival/public event
  • Execute script festival/public event
  • Support artists etcetera
– The dismantlement
  • Execute script disassembly
  • Deliver clean location

B1: Project leader/assistant for publicity
– Reception of the press
– Service to the public
– Public survey

B2: Production leader
– Briefing parties involved
– Coordination scripts
– Budget control / administration

C: The festival/public event
(with construction and dismantlement)

AFTER-CARE / EVALUATION PHASE
(V)
(wrapping up the project)

A: Production leader/project leader
– Execute after-care programme
– Evaluation project
– Any follow-up activities
– Blueprint for possible next time

B1: Project leader/assistant for publicity
– processing survey of participants
– after-care artists/participants

B2: Production leader/project leader
– After-care assistants
– Pay last bills
– Produce final financial statement
– Archive information

C: Evaluation report
(with possible blueprint)

Appendix B4: Phase Model for Stage Productions

For each phase a distinction is made between:
A Product-oriented activities
  (aimed at the development (content and form) of the conference itself)
B Business activities
  (aimed at the support of the product-oriented process)
  1 Communicative activities (marketing, promotion/PR, fundraising, etcetera)
  2 Control-oriented activities (time, money, facilities, quality, information and organisation)
C Phase result/decision making

INITIATIVE PHASE (I)
(idea on paper)

A: Artistic leader/director
 – Project occasion
 – Theme/choice of playing material
 – Project mission/image
 – Target group(s)
 – Objective with respect to content
 – Summary project requirements
 – Possibly obtain text
 – Description of the production (basic concept)
 – Start with the description of the group
 – Type of performance
 – Decision about video registration?

B1: Commercial leader
 – If need be market orientation
 – Communication strategy
   • Product promotion
   • Financing/fundraising
 – Negotiations financiers
 – Contract with places to play

B2: Commercial leader
 – Plan of approach
 – Set-up for the project organisation
 – Overall time schedule
 – Estimate project costs
 – Requirements for the facilities
 – Quality requirements

C: Initiative Report
(possibly with request for subsidy)

PREPARATION PHASE (II)
(development theatre piece)

A: Artistic leader/director
 – Possible writing stage text
 – Dramaturgical contribution
   • research
 – Start with direction concept
 – Role interpretations
 – Auditions
 – Select/make music
 – Possibly choreography
 – Possibly training programme
 – Points of departure for the design of the set
 – First consideration of props

B1: Commercial leader
 – Communication plan
   • Promotion
 – Supplementary fundraising
 – Contracts financiers
 – Contracts with places to play

B2: Production leader/commercial leader
 – Set-up project organisation
 – Contracting actors (cast)
 – Production planning
 – Start with production budget
 – Possibly plan for the facilities

C: Project plan
(with plan for the theatre piece)

Financing/feasibility test

PRE-PRODUCTION PHASE (III)
(prepare production)

A: Director/artistic leader
 – Last adjustments to text
 – Provisional direction concept
 – Possible supplementary training
 – Provisional design
   • scenery
   • costumes etcetera
   • lighting and sound

B1: Commercial leader
 – Communication action plans
 – Promotion action plan
   • Supplementary fundraising
 – Contracts with places to play

B2: Production leader
 – Make rehearsal schedules
 – Arrange rehearsal rooms
 – Arrange rehearsal props/costumes
 – Possibly catering plan
 – Detailed production budget
 – Adjust production organisation
 – Contract technicians (crew)
 – Start premiere plan and travel plan

C: Production schedule
(with, among other things, a rehearsal plan)

PRODUCTION PHASE (IV)
(rehearsal, make scenery)

A: Director/production leader
 – Definitive direction concept
 – Practise lines/rehearsals
 – Dramaturgical contribution
   • Guard the line
 – Definitively design and produce:
   • Scenery
   • Costumes etcetera
   • Lighting and sound
 – Receive/support actors

B1: Commercial leader/production leader
 – Promotional actions
 – Receive/support guests
 – Produce premiere plan
 – Invitations to the premiere

B2: Production leader
 – Overall coordination and organisation
 – (Financial) administration
 – Budget control
 – Organise catering during rehearsal
 – Take care of rehearsal rooms
 – Take care of props
 – Adjustment rehearsal schedule
 – Technical consultation with places to play
 – Planning premiere (week)

C: Programme Play Phase
(with premiere plan)

PLAY PHASE (V)
(performances)

A: Director/production leader
 – Try-outs
 – Premiere performance
   • (Travel and) play in theatre(s)
 – Construction/disassembly/transport
 – Scenery and technical equipment

B1: Commercial leader/production leader
 – Reception guests/press premiere
 – Execute communication action plan
 – Reception/attendance special guests at premiere
 – Programme booklets/merchandising

B2: Production leader/company manager
 – Supporting actors/technicians
 – Monitoring travel/play planning
 – Agreements with places to play
 – Organising transport actors/technicians
 – Calculate/pay accommodation expenses
 – Budget control
 – Quality control performance
 – Produce closing-off programme

C: Closing-Off Programme

CLOSING PHASE (VI)
(disassembly and after-care)

A: Production leader
 – Disassembly/removal/storage
   • Scenery
   • Lighting and sound
 – Evaluation of the performance

B1: Production leader
 – After-care actors
 – Possibly processing of complaints
 – Evaluation attention visitors/media

B2: Production leader
 – Produce final financial statement
 – Evaluation production process

C: Evaluation report

Appendix B5:   Phase Model for Video/Film Productions

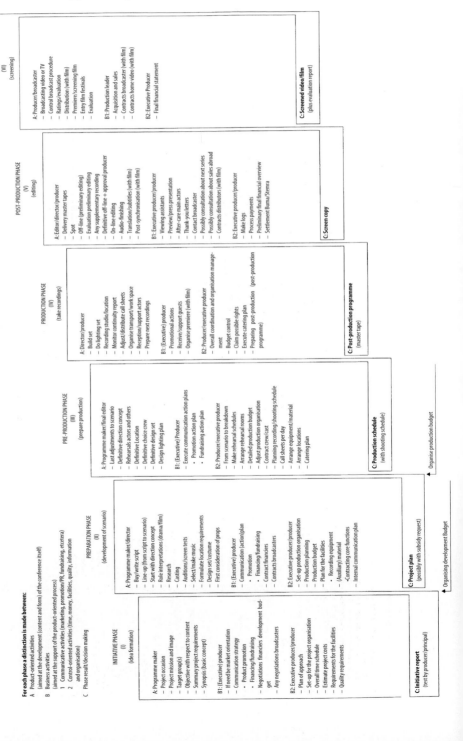

For each phase a distinction is made between:

A Product-oriented activities
  (aimed at the development (content and form) of the conference itself)
B Business activities
  (aimed at the support of the product-oriented process)
  1 Communicative activities (marketing, promotion/PR, fundraising, etcetera)
  2 Control-oriented activities (time, money, facilities, quality, information
    and organisation)
C Phase result/decision making

INITIATIVE PHASE
(I)
(idea formation)

A: Programme maker
– Project occasion
– Project mission and image
– Target group(s)
– Objective with respect to content
– Summary project requirements
– Synopsis (basic concept)

B1: (Executive) producer
– If need be market orientation
– Communication strategy
  • Promotion
  • Financing/fundraising
– Negotiations financiers development bud-
  get
– Any negotiations broadcasters

B2: Executive producer/producer
– Plan of approach
– Set-up for the project organisation
– Overall time schedule
– Estimate project costs
– Requirements for the facilities
– Quality requirements

C: Initiative report
(test by producer/principal)

Organising development Budget

PREPARATION PHASE
(II)
(development of scenario)

A: Programme maker/director
– Buy/write script
– Line-up (from script to scenario)
– Role interpretations (drama/film)
– Start with direction concept
– Research
– Auditions/screen tests
– Casting
– Select/make music
– Formulate location requirements
– Design set/costume
– First consideration of props

B1: (Executive) producer
– Communication (action)plan
  • Promotion
  • Financing/fundraising
– Contract financiers
– Contracts broadcasters

B2: Executive producer/producer
– Set-up production organisation
– Production planning
– Production budget
– Plan for the facilities
  • Recording equipment
  • (Auxiliary) material
– Contracting core functions
– Internal communication plan

C: Project plan
(possibly with subsidy request)

Organising production budget

PRE-PRODUCTION PHASE
(III)
(prepare production)

A: Programme maker/final editor
– Last adjustments to scenario
– Definitive direction concept
– Rehearsals actors and others
– Definitive Location
– Definitive choice crew
– Definitive design set
– Design lighting plan

B1: (Executive) Producer
– Execute communication action plans
  • Promotion action plan
  • Fundraising action plan

B2: Producer/executive producer
– From scenario to breakdown
– Make rehearsal schedules
– Arrange rehearsal rooms
– Detailed production budget
– Adjust production organisation
– Contract crew/cast
– Planning recording/shooting schedule
– Call sheets per day
– Arrange equipment/material
– Arrange locations
– Catering plan

C: Production schedule
(with shooting schedule)

PRODUCTION PHASE
(IV)
(take recordings)

A: Director/producer
– Build set
– Do lighting set
– Recording studio/location
– Monitor continuity report
– Adjust/distribute call sheets
– Organise transport/work space
– Reception/support actors
– Prepare next recordings

B1: (Executive) producer
– Promotional actions
– Receive/support guests
– Organise premiere (with film)

B2: Producer/executive producer
– Overall coordination and organisation manage-
  ment
– Budget control
– Claim possible rights
– Execute catering plan
– Preparing post-production (post-production
  programme)

C: Post-production programme
(master tape)

POST- PRODUCTION PHASE
(V)
(editing)

A: Editor/director/producer
– Delivery master tapes
– Spot
– Off-line (preliminary editing)
– Evaluation preliminary editing
– Any supplementary recording
– Definitive off-line + approval producer
– On-line editing
– Audio-finishing
– Translation/subtitles (with film)
– Post-synchronisation (with film)

B1: Executive producer/producer
– Viewing assistants
– Preview/press presentation
– After-care main actors
– Thank-you letters
– Contact broadcaster
– Possibly consultation about next series
– Possibly consultation about sales abroad
– Contracts distributors (with film)

B2: Executive producer/producer
– Make logs
– Process payments
– Preliminary final financial overview
– Settlement Buma/Stemra

C: Screen copy

PLAY-DISTRIBUTION PHASE
(VI)
(screening)

A: Producer/broadcaster
– Broadcasting video or TV
– Control broadcast procedure
– Ratings/evaluation
– Distribution (with film)
– Premiere/screening film
– Entry film festivals
– Evaluation

B1: Production leader
– Acquisition and sales
– Contracts broadcaster (with film)
– Contracts home video (with film)

B2: Executive Producer
– Final financial statement

C: Screened video/film
(plus evaluation report)

Appendix B6: Phase Model for Fairs

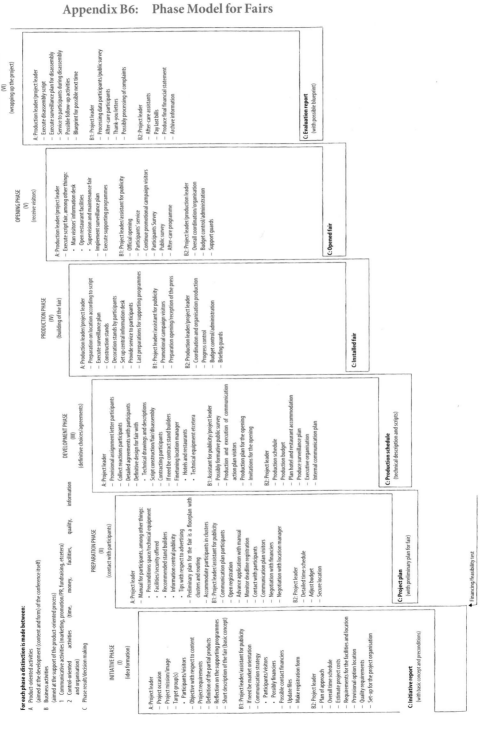

For each phase a distinction is made between:

A Product-oriented activities
(aimed at the development (content and form) of the conference itself)

B Business activities
(aimed at the support of the product-oriented process)
1 Communicative activities (marketing, promotion/PR, fundraising, etcetera)
2 Control-oriented activities (time, money, facilities, quality, information and organisation)

C Phase result/decision making

INITIATIVE PHASE (I) (idea formation)

A: Project leader
– Project occasion
– Project mission/image
– Target group(s)
– Participants/visitors
– Objective with respect to content
– Project requirements
– Definition of the partial products
– Reflection on the supporting programmes
– Short description of the fair (basic concept)

B1: Project leader/assistant for publicity
– If need be market orientation
– Communication strategy
  • Participants/visitors
  • Possibly financiers
– Possible contact financiers
– Update files
– Make registration form

B2: Project leader
– Plan of approach
– Overall time schedule
– Estimate project costs
– Requirements for the facilities and location
– Provisional option location
– Quality requirements
– Set-up for the project organisation

C: Initiative report
(with basic concept and preconditions)

PREPARATION PHASE (II) (contact with participants)

A: Project leader
– Manual for participants, among other things:
  • Preconditions space/technical equipment
  • Facilities/security offered
  • Recommended stand builders
  • Information central publicity
  • Tips with respect to advertising
– Preliminary plan for the fair is a floorplan with clusters and routing
– Accommodate participants in clusters

B1: Project leader/assistant for publicity
– Communication plan participants
– Open registration
– Advance application with manual
– Monitor deadline registration
– Contact with participants
– Communication plan visitors
– Negotiation with financiers
– Negotiation with location manager

B2: Project leader
– Detailed time schedule
– Adjust budget
– Secure location

C: Project plan
(with preliminary plan for fair)

DEVELOPMENT PHASE (III) (definitive choices/agreements)

A: Project leader
– Provisional assignment letter participants
– Collect reactions participants
– Detailed agreements with participants
– Definitive design for fair with
  • Technical drawings and descriptions
  • Script construction/fair/disassembly
– Contracting participants
– If need be contract stand builders
– Finetuning location manager
  • Hotels and restaurants
  • Technical equipment etcetera

B1: Assistant for publicity/project leader
– Possibly formative public survey
– Production and execution of communication action plan visitors
– Production plan for the opening
– Invitations for the opening

B2: Project leader
– Production schedule
– Production budget
– Plan hotel and restaurant accommodation
– Executive organisation
– Internal communication plan

C: Production schedule
(technical description and scripts)

PRODUCTION PHASE (IV) (building of the fair)

A: Production leader/project leader
– Preparation on location according to script
– Execute surveillance plan
– Construction stands
– Decoration stands by participants
– Set up central information desk
– Provide service to participants
– Last preparations for supporting programmes

B1: Project leader/assistant for publicity
– Promotional campaign visitors
– Preparation opening/reception of the press

B2: Production leader/project leader
– Coordination and organisation production
– Progress control
– Budget control/administration
– Briefing guards

C: Installed fair

OPENING PHASE (V) (receive visitors)

A: Production leader/project leader
– Execute script fair, among other things:
  • Man visitors' information desk
  • Implement surveillance plan
  • Open restaurant facilities
  • Supervision and maintenance fair
– Execute supporting programmes

B1: Project leader/assistant for publicity
– Official opening
– Continue promotional campaign visitors
– Participants' service
  • Participants' Survey
  • Public survey
  • After-care programme

B2: Project leader/production leader
– Overall coordination/organisation
– Budget control/administration
– Support guards

C: Opened fair

AFTER-CARE / EVALUATION PHASE (VI) (wrapping up the project)

A: Production leader/project leader
– Execute disassembly script
– Execute surveillance plan for disassembly
– Service to participants during disassembly
– Possible follow-up activities
– Blueprint for possible next time

B1: Project leader
– Processing data participants/public survey
– After-care participants
– Thank-you letters
– Possibly processing of complaints

B2: Project leader
– After-care assistants
– Pay last bills
– Produce final financial statement
– Archive information

C: Evaluation report
(with possible blueprint)

Financing/feasibility test

Appendices C
Models of Decision Documents

Appendix C1:   Model of a project proposal for an events
project

The project proposal (or initiative report) consists of all the points of departure
and *preconditions* for the events project.

The project proposal serves as a *starting document* for the events project and
it serves as a gauge for monitoring the process of the whole track that follows.
When working on 'a commission' the project proposal is the first decision
document that is shown to the client. In order to comply with this decision-
making process the project proposal should contain sufficient information so
that a realistic picture can be presented of the *project result*, or in other words,
how the event will generally look by the end of the project, including all of the
consequences.

In the themes presented in the model, the steps which are described in Section
5.1 *Step-by-step plan for the initiation phase* are referred to as much as possible.
For further instructions concerning the writing of a project proposal, see Step
8 in the step-by-step plan found in Section 5.1.

Warning 1: It is definitely *not* a good idea to list all of the answers from the steps
in the step-by-step plan, and then to bind them together using a cover! Write
new (concise) texts, which indeed have also been based on the answers you formulated to match the steps.

Warning 2: When writing the project proposal keep in mind what this first decision document's objective is (See above). It is therefore not meant that you
jam *all* of the information gathered into this first document. Remember that
managers have a great preference for very concise management information in
regard to decision making!

Cover

- (working) title plus possibly a sub-title of the project and a project logo
- type of report (Here: Project proposal/Initiative report or Project contract)
- possibly the name and logo of the client and/or agent

Important details (point-by-point information on the title page, the page
after the cover)

- (working) title plus possibly the subtitle of the project / type of project
- type of report (See cover)
- date of report
- important data regarding project (opening, completion date or opening performance date and closing date)
- number of times that the event will possibly be held, and the number of visitors/participants
- client or initiator (including contact details)
- maker(s) of the report, project team and project leader (including contact details)
- possible legal form of the project and possible partner(s) for cooperation

Table of contents (including chapters, sections, appendices and page numbers)

1 Introduction

- Who is the client and which other parties might be involved (for example future users, collaborative partners)?
- What is the reason for the project? (Step-by-step plan, Section 5.1, Step 1b)
- What is the context of the project (Does it take place within an organisation, and if so, what does this organisation do? Is the project connected to other projects? In what way does it distinguish itself from other projects, or what is the added value of this project?, etc.) (Step 1b)
- What does the client want to achieve in the end? (This is the client's goal) (Step 2a)
- What does the client actually require from the agent? (This is the presentation of the question or the phrasing). (Step 2)
- What kind of report is it, for whom is it intended and what is its objective?
- What can the reader expect from the report? (brief outline of the report)
- What is the status of the report (for ex. the idea, final draft, approved, etc.)? It is not referred to as the 'Project contract' until it has been approved.

2 Intrinsic points of departure
- Description of the project mission, project image and legitimacy, as response to the question of the client. (Steps 3a, 3b en 3c)
- Who is the target group(s) for the project, and how large will it be? (Step 3d)
- What are the target group's(s') objectives for this project? (try to measure them as much as possible!(SMART)). (Step 3e)
- What might the possible positive or negative spin-off be (side effects) of the event? (Step 3f)
- Description of the project's constraints. (which phases (length) and which parts (breadth) do not belong?) (Step 3g)
- Summary of the project requirements and criteria. (Step 3h)

3 Project contents
- General description of the project result in the form of a basic concept, including the motivation used to make choices. (Step 4)
  The basic concept:
  - gives a general but clear picture of the project result
  - provides an answer to the client's question
  - is interesting, attractive and has 'staying power'
  - the possible parts have a good intrinsic coherency
- short atmospheric description, which is a vivid description of the way in which the project result will be experienced by the prospective visitor or participant. From this the 'entertainment value' of the event can be determined.
- short piece of information regarding the project result (PMCs) and the link between them. (Steps 4d and 4e)
- description of the most important consequences from having chosen this form (event). (Step 4c)

4 Project approach
- Motivation for having chosen the approach (Step 5a)
- Point-by-point description of the activity plan, (general) breakdown. (Step 5b)
- Description of the project structure, i.e. a sound phase model including milestones in which decision documents are to be delivered that have been required for the decision making by the client. (Step 5b)
- Description of what type of information the decision documents con-

tain, based on the conclusions of the phases that will be provided to the client. (Step 5b)

5 **Project marketing and communication**
- Description of the strategic issues (the conclusion of the SWOT-analysis). (Step 6a)
- Description of the communication strategy. Divided into three different target groups: project target groups, fundraising target groups, other communication target groups. (Step 6b)
  (Means of communication, pertaining to the following phase.)

6 **Control aspects** (QOFTIM)
- Quality; describe how the quality of the project result and the project process are to be guaranteed (formulation of the quality requirements and procedures). (Step 7a)
- Organisation; make a set up for the project organisation (formal allocation of tasks and authorisation given to the parties concerned, depicted in an organisation flow chart). Describe the allocation of tasks within the project team, linked to the (main)activities set down in the activity plan. Describe the consultative structure and possible legal rights to the project. (Step 7b)
- Facilities; formulate the facilitary points of departure, including requirements concerning the venue. Likewise, draw up a statement regarding liability. (Step 7c)
- Time; set up a general *time sheet* in the form of a bar chart that shows the entire phasing and the most important activities per phase (the next phase more extensively and the following phases more generally). (Step 7d)
- Information; describe the system used for distributing and keeping records of the project information. Possible description used for registering hours. (Step 7e)
- Money; setting up a framework for *project costs and insurance plan*, and when applicable, send separate clarification per post. (Step 7f)

7 **Risk analysis** (Step 7g)
- Take stock of the most important risks which might impair the project's success (failure factors).
- Describe the measures that should be taken in order to reduce or eliminate the possible risks.

> **Appendix**
> In many cases a survey, text or graph (for example, a time sheet, financial scheme and organisational chart) as an appendix to the project proposal are enclosed. This increases the report's readability. The essence or summary of an appendix should be included in the main text, where naturally a reference should be given that refers to the corresponding appendix. It is only advisable to include such a survey, text or graph in the main text when it forms an indispensable component in the line of thought, which is of vital importance.

Appendix C2:   Model of a project plan for an events project

The project plan should, among other things, contain sufficient information for the client in order to provide him or her with an *exact* picture of the events project, including all of the possible consequences, in order to further the decision-making process.

Reference has been made as much as possible to the steps that are described in Section 5.2 *Step-by-step plan for the preparation phase* for the themes shown in the model. For further instructions concerning how to write a project plan, see Step 12 of the step-by-step plan in Section 5.2.

> **Cover** (See remarks in Appendix C1)
>
> **Important details** (See remarks in Appendix C1)
>
> **Table of contents** (See remarks in Appendix C1)
>
> **1 Introduction**
> - The recapitulation of a question or assignment formulated in the project proposal.
> - What kind of report is it, for whom has it been written and what is its objective?
> - What is its relationship to other decision documents? (something about phased decision making).

- What is worth mentioning since the last decision document appeared?
- What can the reader expect from this report? (brief outline of the report).
- What is the status of the report (for example the draft, final version, approved copy, etc.).

2 Project contents
- Short description of the general points of departure or the basic concept that has been chosen based on the plan or design that is made during this phase.
- Precise description of the actual project result rendered in the form of a detailed plan or design. (Step 9b) It should show the exact times, programming/names, sizes, specific places, locations, etc..If necessary, it should provide drawings of the design with explanations included. For each programme or part of the project (for ex. opening, party, workshop, competition, etc.) make a corresponding description and/or design.
- Atmospheric sketch, this is a vivid description of the way in which the project result can be experienced by the prospective visitor/participant. (Step 9c)
- If applicable, a general description of the production methods and performance aids (qualitative), (extensive production details follow later in the production programme). (Step 9d)
- Possibly further explanations, remarks, particulars.

3 Project marketing and communication
- Description of possible adjustments to be made in regard to communication strategy following the project proposal.
- Description of Marketing plan. (Step 10a)
- Description of Fundraising plan. (Step 10b)
- Description of Communication plan. (Step 10c)

4 Control aspects (QOFTIM)
- *Note in advance:* in the description of the aspects to follow, you should still indicate the points of departure that have been altered in regard to the approved project proposal.
- Quality; possible remarks concerning quality control. (Step 11a)
- Organisation; make an adjusted layout for the project organisation (organisation chart), to be used during the next phase. (Step 11b)

- Facilities; (Step 11c) can be divided into:
  - venue plan, with motivation for having chosen the venue, layout plan and description of all the practical matters in regard to the venue
  - facility plan, detailed description of the necessary facilities, and how these can be made available
  - Legal plan or permit, with an overview of the necessary permits/approvals/acquired rights, etc. and how it will be approached.
- Time; setting up of a general time schedule in the form of a bar chart, starting at the end of the preparation phase up until the end of the project. With an extensive overview of the activities concerning the First phase to follow (development phase). (Step 11d)
- Information; possible adjustment of the monitoring system for the project information. (Step 11e)
- Money; setting up a budgetary plan and insurance plan, possibly in combination with a budget report. Both the estimate as well as the budget report should be accompanied by a separate explanation by post. (Step 11f)

Appendix
(See also the general remark given in Appendix C1)

Appendix C3:   Model of a production programme for an events project

The production programme is not really a regular report, but instead it forms actually more of a compilation of separate pieces of production information, which help the execution team to carry out the events project. In addition, the production programme is also the final decision document, upon which the client can give the final go/no-go-decision for the events project.

Reference is made whenever possible to the themes used in the model that correspond to the steps that are described in Section 5.3 *Step-by-step plan for the production phase*. For further instructions concerning the writing of a production programme, see Step 16 from the step-by-step plan in Section 5.3.
See the general information given on the production programme as a report.

Cover (See remarks made in Appendix C1)

Important details (See remarks made in Appendix C1)

Table of contents (See remarks made in Appendix C1)

1. Introduction (as concise as possible)

- The recapitulation of a question or an assignment formulated in the project proposal.
- A short summary of the most important points in the project plan
- What kind of report is it, and what is its objective (in regard to the other decision documents)?
- What is worth mentioning since the last decision document appeared?
- What can the reader expect from the report? (brief outline of the report)
- What is the status of the report (for ex. the idea, final draft, approved, etc.). It is not referred to as the 'project contract' until it has been approved.

2. Project contents
- General description of the actual project result, in other words, how the event will look later (the plan or design), (describe as well the possible intrinsic deviations in regard to the approved project plan, which should be mentioned to the client)
- Describe all of the intrinsic and production technical information for the actual/production/execution of the project. In other words, take stock and describe which information the people who are going to actually set up and take down the event will need. Think things through in a very practical way! (Step 13)
  Note: Include all of the separate lists in the appendices, but mention them in this chapter as well.
- Add as appendices the operationalisation programme and the after-care programme. (Steps 13c and 13d)
- Any further information, remarks, particulars.

3. Project marketing and communication

Note in advance: In many cases it is recommended not to include this part as a chapter, but as a separate appendix instead, which can be attached to the production programme because this information is only relevant for those people who are responsible for project communication.

- Describe any possible adjustments that have been made to the marketing plan, fundraising plan and communication plan after the project plan.
- Describe the plans of action, if this has not already been done, (Step 14a) for:
  - Marketing
  - Fundraising
  - Communication
  All of the activities in these plans of action have been included in a kind of script.
- Describe the main theme in a possible research survey: if it is decided to conduct an evaluation public survey during the event, a separate research survey should be drawn up. In this chapter the main themes of the research survey should be described briefly. (Step 14b)

4. Control aspects

Note in advance: When describing the following aspects, you should begin each time by mentioning the possibly adjusted points of departure in regard to the previously approved project plan.

- Quality: possibly describe comments made in regard to monitoring the quality aspect during the production. (Step 15a)
- Organisation: make a plan for the production organisation (expand organisational chart to include production roles). Make possibly timetables for using in the following phase(s), etc.. (Step 15b)
- Facilities: make a facility plan of action (Step 15c), and include among others:
  - plans of action for making available facilities, etc. (order lists, rental lists, list of suppliers, etc.)
  - signposting plans, etc.
- Time: make scripts for the three sub-phases of the development phase (Step 15d), namely:
  - Script for setting up (production phase)
  - Script for the event itself (operationalisation programme), (some-

times for parts separate from the script, for ex. the official opening)
– Script for dismantlement

Possibly extended to include planning capacity for people, space, machines, and so on.

Note: The scripts are the most important part of the production programme. Sometimes it is more practical to deliver the scripts as independent work documents.

- Information; possibly adjust the monitoring system for project information. (Step 15e)
- Money: set up a working budget and budget control system during the execution. (Step 15f)

Appendices

All of the separate lists, maps and overviews should be included as an appendix! Often the *operationalisation programme*, the after-care *programme*, but also the *communication plan* and the *scripts* are included as appendices to the production programme.

See as well the general remark given in Appendix C1.

Bibliography

Amelsvoort, P. van en Scholtes, G., *Zelfsturende teams, ontwerpen, invoeren en begeleiden*. Oss 1994.

Beers, B. van e.a. *Projectmatig communiceren bij veranderingen*. Deventer 1998.

Berge, A.P. van den, Boer, A.J. de en Klootwijk, J.W., *Werkboek conferenties*. Utrecht 1994.

Blom Stef e.a., *Effectief projectmanagement*. Groningen.

Boer, H. de, *Schriftelijk rapporteren*. Utrecht 1974.

Boer, P. de, Koetzier, W. en Brouwers, M.P., *Basisboek bedrijfseconomie*. Groningen.

Bos, J., Harting, E., Projectmatig creëren 2.0. Scriptum 2006.

Buuren-Verwaijen, M. van, Werkwijzer Succesvolle evenementen. Kluwer 2002.

Chan, P. Y., Praktische handleiding voor projectmanagement. ThiemeMeulenhoff 2006.

Damiaens, E., Evenementen organiseren. Garant 2007.

Dieho, B., Hagoort, G. en Olink, H., *De achterkant van de Theaterpraktijk*.

Eco, U., *Hoe schrijf ik een scriptie*. Amsterdam.

Eyzenga, G.R., *Trends in management*. Groningen.

Gerards, H. en Lubberding, J., *De bestaansvoorwaarden, inleiding in de organisatiekunde*. Wolters-Noordhoff.

Gevers, T., Zijlstra, T., Praktisch Projectmanagement 1. Academic Service 2001.

Gevers, T., Zijlstra, T., Praktisch Projectmanagement 2. Academic Service 2003.

Goldratt, E., De zwakste schakel, De internationale bestseller over projectmanagement. Spectrum 2007.

Gritt, R., Projectmanagement, een praktisch handboek voor projectmatig werken. Groningen 1994.

Gritt, R., Projectmanagement. Noordhoff Uitgevers 2008.

Hagoort, G., *Cultureel ondernemerschap*. Culemborg 1992.

Hagoort, G., *Strategische dialoog in de kunstensector, interactieve strategievorming in een kunstorganisatie*. Utrecht 1998.

Heide, van der en Rottger, *Succesvol deelnemen aan beurzen en tentoonstellingen, handleiding voor effectief exposeren*. Amsterdam.

Hendriks Brigit e.a., *De kleine Prince 2, Projectmanagement methodiek voor kleine en middelgrote projecten*. Pink Elephant 1997.

Heuvel, G. van den, *Alweer een verslag*. Baarn.

Hildebrand, N., *Een evenement als bron van inkomsten*.

Honert, A. van den en Broersma, H., *Projectmanagement*.

Hummel, H., Slootmaker, A., Berkhout, J. Projectwijzer. Noordhoff Uitgevers 2003.

Jans, R., *Een goed rapport*. Baarn.

Jutte, B., Handboek Projectrisico's. Concilio 2006.

Kingdon, D.R., *Matrix-organisatie, integratiemogelijkheden voor grote organisaties*. Alphen aan den Rijn 1977.

Kop en Mierlo, van, *Reader Vrijetijdskunde: Organiseren van evenementen*. Breda.

Kraan, Ph., *Verslag van lezing over sponsoring binnen training 'Projectmanagement'*. Hoorn/Zwaag 1992.

Kroonenberg, H.H. en Siers, F.J., *Methodisch ontwerpen*. Culemborg.

Lamers, H.A.J.M., *Handleiding voor pr- en reclameteksten*. Muiderberg 1991.

Lange, H., *Motivatie in organisaties*. Deventer 1991.

Launspach, N., *De organisatie van evenementen*. Arnhem 1994.

Lazeron, De krachtenveldanalyse. In: *Opleiders in Organisaties* (capita selecta). Deventer 1995.

Lievegoed, B.C.J., *Organisaties in ontwikkeling*. Rotterdam.

Mahieu, J., Evenementen en kostenbeheersing. Kluwer 2005.

Mannes, B., *Kaap Helder publieksonderzoek*. Haarlem 2003, Kunst en Cultuur Noord-Holland.

Meyenfeldt, F. von, *Basiskennis projectmanagement*. Schoonhoven 1999.

Misteli, J.M., Oosten de Boer, P.F. van, *Ondernemerswijzer, De praktische gids voor elke ondernemer*. Deventer 1993.

Neumann, R. en Bredemeier, K., *Projectmanagement van A tot Z*. Amsterdam 1998.

Noordman, D., *Kunstmanagement, hoe bestaat het*. Amsterdam 1989.

Onna, M. van, Koning, A., De kleine Prince 2, Gids voor projectmanagement. Academic Service 2007.

Oosthoek, E. en Revoort, A., *Basisboek televisie maken*. Groningen.

Poel, H. van der, *Tijd voor vrijheid, Inleiding tot de studie van de vrijetijd*. Amsterdam 1999.

Portny, S., Projectmanagement voor dummies (pocketeditie). Addison Wesley NL 2003.

Quant, P., Je project op de rails: In 15 stappen. Thema 2006.

Regterschot, J., *Facility management*. Deventer 1989.

Ranshuysen, L., *Handleiding publieksonderzoek voor podia en musea*. Amsterdam 1999, Boekmanstichting.

Schot, T., *Praktijkhandboek voor communicatief exposeren*. Deventer 1985.

Seijner, M., De competente projectleider. Noordhoff Uitgevers 2007.

Stapele, M. van, *Checklist conferentie organisatie*.

Stern, M., Het evenement als sales instrument. Media Business Press 2003.

Theunissen, J., Handboek publieksveiligheid bij evenementen. Kluwer juridisch 2008.

Timmer, Bureau, *De Grote Klapper*. 1991.

Verhaar, J.P.M. en Meeter, J., *Projectmodel Tentoonstellingen*. Amsterdam.

Verhaar, J.P.M. en Meeter, J., *Projectmodel Exhibitions*. Amsterdam.

Verhaar, J.P.M., *Strategisch Bedrijfsplan, handleiding voor het maken van een strategisch bedrijfsplan voor kleine en middelgrote culturele instellingen*. Hoorn/Zwaag 1995.

Verhaar, J.P.M., *Managementvaardigheden voor projectleiders*. Amsterdam 2007.

Verhaar, J.P.M., *Het project*. Amsterdam 2007.

Verhaar, J.P.M., *Eventmanagement: cases*. Amsterdam 2008.

Verhaar, J.P.M., Project *Management*. Amsterdam 2005.

Verhaar, J.P.M., Projectmatig werken. Amsterdam 2005.

Verhaar, J.P.M., *Aanpak Adviesprojecten in de culturele sector*. Hoorn 2000.

Verhaar, J.P.M., IKO-model, een dynamisch diagnose-instrument voor het begrijpen en beschrijven van organisaties als levend systeem. Hoorn 2000.

Verhage, B. en Cunningham, W.H., *Grondslagen van de marketing*. Leiden/Antwerpen 1989

Vlist, R. van der, (red.), *Visies op organisatiecultuur*. Utrecht.

Walters, G., *Management van projectmanagement, het managen van multiprojecten en programma's*. Culemborg 1999.

Watts, H., *On Camera, how to produce film and video*.

Weeda, N., (red.), *Handboek Personeelsactiviteiten en Bedrijfsevenementen*. Alphen aan den Rijn.

Wijnen, G., Renes, W. en Storm, P., *Projectmatig werken*. Utrecht 1988.

Wijnen, G., *Multiprojectmanagement*. Schiedam 1997.

Wijnen, G., Tak, T. van der, Projectmanagement, Sturen op samenhang. Kluwer 2006.

Wijngaards, N.M., *Probleemoplossende technieken*. Utrecht 1989.

Wolbink, R., *Problemen in organisaties, handboek voor probleemoplossers*. Baarn 1993.

Subject Index

About the Authors

Iris Eshel

After graduating from the Amsterdam College of Arts with a degree in Cultural Management, Iris Eshel began to specialise in project management and production of events and played a significant role in the professionalisation of the Dance Music Industry in the Netherlands. She started as a programmer and project manager at *Mojo Concerts* (concert promoter in the Netherlands, now owned by *ClearChannel*) and followed this by setting up her own business involved in the production of large festivals such as the *Awakenings Festival* and *Dance Valley*. She also programmed and produced internationally renowned and successful concepts in various clubs and pop venues in the Netherlands and beyond. The project management method gave her the opportunity to excel and make a difference in a starting and blooming industry. She is currently a lecturer in Event and Project Management at the INHolland University in Haarlem at the Media & Entertainment Management department, a trainer in Project management for the Master in Event Management programme, an advisor for the Festival Department of the National Fund of Performing Arts and co-author of a current publication about event management. Her major professional interest is training students and professionals by giving them a practical approach to event management and empowering them so that they can control the event process.

Jan Verhaar

After receiving his degree in architecture and the economics of civil engineering, Jan Verhaar (1949) took a great many study and training courses in the field of management and organisation theory. He worked in a senior position at a large city council in the Netherlands and he held several management positions in the creative industry as a project manager at an engineering firm. He runs his own consultancy firm, MENS&ORGANISATIE, Agency for Project Management and Development Issues. The agency MENS&ORGANISATIE gives advice and support, and arranges management training courses for a very wide field of businesses. Training and coaching the application of the project-management approach in the participant's own work situation is part of this. He is/was also a part-time teacher of management at the Reinwardt Academy, the Department of Cultural Management and the Netherlands Film and Television Academy of the Amsterdam College of Arts, the Center for Art & Media Management at the Utrecht School of Arts, and the Netherlands Institute for

Art and Management, Media-and-Entertainment-Management course at IN-HOLLAND University, Haarlem. He is the author of several publications in the fields of project and innovation management. His major professional interest is innovation within organisations and its relationship to the people who work within them.

Agency for Project Management and Development Issues
Established in Zwaag/Hoorn-NH, Netherlands
e-mail: j.verhaar@mensenorganisatie.nl
internet: www.mensenorganisatie.nl